RACE

AND

FOOTBALL

IN AMERICA

RED ⚡ LIGHTNING BOOKS

RACE

=== AND ===

FOOTBALL

IN AMERICA

THE LIFE AND LEGACY OF
GEORGE TALIAFERRO

Foreword by Delise S. O'Meally
Foreword by Bob Kravitz

DAWN KNIGHT

This book is a publication of

Red Lightning Books
1320 East 10th Street
Bloomington, Indiana 47405 USA

redlightningbooks.com

Manufactured in the United States of America

ISBN 978-1-68435-095-7 (hdbk.)
ISBN 978-1-68435-066-7 (pbk.)
ISBN 978-1-68435-068-1 (web PDF)

1 2 3 4 5   24 23 22 21 20 19

To Jon, AJ, Taylor, and Mackenzie;
To Dad;
To George Taliaferro, may your legacy continue to inspire others; and
To those willing to challenge the status quo to fight for social justice

CONTENTS

FOREWORD

NELSON MANDELA ONCE SAID, "Sport has the power to change the world, it has the power to unite people in a way that few other activities can." For those of us who have made sport our life's work, we know this to be true. We have seen sport unite communities after tragedies, natural disasters, wars; we have seen sport form unity among people with differing beliefs and values. We have seen sport bring hope in areas of society where hopelessness has taken root. The power of sport also can be seen through the impact and influence of athletes at all levels of the game. Throughout history, because of their enviable skills on the playing field, athletes have held positions of high regard in our culture. Some, like LeBron James, Serena Williams, and Roger Federer, transcend sport and achieve celebrity status, with a global ability to affect and influence. Others may have impact on a more local level, in high schools or colleges, youth groups or communities. Regardless of the sphere of influence, sport presents the opportunity to make a positive mark on society and change the world for the better.

Many athletes have stood in support of a cause—or in opposition to injustice and oppression—in iconic moments in history, from the raised fists of John Carlos and Tommie Smith to the bended knee of Colin Kaepernick; from Muhammad Ali's resistance to the Vietnam War and his fight for African American rights to Billie Jean King's fight for equal rights and opportunities for girls and boys. Athlete activists have spoken out privately and publicly; have lent their images, their celebrity, and their resources to a cause; have given voice to issues where those most directly affected have no voice; and have endured humiliation and vilification in order to pave the way for others. George Taliaferro is one of these heroes.

As author Dawn Knight so eloquently and movingly portrays, Taliaferro's life represents triumph through adversity and the courage to stand up for what was right when what was right was not popular. Years later as a professor at Indiana University, Taliaferro would write his favorite saying on the chalkboard in his classes: "All sickness ain't death," a phrase that speaks to perseverance, determination, courage, and commitment during difficult times. George Taliaferro lived a life of perseverance, from his early years in Gary, Indiana, where segregation and oppression limited his educational and athletic opportunities: His determination while at Indiana University to be educated despite daily doses of racism and prejudice. His willingness to use his status as an athlete to integrate the Bloomington, Indiana, community in an effort to make life better for others. His courage and fortitude during his time in the armed forces, representing a nation that at times did not embrace him. His years in the NFL as one of only a few African American players. His enduring commitment over seven decades to fighting oppression and injustice.

At a time when America was black and white—or rather white and "not white"—George Taliaferro leveraged his platform as a great athlete and humanitarian to change hearts and minds. His influence in college sports, in the NFL, and in the very fabric of American life is still felt today. Regardless of whether you support the causes championed by today's athlete or agree with their methods of protest, the fact is that the Constitution guarantees all of us the right to speak and protest those injustices that affect our lives and the lives of others. The very freedom we fight for includes the freedom to speak out when change is needed. George Taliaferro's courage and perseverance (all sickness ain't death) paved the way for others to stand (or kneel) against oppression.

As I immersed myself in Taliaferro's story, I found the inevitable commonalities that we all can find if we take the time to learn more about each other. Our paths crossed in history when I first walked onto the campus of Morgan State University as a young tennis student athlete in the early 1990s—the same Baltimore, Maryland, campus for which Taliaferro served as dean of students and volunteer football coach more than twenty years before me. Legendary Morgan State Coach and Athletic Director Earl Banks retired just five years before I arrived on campus. Banks was the friend who broke the news to Taliaferro, in that Chicago restaurant in 1949, that he had been selected by the Chicago Bears as the first African American drafted into the NFL.

What George Taliaferro stood for more than seventy years ago, and continued to stand for throughout his youthful ninety-one years, is the idea that with celebrated status comes the responsibility to use your platform to bring attention to the social issues of our times. On April 4, 1967, exactly one year before his assassination in Memphis, Martin Luther King Jr. delivered a speech entitled "Beyond Vietnam: A Time to Break Silence." He led with this statement: "A time comes when silence is betrayal." In recent times, athlete activism has increased at all levels of sport. While much attention has focused on NFL players, athletes, both male and female, in all major sports have been at the forefront of many of these issues. By taking a stand, by refusing to be silent in the face of criticism, a new generation continues to fulfill the legacy of George Taliaferro. All sickness ain't death.

Delise S. O'Meally
Executive Director,
Institute for Sport and Social Justice

FOREWORD

WHEN I ARRIVED ON THE Indiana University campus in 1978, I was a typical freshman whose only two goals were to cover Bob Knight and have as much fun as humanly possible—and not necessarily in that order.

By my sophomore year, though, I had learned that there was a whole lot more to IU than the basketball coach and Nick's English Hut. That's when I began covering IU basketball for the student newspaper, the *Indiana Daily Student*, and that's about the same time I started getting sideways with a certain legendary but crusty college basketball coach.

Enter George Taliaferro.

He didn't know me from Adam, but whenever I criticized Knight in print, he always went out of his way to send me a note or call me to tell me to stick by my guns, to always stand on principle. Quite honestly, I don't know to this day how he truly felt about Knight; I just knew that he seemed to appreciate the fact that I was a budding contrarian who took on one of the most powerful people, if not *the* most powerful person, on the campus.

Now that I'm older and presumably a bit smarter, I can understand why George embraced the notion of taking on the established order. George wasn't just a great athlete who became the first black man ever to be drafted by the National Football League; he was also an agent of social change. In so many ways, he was far ahead of his time.

It's astonishing to me, as I read this book, that my parents used to take me out to the Gables for special dinners when I was a student at IU. This restaurant, like so many establishments throughout Bloomington, was segregated during George's time in school. He would not accept the status quo, though, and over time, he was central to desegregating several areas of the campus—the pool, dining establishments, and the list goes on.

I can't possibly recommend Dawn Knight's book enough. I wish it had been written back in the late 1970s or early 1980s, when I was still in school. I would have had a greater appreciation for what Mr. Taliaferro meant to the campus and to the history of college and professional football. Again, though, it's never too late to understand what a huge change agent Mr. Taliaferro was, or what a fine, principled man he was. I am supremely fortunate to have crossed paths with him many, many years ago and to feel as if he's part of my life to this day.

Bob Kravitz
Indianapolis sports personality

PREFACE

"LIVES OF GREAT MEN ALL REMIND US / We can make our lives sublime," transcendentalist Henry Wadsworth Longfellow writes in the poem "Psalm of Life." The poem continues, telling us that we, having been inspired, can inspire someone else, leaving "footprints on the sands of time." George Taliaferro's life left and inspired indelible footprints. I was a sophomore at Indiana University in 1991 when, at the unrelenting prompting of my roommate Lori, I added an introductory social work course to my schedule. Not a morning person, I avoided early classes, so I had resisted at first. Eventually, her persistence, and the fact that I needed another elective anyway, prompted me to enroll. I'm sure I was thinking something along the lines of *this better be good* as I crutched my way to Ballantine Hall that first day of class (I was dealing with a knee injury). As I made my way along a trail that ran through the heart of Indiana's sprawling campus, my stunning surroundings of trees, limestone buildings, and a winding creek probably did little to improve my attitude. When I entered the classroom several minutes later, George Taliaferro took in my crutches and said, "Well, there's One Hung Low!" His contagious laugh made me laugh, and I knew already he was someone special. One Hung Low remained my nickname until I was finally rid of the crutches. (Years later, when my married name became Dawn Knight, he gave me a new nickname, A.M. P.M.)

In class, Taliaferro lectured that everyone has worth and dignity and deserves respect. Although this was something that I had recognized in others, it had not translated to myself until that class. The discovery that I too had worth and dignity and deserved respect was profound and powerful. There were other lessons too. On exam days, before handing out the source of dread for countless college students, the blue book, Taliaferro would write on the board, "All sickness ain't death." He never explained—just wrote it on the board for us to contemplate. At first I laughed, thinking it was meant as a joke about test anxiety or our ability to perform on the exam. It wasn't until later, when I began to piece together Taliaferro's story, that I realized it meant much more.

Before we began the exam, Taliaferro reminded us to spell his name correctly on the blue book cover or he wouldn't bother to grade the exam. When he said it, although the laugh lines would appear around his eyes again, we couldn't be sure that he was joking. For this reason, early in the semester, we had each memorized the correct spelling and had cautiously printed it on the cover of every exam since, just in case. I still don't know if he would have actually carried out the threat, but I do know that the name is important to him—that it has a rich history. Taliaferro's great-grandfather was a slave owned by an Italian physician with the surname Tagliaferro (silent *g*), and his life was changed dramatically when on September 22, 1862, President Abraham Lincoln declared freedom from slavery in the Emancipation Proclamation. His owner told the former slave he could keep the name if he wanted, and Taliaferro's great-grandfather did, but he dropped the *g* to make the name more his own. Over one hundred years later, George Taliaferro, on an Alaskan cruise ship with an Italian crew, learned that the name meant "ironworker," an appropriate name for a man who grew up in a steel town and who played seven football positions during its iron man days.

Long after he retired from the NFL, at an event for the league, Taliaferro heard another anecdote regarding his name. Ralph Guglielmi, another retired player, told Taliaferro that his father, an Italian immigrant, would brag at the local barbershop about the great Italian kid playing football at Indiana University, George Taliaferro. He went so far as to brag that he knew the family—a good Italian one—well. Guglielmi's constant bragging prompted one of his friends to write to the university to get an autographed picture for him. Needless to say, upon its arrival, they were all surprised to see the smiling face of George Taliaferro, who didn't look, well, Italian.

Taliaferro's name had a history, one that was a part of who he was. In a class about listening to the stories of others, it was important that we knew how to spell the name, that we had listened, that we understood that it was part of him. Still, he didn't tell us his story. It wasn't until a couple of years later that I would begin to learn it. Instead, he continued teaching us lessons inherent to social work, like the idea that all human beings have the right to self-determination. His lessons revolved around learning to see others differently and ourselves differently too, about understanding our place in the world and taking an active role in making it better. One day he wrote on the board, "May our complacency disturb us profoundly today," again leaving it there for us to ponder. Although his story was still untold, it had become clear that his lessons on worth, dignity, and equity had not come from a mere textbook.

Taliaferro had a keen sense of humor. If someone fell asleep in class, his policy was to whisper, "Hip hip." That was the cue for the rest of the class to tiptoe to the guilty party and yell, "Hooray!" It only happened once. His humor, which was a part of nearly every lesson, did not diminish the serious nature of the subject matter. Rather, it taught us the importance of balance. In a field where workers often see humanity's worst, it is a reminder that we must still seek joy. I realized later that the Dalai Lama, who fled Tibet and saw countless horrors done to his people, embodied this same philosophy. Taliaferro would signal the end of class by telling us, "Grab your hats!" We were usually surprised it was already time to leave. By the end of the semester, Taliaferro's class had left an impression on me. This time, I joined Lori in persuading our other roommate, Michelle, to take the class. She didn't even bother to argue, and as we had, she ended her semester with some profound realizations about herself and the world around her. In appreciation, and for putting up with us for three straight semesters, we invited Taliaferro to "break bread," as he put it, at Macri's Deli, just down the street from College Mall. He accepted.

When we approached the hostess stand, three white college students and a black man in his sixties, the hostess asked, "Will there be four of you dining tonight?"

"Yes, I'm dining with my daughters," Taliaferro replied. The hostess laughed.

"What? You don't think they can be my daughters?" Taliaferro asked, his tone clipped.

The hostess gaped, no words escaping her open mouth. Clearly mortified, she began to stammer an apology. Before she could, Taliaferro's stern face melted into laughter, the familiar laugh lines reappearing. The hostess, finally joining the rest of us in laughter, showed us to our table. Even before we had a chance to sit, though, Taliaferro was trying to give us away to the army recruiter at a nearby table. "My daughters could use some discipline," he explained.

What began as an appreciation dinner turned into a tradition (which often included his wife, Viola) that continued long after we had graduated. It was during one of these dinners that I began to learn some of Taliaferro's story. This time, we were seated at a fairly long table because some of Taliaferro's friends had joined us. There were several conversations going on at once, but I heard a fraction of one that warranted my attention. Someone had said something about "when you played football here" to Taliaferro.

"Wait? What? You played football at IU? You never told us that," I whined.

"It had nothing to do with social work." He laughed. His friend, realizing how little we knew, filled us in on a few more important details. Taliaferro had also played in the NFL, and he was the first black man drafted by an NFL team. I was dumbfounded. How had I not known this? Taliaferro had taught us that everyone has a story. How had we not bothered to learn more of his? We heard a little more that evening, but he wasn't offering a lot of details.

After graduation, I became a high school English teacher. I began inviting Taliaferro to speak to my classes about being an NFL trailblazer. There were numerous visits, for which he would make the drive from Bloomington to Indianapolis to speak to my students. While some of his speech was about his role in black history, it went beyond that. He encouraged the students to *do something*—to find something they love and to do it. To be successful. Being a follower, he explained, doesn't work. He stressed the importance of not yielding to social pressure, of avoiding drinking or doing drugs. You can never be as good at being someone else as you can at being yourself, he explained. "I will do whatever it takes to be the best me I can be," he told one group, urging them to do the same. He told them that the reason that he weighed nearly the same sixty years later as he did when he played football is that he took care of himself. "I'm not waiting on you to love me—I love me," he explained. At the end, he talked about the danger of being complacent as he held up the "Colored" sign he had taken decades earlier from a movie theater. He finished his lecture, looking out at the high school students and saying, "If you need to, come stand on my shoulders because the sky won't be too far away, and the sky's the limit." There were new stories with every visit.

As years passed, several thoughts that had occurred to me at different moments over the years began to come together. There were more stories I needed to hear. Taliaferro was not only a Hoosier treasure but a national treasure. He would not be around to tell his stories forever. I picked up the phone and called him.

"Has anyone ever thought about writing a book about you?" I asked when he answered.

"Who would want to write a book about little old me?" he asked, laughing.

"I would," I said. He told me I could if I wanted to, but his tone was like that of a parent appeasing a toddler. I'm not sure he actually thought I would do it.

It took copious amounts of research and coffee and several years to write *Taliaferro: Breaking Barriers*, which was published in 2007. As we worked on the book—eventually he realized I was serious—he would sometimes digress to lecture me about other topics too. During one phone conversation, when my children were small, my youngest came into the room to tell me good night. I asked Taliaferro to wait for a second, and I put the phone down and gave a good night hug, kiss, and "I love you" to my daughter. When I picked the phone back up, I apologized, explaining the interruption.

That was all it took for him to launch into a lecture. "You and Jon have built a beautiful foundation for your kids," he told me. "You are not only Mom; you are someone they can always turn to." Kids have to be confident in knowing that there isn't a subject they can't discuss with us, he told me. I had to be available at any time to talk to them about any subject. He said, "I will remind you as long as I live of that obligation." This was the foundation he and his wife built for their own family, one of unconditional love and open communication. When their daughters were teens, the Taliaferros created contracts with them, asking them to set goals for themselves.

My youngest, who was supposed to be in bed, interrupted the conversation three more times during this lecture. I stopped each time to give her hugs and tell her I love her.

It wasn't just reminders of lessons like this one that went on for years after I sat in his classroom in Ballantine Hall. Taliaferro continued regaling me with his stories too, even after the book was published. In fact, by the time the book was on the shelves, I already had a list of new stories that had come out at book signings and events or just while we were breaking bread together. In 2010, Taliaferro and I were asked to participate in the Pop Lloyd symposium in Atlantic City, he as an award recipient, me as a presenter. The yearly symposium is in honor of Negro League baseball star and Hall of Famer John Henry "Pop" Lloyd's historic contribution to baseball, and it celebrates his humanitarianism. In attendance were Negro League players like Hall of Famer Monte Irvin and 105-year-old Emilio Navarro, a member of the Puerto Rican Baseball Hall of Fame. My husband and I sat at dinner one evening during the symposium. The Taliaferros, Monte Irvin, and another Negro League player sat with us. For over an hour, my husband and I tried to keep our chins off the table as we listened in awe to the shared experiences of those around that table, including references to time they spent with Joe Louis and Jackie Robinson.

While I was honored to be a part of conversations like that one, I regretted stories that I had discovered too late to include in the book. For this reason, I have wanted to update it for some time. I just had not made it a priority to do so. Then, San Francisco 49er quarterback Colin Kaepernick sat during the national anthem during a preseason football game in August 2016. The polarity of the reaction to what eventually became known as the national anthem protests finally prompted me to write the update. I wondered at the absolutism of the responses, at the lack of an attempt to understand one another. In so many ways, it reminded me of Taliaferro's story. This book goes beyond telling the story of

George Taliaferro. It also tells the story of the history of race and the NFL as a vehicle for social change. Hopefully, Taliaferro's story will provide some context through which we can explore race in America and will encourage honest discourse about what that means today.

Dawn Knight
January 24, 2018

ACKNOWLEDGMENTS

WITH MUCH APPRECIATION TO MY family, whose unending support enabled me to write the original version of this book and this update to it. At times both took precedence over them, but their support never wavered. To my sister, Michelle, for listening to me ramble on about this book—again. To my IU roommates Lori Tragesser and Michelle Hood Klein, for making me take George Taliaferro's class and for all the dinners together with him after—and for continuing to be an important part of my life almost thirty years later. To Helen Petersen for the adventures and conversations on our road trips to visit the Taliaferros. To John Dudeck for the countless hours on the phone to tell me his Taliaferro story. To Bob Kravitz and Delise S. O'Meally, who took the time to read the manuscript and write a foreword, even though we had never met. To Indiana University Press, especially to Ashley Runyon and Peggy Solic, for believing in my idea for an updated version, for patiently answering my questions (sometimes twice), and for extending deadlines. Thanks for a second time to Brad Cook at the Indiana University Archives, who not only found the pictures I requested but also sent them directly to IU Press. To the English Department at Westfield High School in general, but especially to Roger Wachtel, Dawn Grinnage, Holly Wheeler, and Jennifer Yoder for your insight, ideas, and inspiration. Thank you to my students, who remind me that there is much hope for the future. And to those of you who could have chosen to read anything but chose this. I am grateful.

RACE

=== AND ===

FOOTBALL
IN AMERICA

ONE

—ᴡ—

OCTOBER 2005:
TRICK OR TREAT

"THANKS, NIGGER," THE LITTLE BOY said, not viciously, but in the same tone anyone would use to genuinely thank someone else.

George Taliaferro had opened the door with one hand and balanced a large bowl of candy in the other. He was greeted with the customary "Trick or treat!" Three young trick-or-treaters, a girl about ten and her two younger brothers, probably about five and seven, stood on his doorstep, arms holding bags extended in anticipation. They were wearing all white, the girl in some kind of princess costume; the boys in white short-sleeved shirts and white pants. It was a warm October in southern Indiana, so none of them were wearing jackets. Taliaferro wasn't sure what they were supposed to be. *Maybe they're ghosts*, he thought.

"Do I get some of yours, or do I give some to you?" Taliaferro had teased. The kids didn't hesitate to explain—it was his job to provide the treat, of course. Taliaferro had obliged, bending to put a good-sized handful into each bag.

"Thank you!" the two oldest had said.

"Thanks, Nigger," the third, the youngest, had said.

It came out as naturally as *ball, car, peanut butter*, or any other word young boys often said. But it wasn't like that at all, because those words didn't surprise Taliaferro; they didn't hurt; they were expected.

Maybe I heard it wrong, Taliaferro told himself. Maybe that wasn't what the boy had said after all. But before he could convince himself, the boy's sister shushed him, confirming what Taliaferro had known but didn't want to believe. He shut the door. It was 2005. Of course racism still existed, still exists. Taliaferro knew that as well as anyone. But it was Halloween; there were kids and costumes and candy. Princesses and pirates were giggling, glowing necklaces guiding their way as their parents pulled younger siblings in wagons. The word was unexpected, especially from the mouth of a sandy-haired five-year-old in a Halloween costume on a warm night in an upper-middle-class neighborhood in Bloomington, Indiana.

Taliaferro had experienced racism in Bloomington before, but significant changes, some inspired by him, had occurred since he had played football for Indiana University in the 1940s and lived in a segregated Bloomington. This neighborhood was also different from the working-class world he had lived in when he played football for all-black Gary Roosevelt High School in Gary, Indiana. It was in that neighborhood, however, that Taliaferro was first recognized for his football prowess, and it was football that had removed him from the relative shelter from racism that his Gary neighborhood had provided.

1944–45: TALIAFERRO'S FOOTBALL ROOTS

"I WANT TO BE A boxer," George Taliaferro told his mother. Young boys often want to emulate their favorite professional athletes, but in the late 1930s, the only African American professional athletes were boxers and baseball players, and the baseball players could only play in the segregated Negro league. Jackie Robinson hadn't yet shattered the barrier that kept young African American boys from dreaming. Naturally, then, Taliaferro wanted to be a boxer. His mother had heard him and probably would have preferred to ignore him, but knowing that young boys don't let go of an idea once they have one, she needed a different tactic. So Virnater Taliaferro looked at her son, who was already getting bigger than she was, with the knowing look all moms give when they know ahead of time that they've won an argument.

"You can be a boxer, but you can't live in this house," she responded matter-of-factly. She had him, and she knew it. He had learned long ago that when his mother said something, "you don't try to reinterpret it—she meant what she said." In this case, Taliaferro determined that leaving the source of "three squares and a flop" could only be bad decision-making. So he turned his sights to the unattainable. He would be a professional football player instead. But, as in baseball, at the time there was a pronounced color line in professional football. Growing up in an integrated neighborhood had left him unaware of this. Someday, he decided, he was going to play for the Chicago Bears. Luckily, no one told him how unlikely that was.

If he was serious about becoming a football player, he was going to have to get his hands on a football. So Taliaferro enlisted the help of his friends, and together they scoured their Gary, Indiana, neighborhood for cans and other items they could sell. Their persistence paid off, and eventually they had the money to buy the prized possession. They spent an entire afternoon testing it out, laughing as they played catch, made tackles, and planned strategy. When it was time to go home, they had a tough decision to make: Who would get to take the ball home? In Gary, streets on the east side of town were named after states, in the order of their entrance into the union. Streets on the west side were named after the presidents, in chronological order. After much discussion involving taking turns and flipping coins, they decided that the Taliaferro house, located on the 2600 block of Madison Street, was the most centrally located. One of Taliaferro's friends lived on the 2400 block; the other on the 2800 block. Keeping the precious commodity at his house would make it easy for all of them to retrieve the ball when they needed it. Not that there would be too many times when they weren't playing with it together anyway.

Football quickly replaced other sandlot games, like Cock the Rooster, a game involving any number of kids who had to remain inside a set of drawn boundaries. One person, the rooster, had to tackle as many people as he could. Anyone who was tackled or who ran out of bounds became a rooster too. There was no other organization to it, but Taliaferro partially credited this childhood game with the style of running he developed later as a football player. He often won Cock the Rooster by avoiding tackles until he was the last one remaining, and Taliaferro believed it was good preparation for his football career. "Just add a ball and some equipment, and you have a halfback," he said.

While he and his friends occasionally still played Cock the Rooster, football became the game of choice. They named their sandlot team for the street they lived on; the Madison Street Tigers did not limit themselves to football, though. They also played baseball and basketball at Circus Field against other sandlot teams in their neighborhood. Sometimes Taliaferro would be so excited to get up and play the next morning that he would get out of bed at nine thirty or ten o'clock at night and ask his mother, "Is it morning yet?" Shaking her head, she would send him back to bed and tell him to wait until morning. It was hard to fall asleep on those nights of football dreams.

It is not surprising that these sandlot games were a source of entertainment for Taliaferro and his friends. Their neighborhood was made of modest one-story homes in the heart of Gary, a steel town located just thirty miles east of Chicago on the shore of Lake Michigan. Gary, Indiana, was actually created by the US Steel Corporation in 1906 for the sole purpose of steel production. It was even named after the corporation's chairman of the board, Elbert H. Gary. During Gary's development, the steel industry focused on the mills themselves and not on planning the town, which was thus left largely to land speculators. It didn't take long for slums to develop. The steel mill workers, mostly immigrants and African Americans, populated the city, which was defined by the relationships among the various ethnic groups and the city's dependence on the steel industry. This dependence left Gary particularly vulnerable during the Great Depression. The decline of the steel industry continued well into the twentieth century, and by the late 1980s and 1990s, Gary had become a city with one of the highest murder rates in the world, a fact Taliaferro attributed to the loss of the steel mills and the increase in drug use on the streets. This, however, was not the town of George Taliaferro's childhood. Although the Depression meant financial difficulty at times, the Gary of Taliaferro's youth was a much different place.

Taliaferro was born on January 8, 1927, in Gates, Tennessee, where he lived just down the street from *Roots* author and Malcolm X biographer Alex Haley. When he was just an infant, his family moved to "the region," as Gary and other northwestern Indiana cities are sometimes called because of their close proximity to Chicago. Life in Gary for the Taliaferros and other steel mill families often meant financial hardship, but it also allowed for a unique interaction of various ethnic groups. Despite the economic struggles, Taliaferro said his completely integrated neighborhood was "the way all towns ought to be." It may have been the socioeconomic equality of the people in the neighborhood or the fact that those who weren't black were immigrants, sharing similar experiences, having come from Italy, Germany, Croatia, Poland, Serbia, and other mainly European countries. They all got along. Pig roasts, an important part of Serbian culture, became a regular part of life for all of the neighborhood families. A Serbian family would slowly roast a pig on a big spit, and the rest of the families would bring side dishes. It didn't matter that the kids were of different races; they were friends. The kids played together without incident while the adults cooked and talked, often about sports and local athletes. "It was a melting pot," Taliaferro said.

Like the Taliaferro home, most homes were modest one-stories. The only exception was the home directly across the street from the Taliaferros'. It was the biggest home in the neighborhood, with two stories and a basement, but unlike most it was shared by two families. The Callaways, who had eight children, resided on the first floor and in the basement. Another family lived on the second floor. Like the other homes in the neighborhood, the Callaway home was well kept. Although the homes were small, a lot of pride went into keeping the lawns neatly trimmed and into applying fresh coats of paint when needed. There weren't any apartment buildings in the neighborhood, but there were two grocery stores, small mom-and-pop stores whose owners were neighbors themselves and knew each of their patrons by name. Most of the homes belonged to two-parent families. The only kid Taliaferro knew who belonged to a single-parent home was his close friend Chester "Chet" Davis. Since everyone looked out for everyone else, Chet still had a lot of adults in his life. As Chet said, "Mrs. Taliaferro used to yell at me all the time." Even the teachers at Taliaferro's school lived in the neighborhood and knew the kids by name. He and his friends used to climb onto a fence to reach the cherries on a neighbor's tree. When the adults discovered what they were doing, they found a unique way to discourage the theft. They baked a cherry pie for the kids, but they added an extra ingredient: castor oil. Even into adulthood, Taliaferro did not like cherry pie.

In his neighborhood the children had to obey all of the adults, not just their own parents. Taliaferro recalled, "If Mrs. Callaway told me to do something, it was done. If not, she would call Mom and Dad, and I'd be dead anyway." Chores were another expectation of Gary youth. Taliaferro, who was the second oldest, shared chores with his four siblings: older brother James and younger siblings Rozell, Claude, and Ernestine. The chores were divided, not equally but based on their ages and abilities, so Taliaferro and James had the bulk of the work. A strong work ethic, developed throughout his youth, became an important part of George Taliaferro's character.

He still vividly remembers the time his father asked him to dig out a garden in the backyard by the time he returned from work, and the disappointment in his father's voice when he failed to do so. He had planned on doing it, but before he could start digging, friends came by asking if he wanted to go to the neighborhood pool. Youth, heat, and humidity made it impossible for him to resist the temptation, but he rationalized that he could get back in time to dig the garden because his father wouldn't be home until four anyway. He went, and after swimming for a while, he lay down by the pool to dry off. What he hadn't planned on was falling asleep. He woke with a start.

"What time is it?" he asked the lifeguard nearest him. It was almost four. There was no way he would get it done. Still, he jumped up and ran as fast as he could, but he was only home a few minutes before his father arrived.

"A man is only as good as his word," his father said when he saw that the garden had not been dug. Stung by his father's disappointment, Taliaferro decided to make it right. He grabbed a shovel and got started. He wasn't finished when the sun set, so his mom held a lantern for him while he worked. He dug until he finished, having learned a lesson he would take with him for the rest of his life.

When Taliaferro was twelve or thirteen, he was a golf caddy at the North Gleason Golf Course in Gary. That is where he first met the man who had inspired him to tell his mother he would be a boxer someday. Apparently, Joe Louis was almost as good at golf as he was at boxing. When he golfed in Chicago, he would first come to the course in Gary to hone his skills. He always chose Taliaferro to be his caddy, for a couple of reasons. "He chose me because I did the job the way he wanted," Taliaferro said. Taliaferro didn't swing Louis's clubs or set his bag down where he didn't want it, and he had a knack for finding the balls. Louis also preferred the "Little Big-Head Boy," as he referred to Taliaferro, because, as Taliaferro explained, "I was always clean. I didn't wear new clothes, but they were clean." The fact that Louis would choose him over other caddies said something to Taliaferro. It told him, "You are somebody." His parents and Joe Louis had done that for him—instilled in him that he had worth, something he would spend decades of his life doing for others. Taliaferro didn't like playing golf then—caddying was just a job. In fact, he said that at that age, he "would rather go to hell than swing a golf club"—but that when he got older and "understood the practice and knowledge involved," he "couldn't stay away."

When they weren't doing chores, Gary's youth managed to keep themselves busy and out of trouble with outdoor activities like climbing trees, swimming, and playing sandlot baseball and football games. While they kept themselves entertained, adults also needed an escape from the financial struggles they faced, especially during the Depression. It is no surprise, then, that Gary residents took a keen interest in high school athletics and in their star high school athletes, an inexpensive interest that generated a strong sense of community pride. Having developed his skills in the sandlot games, Taliaferro became one of those stars when he attended all-black Gary Roosevelt High School. Although his neighborhood was completely integrated, the schools were not. Taliaferro attended Gary Roosevelt, which was an elementary, junior high, and high school. Despite living only a couple of blocks from Gary Roosevelt, one of Taliaferro's best friends, Nick Miller, had to be driven to all-white Emerson High School by his father. Placement in the three schools was based on geography. The northern district was all-white Emerson High School; the central district was all-black Gary Roosevelt; and in between was integrated Froebel, a school that would soon make national headlines.

By the time Taliaferro was in his freshman and sophomore years of high school, the Depression had been over for a while, the world was once again at war, and Gary Roosevelt was permitted to compete against all-white schools in track and field because it was a noncontact sport. However, football, a full-contact sport, was still segregated. This made it difficult for the Gary Roosevelt football team, which often had to endure long road trips in order to compete against other all-black schools. Wendell Phillips and DuSable, all-black schools in Chicago, were among the closest. Indianapolis's Crispus Attucks High School was a couple of hours away but still closer than Vashon and Sumpter High Schools in St. Louis and Lincoln High School in Evansville, Indiana. One of the longest road trips actually took the Gary Roosevelt football team about eight hundred miles to Tuskegee, Alabama, for a game.

World War II increased the difficulty of these long road trips. Gas rationing and the fact that there were no buses meant the team had to pile into the cars of coaches and teachers, adults who were painfully aware of the reason they had to travel so far for the games. The teenagers on the football team, excited to be doing what they loved, took little notice of it or of the fact that they dressed in hand-me-down uniforms donated by Northwestern University. Taliaferro's uniform hung from his lean frame. It was so big, in fact, that it was literally taped to his body, a stark contrast to the new, perfectly fitting uniforms worn by players in the area's all-white high schools. Since they didn't play against those teams, though, his team members were unaware of the contrast. The Gary Roosevelt players had not known any other world than the sheltered lives they led in their Gary neighborhoods. (This would change during Taliaferro's junior year, when "colored" and parochial schools were admitted into the Indiana High School Athletic Association and black and white schools were permitted to compete against each other.)

Besides, Taliaferro was more focused on the thrill of competition and the recognition it brought than on the segregation that forced his team to travel. He reveled in the attention that came with being one of Gary Roosevelt's elite athletes. His athleticism wasn't limited to football, although that was the sport that would eventually take him somewhere. He was also a swimming champion and a part of Gary's state championship track teams of 1944 and 1945. He even set a record on the pole vault of twelve feet, six inches, which stood for fifteen years. On top of that he lettered in football, baseball, basketball, and track all four years of high school, earning sixteen letters in all. He was basking in the spotlight, enjoying his status as a star athlete.

Natural athletic ability like that which Taliaferro possessed was recognized in Gary, a town some people considered to have one of the best athletic programs in the nation. His success made him a local celebrity. That was especially true at school. Of this attention, Taliaferro said simply, "Everybody in that school loved me for one reason: because I was George Taliaferro." One such admirer was Sydney Cummings, who lived across the street and followed his hometown hero around. A couple of years younger, he would follow Taliaferro home from school and offer to carry his shoes for him just so he could spend time with his hero. Cummings couldn't have realized what a special honor it was that Taliaferro allowed him to do so. Taliaferro shined those cleats every day, considering them his life. And, he would point out later in life, knowing the opportunities his football career had afforded him, he was right to think so.

On school nights, Sydney Cummings would be sent to bed early by his mother, who wanted him to be well rested for school. She didn't realize that he couldn't go to sleep anyway, not until he heard Taliaferro coming home. He would lie in bed, staring at the ceiling and listening for the familiar sound of Taliaferro's whistling. It was so quiet on their street, he could hear it from halfway down the block. "That whistlin' thing is what got me. I just got happy when I heard it," Cummings said. He would wait until Taliaferro got closer; then he would yell from his window, "Hey, Fat!"—Taliaferro's high school nickname—"How you doin'?" Taliaferro would always respond, usually gently reminding Cummings that he should be getting to sleep. Then, and only then, could Cummings fall asleep. His interest in Taliaferro's football success was so keen that he even decided to become a mascot for the team.

Cummings was just one example of the Gary Roosevelt Panthers' fan base. To satisfy these hardcore football fans, Norman S. Werry, sports editor for the *Gary Post-Tribune*, wrote weekly updates about the exploits of their beloved football team. Werry often referred to Taliaferro in his articles. Even when Gary Roosevelt High School did not win, Werry wrote rave reviews about Taliaferro's performances. A shutout by Hammond Catholic Central in his senior year was just one example. Werry wrote after that game, "Central intercepted a Roosevelt pass and then got a completion before the Panthers could put on the brakes and give Taliaferro a chance to get off one of several booming punts which were a major factor in keeping the Panthers in the game." After another loss against Horace Mann, Werry described Taliaferro's contribution to the team. "The Panthers wasted no time getting their touchdown starting the third quarter when George Taliaferro ran the kickoff back 35 yards to the Mann 40. . . . Then Taliaferro swung wide at his right end on a weak side sweep for 12 yards and a first down on the Mann 20," he wrote.

Werry's references were even more glowing, of course, after the many Gary Roosevelt wins, to which Taliaferro was always a major contributor. After the Froebel game, for example, Werry wrote, "The Panthers did not count until the third quarter when George Taliaferro ripped over his right guard from three yards out after gaining 15 yards on a pass from Cornelius Sneed. . . . Taliaferro added the extra point with a perfect placement to complete the scoring in one of the wackiest games ever engaged in by any Steel City rivals." *Ugliest* might have been a better term for the game, as there were fourteen total fumbles. Still, Taliaferro's impressive performance earned the team a 7–0 win over Froebel.

Tom Kennedy also wrote about Taliaferro's performances. After another win against South Bend Central, he wrote, "Hard hitting George Taliaferro turned in one of his customary bang-up performances on the turf of Gleason field. . . . Taliaferro put Roosevelt out in front at the outset when he whipped a nifty 21-yard pass to quarterback Charles White. . . . Roosevelt came up with its best drive in the fourth period to account for its final score. It covered 62 yards and ended with Taliaferro going six yards on a center smash to score standing up. On the previous play he had passed 21 yards to Johnny Nickols for a first down."

In the last game of the season, against Tolleston, Taliaferro contributed with three major punts, including a sixty-four-yarder into the end zone and a seventy-six-yarder. It wasn't just Taliaferro's punts that were impressive that night, however. Taliaferro "cut sharply over his left tackle and out-ran the Raider secondary for a 56-yard touchdown," Werry wrote. With two touchdowns and an extra point, Taliaferro had earned a position of third in points in the state, and Gary Roosevelt came off the season with its best record in years, at five wins and three losses.

Panther fans, excited about their winning season, showered the team and its stars with attention. While all of the accolades should have been satisfying for Taliaferro, instead he found himself frustrated by a system he was just beginning to realize was keeping him from achieving everything he was capable of. Sure, he was enjoying the recognition his star status brought, and Werry and other sportswriters had eloquently praised him all season for his football prowess. He had even managed to draw the attention of some college recruiters. Taliaferro was beginning to see beyond the immediate gratification his ability brought, however, and to recognize the reality of a system of racism that kept him from achieving his full potential. Taliaferro was not satisfied because when recruiters asked if he had won any awards, he could only give a negative reply.

This would have been easier for him to swallow if it had been a lack of ability or a lack of motivation on his part that kept him from earning these honors. But it simply was not the case; the numbers spoke for themselves. Most frustrating to Taliaferro was that he lacked not the skill but the skin color for receiving these honors. Because they attended an all-black school, Gary Roosevelt's athletes were not eligible for any postseason honors, and the team was not permitted to play in any postseason tournaments. "We were not recognized, because we were black. For no other reason. And this frustrated me," Taliaferro said.

Taliaferro wasn't the only person who thought he was deserving of an award. Sportswriter Bob Hammel, Indiana's first Mr. Football, also believed that was the case. In a 1995 *Bloomington Herald-Times* article, Hammel wrote about past football players he thought would have been named All-State if that honor had existed when they were playing. On his list, Hammel included Les Bingaman of Gary Lew-Wallace, who went on to be an all-pro center for the Detroit Lions, and George Taliaferro. Although he was flattered by Hammel's recognition, Taliaferro also felt compelled to correct him. He would not have been considered for the honor even if it had existed, he explained to Hammel, simply because the color of his skin would have made him ineligible.

In a time of blatant segregation, it was Taliaferro's football prowess that was going to create opportunities for him, though he was unaware of that at the time. His unique ability to run, pass, and kick, and do it all well, made him a triple threat on the football field. Often, he would score the touchdown and then follow it by earning the extra point. This, he said, was what made him such a valuable player: "They [opponents] never knew what I was going to do with the ball, and I could do anything that needed to be done. I could throw it. I could kick it. I could catch it. I could run with it. And the defenses that were set up specifically to stop me were not what they would have set up for anybody else. They could not take risks when the ball came to me. So, what they had to do was to spread out and keep me from darting through the holes."

Not only was Taliaferro a triple threat on offense, but he was equally skilled on defense. This, and a little luck, started him on the road to trailblazing. His most notable game of the season finally earned him some real attention outside of Gary, attention that also led to a football scholarship. Ironically, it was a game Gary Roosevelt was never anticipated to play. This game, which was never on the schedule, went against the status quo because it pitted all-black Gary Roosevelt against an all-white school. The product of a fluke chance, this game, against football powerhouse East Chicago Roosevelt, changed the course of George Taliaferro's life.

East Chicago was not the average high school football team. It was quite the contrary. In fact, in the early 1940s, "East Chicago Roosevelt was," according to an article by sportswriter Mike Whicker, "the Goliath of Indiana high school football." The undefeated Rough Riders "owned the gridiron. [They were] The colossus no one could beat." Whicker advised their potential opponents, "Don't even try. Just take your lumps and be thankful you walked away." Gary Roosevelt, it seemed, would be attempting to do the impossible.

An open date at the end of the schedule would not offer the kind of preparation East Chicago's coach, Pete Rucinski, wanted for his championship-bound team. He worried that not playing for two weeks would soften his players. He wanted them to remain sharp and focused, so he decided to schedule a game that would challenge his team and keep them geared up for the championship game. Gary Roosevelt High School was the perfect solution. Being ineligible for postseason tournaments because it was an all-black school, Gary Roosevelt would be available to play an unscheduled game. However, it was also a first-rate team that would provide sufficient challenge to his players. Pete Rucinski contacted Gary Roosevelt's coach, Bo Mallard, and asked if his team would do it. Mallard agreed to the scrimmage, and they set the date. At the time, neither coach realized the impact that conversation would have. It set into motion events that not only would change the course of one young man's life but would ultimately have an impact on the system of segregation and the sport of football as a whole.

Rucinski and Mallard scheduled the game for October 6, 1944. The Gary Roosevelt Panthers were geared up and ready to play. The game afforded them the opportunity to compete against a school that had previously been off limits to them as an opponent; it was their chance to prove themselves. They understood what a football power they were facing, but they did not let it discourage them. Although Taliaferro was ready, he couldn't help but be nervous. He knew they were playing against a notorious East Chicago football team that would provide more competition than he and his teammates had ever faced. This time there would be no long road trip to get there; the game was practically in their own backyard. There would be a lot of people he knew, probably his entire neighborhood, watching this game.

Before the game, Coach Mallard launched into his usual locker-room pep talk. He wanted to get his team mentally prepared for the challenge they were about to face. "Football is a team sport," he told them, "but each member has to fight an individual battle as well. If one person makes a good block, then another one can score." He continued, stressing the importance of the fundamentals, like blocking and tackling. When Coach Mallard finished his pep talk, his Panthers ran onto the field to face the heavily favored East Chicago Rough Riders, a team that Whicker wrote was "devouring their foes like some hungry behemoth."

No one, including the players, was surprised when East Chicago took an early lead. Their first score came on a fifty-yard drive, and it didn't take long for them to add two points to their lead with a safety when the Panthers had trouble fielding the kick-off. At the end of the first quarter, the Panthers found themselves already trailing the Rough Riders by nine points. Getting behind early to East Chicago made an already impossible task even more unlikely. Somehow, they managed to keep their hearts and heads in the game despite the fact that many of the spectators had already counted them out of it. Their steely resolve paid off about halfway through the second quarter when Leroy Allen scored on a fifty-yard drive, as *Gary Post-Tribune* sportswriter Joe Kutch wrote, through "the entire East Chicago defense."

The Panthers heeded Mallard's locker-room advice and focused on basic blocking and tackling, somehow managing to keep the Rough Riders from scoring the rest of the game. There were some lumps involved in this defensive matchup. According to Kutch, "Play had to be stopped on several occasions to revive some of the boys who got hit a little too hard." Gary Roosevelt's offense managed to sneak in a touchdown, making the score 7 to 9. Then, Gary Roosevelt got possession of the ball back with an opportunity not only to close the gap but also to take the lead from their new rivals. This is when, "taking advantage of the edge which the versatile Taliaferro gained with his booming punts, the Gary Gridders found themselves on the Twin City men's twenty-two yard line," as Kutch wrote. Taliaferro hadn't done it alone. Coach Mallard managed to pull one over on East Chicago's Coach Rucinski the final play of the game. Cornelius Sneed, the quarterback, threw the ball to Taliaferro, who usually played tailback. Kutch described what happened next: "Taliaferro snagged the ball on the two-yard line and then argued with a host of Rider tacklers before ending up on the seat of his pants with the upset victory in the bag."

In Indiana high school football history, East Chicago Roosevelt High School is in the record books for winning thirty-four straight games from 1944 through 1948. The game against Gary Roosevelt's Panthers, an unscheduled game against an unlikely rival, did not count. To Taliaferro, however, this mattered very little. To him the satisfaction of beating the state's powerhouse was still an overwhelming feeling, even if his team wouldn't get formal recognition for it. "A fighting Gary Roosevelt football team which wouldn't believe what everybody was saying about that powerful East Chicago Roosevelt eleven went out to the lair of the Rough Riders last night and didn't start home until they had licked the previously unbeaten boys 13 to 9," Kutch wrote. He had to preface the article title with a statement about his honesty, just in case anyone doubted him. The article, "No Foolin', Panthers Trip Rough Riders, 13–9," came out the next day.

The title is not surprising given the fact that even Gary Roosevelt's football players couldn't believe they had won. "It was hard to imagine that Gary Roosevelt had beaten East Chicago Roosevelt," Taliaferro said of his and his teammates' initial reaction.

Although it was the most important game he had ever played, his parents were not there to see his game-winning touchdown. He hadn't expected them to be, though. They had never seen a single game of their college-bound son's high school football career. It wasn't that they didn't care; they just didn't understand the game, Taliaferro said.

Virnater Taliaferro, a heavyset woman with a sixth-grade education, had almost kept her son from playing football. It was a dangerous sport, and one she did not want to see her son playing. When he had first brought home a permission slip for her to sign so he could play, she had refused to do so. It wasn't like the sandlot games he and his friends had played, she thought. They had been just kids then, and they hadn't needed any pads. She didn't like the idea of him playing on the school team, which she felt would be more dangerous. But Taliaferro, who was determined to play, wouldn't accept no for an answer. He continued to press her until she finally agreed to sign under certain conditions. First, she said, he had to submit to a physical exam, one that she, the family "doctor," would give Taliaferro herself. Taliaferro said that it was an exam that "few human beings and no animals could pass," and it was a ritual for the four years he was in high school. The other condition was that Taliaferro had to get a copy of the rules and requirements for the football team from Coach Mallard.

Once Taliaferro had satisfied all of her conditions, his mother finally acquiesced and gave him permission to play. He took a lot of pride in this, and every night he came home from practice with his jockstrap, underwear, and socks for her to launder. Then he would sit down and shine his football cleats. Football had become his life, and it showed. He was tearing up the field every game. In a 1993 article by Al Hamnik, Taliaferro's Gary Roosevelt teammate J. Donald Leek described him: "He could really take care of business. He'd run by you, over you, whatever was required. George played for every game, every down. We didn't platoon in those days. You played until the game was over or you got hurt, whichever came first."

The East Chicago game was no exception.

Taliaferro's performance and game-winning touchdown had not disappointed his loyal Gary fan base. Werry, as usual, reported on the game. "This one goes into the book as one of the all-time upsets in Calumet schoolboy football," he wrote. Taliaferro, who was still having a hard time believing they had won, kept playing it over and over in his head. He remembered cradling the ball, dropping on his butt in the end zone, and holding on to the ball "as if it were life itself." In an interesting twist of fate, it was, because it was his performance during this game that would change the course of Taliaferro's life forever. Taliaferro, though not yet famous for his triple-threat abilities, had played the game of his life. Kutch wrote, "Leading the Panther gridders was Taliaferro, a young man who can do anything a star should be able to do. His bone-crushing tackles, powerful running and long-distance booting would make any coach smile with satisfaction." Any coach but the other team's, that is. Taliaferro had not gone unnoticed by East Chicago coach Pete Rucinski.

"Rucinski became my greatest admirer," Taliaferro said. Rucinski had even joked that his team would never play Gary Roosevelt again. But Rucinski was altogether serious when he contacted a personal friend, Indiana University coach Bo McMillin, to tell him of his discovery. Taliaferro explained that Rucinski told McMillin, "There is a kid in Gary, Indiana, that you really need at Indiana University." He described Taliaferro's prowess, the triple-threat performance against his own previously undefeated Rough Riders. There was no better tailback in the state of Indiana, he said. The only problem was that Taliaferro was black. According to Taliaferro, McMillin replied, "He can be purple if he can do the things that you just told me he can do."

In fact, Bo McMillin was so convinced that he wasted no time in dispatching recruiter J. C. "Rooster" Coffee to Gary to talk to

Taliaferro and Gary Roosevelt coach Bo Mallard. The trio met in Mallard's office. Coffee, a guard, was one of just a handful of black players on Indiana University's football team. As a student at Indiana University (IU), Coffee had also helped President Herman B Wells integrate the gymnasium pool. According to Bob Cook, a former Indiana University athletic director and McMillin biographer, Wells had asked for the most popular black athlete and had been told about Coffee. According to Taliaferro, Wells urged Coffee to just "go in [the pool] and don't ask anybody." Coffee obliged by jumping naked into the whites-only pool. Nudity was considered more hygienic and better for the pool filters, which were not as efficient as they are today. Plus, the material that made up the swimsuits was heavier and harder to filter. So nudity in pools was fairly common, but integration of pools was not. Still, no one seemed bothered when Coffee jumped in. While Coffee was not the first black man to jump into the pool, he was the first to do it successfully. According to Taliaferro, another black man, J. B. Clark, jumped into the pool once but was immediately kicked out. Subsequently, the pool was drained of its water, to be replaced by fresh, new water, presumably that had not touched the skin of a black man. It was an altogether different story when Coffee, the popular athlete, jumped in. No one complained, other black students also began to use the pool, and soon it was integrated without incident. Coffee's status as an athlete and his dynamic personality probably had a lot to do with the pool's successful integration.

In the McMillin biography, Cook writes of a time when McMillin was having the team work on a new offensive maneuver and was becoming frustrated with the lack of progress. McMillin had said, "Daggone it. This play could be a topper, and we're going to work on it until we're black in the face." According to Cook, Coffee responded, "Well, Coach, I guess that means I can go in." Everyone laughed. Coffee, then, was an ideal candidate to visit Taliaferro, who could relate to another popular black athlete.

Despite Coffee's help in recruiting Taliaferro, there was a lot of doubt about whether he would actually play for the Indiana University Hoosiers. There were a lot of forces working against such an outcome. One obstacle was Taliaferro's Gary fans. Some people from his predominantly African American community were vocal in their reservations about him attending Indiana University. They were suspicious, Taliaferro said, because Coach McMillin hailed from Texas, a place they associated with intense racism. Moreover, Pat McPherson, another popular black athlete from Gary, had attended IU in the 1930s, only to transfer to all-black Wilberforce in Ohio because of the extreme racism he had faced in Bloomington, Indiana. Gary fans did not want Taliaferro to face a similar fate. Indiana University, they felt, was just not the right place for their star athlete.

Racism wasn't a big concern for Taliaferro. He had lived most of his life in that Gary neighborhood, where he had been relatively sheltered from the harsh reality of racial discrimination and intolerance. The only advice about racism that his parents had ever given him was to just behave himself, not to give anyone a reason to harm him in the first place, advice that parents more than seventy years later are still giving to young black men. Still, Taliaferro knew racism existed. He still remembers playing against Horace Mann. After the game, the two teams went directly to their locker rooms, forgoing the usual handshakes. Before he left the field, though, Carl Biesecker, one of Horace Mann's players, crossed over to shake George's hand.

"It was a pleasure to play against you," Biesecker said.

Taliaferro was shocked. Later, he explained, "Mother and Father always told me I was somebody. I wish everybody did that for their child." Joe Louis had made him feel that way too. But this was different. This was a white player telling him he was somebody. Taliaferro would never forget that moment. He didn't know it yet, but football would throw him and Biesecker together again, leading to a lifelong friendship.

Gary residents were not the only obstacle coming between George Taliaferro and Indiana University. Other schools, like UCLA and Illinois, were also actively recruiting him. In addition, Taliaferro was giving serious consideration to attending North Carolina Central, an all-black college. The transition from an all-black high school to a historically black college (HBC) was a natural choice. Like so many high school seniors, he had a difficult decision to make. Unlike today's high school seniors, however, he had to contend with World War II, which played a major role in determining where he would end up going.

Although World War II was coming to an end, the draft was not. Mrs. Parham, the Taliaferros' next-door neighbor, was on the draft board. She explained to Robert and Virnater Taliaferro that their son would have a better chance of being deferred from the draft if he remained in Indiana while attending college. In other words, if he attended Indiana University, he would be less likely to be drafted than if he attended any of the other schools he was considering. Of course, the Taliaferros preferred not to have their son fight in the war and encouraged him to take Mrs. Parham's information into serious consideration as he made his decision. So it was Mrs. Parham who became IU's best recruiter, sealing the deal for Coach Bo McMillin.

Another Gary resident, Ora Wildermuth, would have played a key role in Taliaferro's decision if Taliaferro had been aware of Wildermuth's feelings on integration. Wildermuth was on IU's board of trustees, where he was very vocal about his opposition to integration. Taliaferro was unaware of this, however. He just knew that his neighbor, William Downs, was a domestic worker for Wildermuth and that Downs said Wildermuth was a fan of his. Taliaferro had no idea that the powerful alumnus and board of trustees member was trying to prevent integration at Indiana University. Tom Graham and Rachel Graham Cody's book about the Big Ten's first black basketball player, Bill Garrett, describes Garrett's experiences at Indiana University and Wildermuth's fight to keep segregation. They quote a letter from Wildermuth to the board's treasurer: "I am and shall always remain absolutely and utterly opposed to social intermingling of the colored race with the white." Wildermuth went on to write, "If a person has 1/16th colored blood in him, even though the other 15/16ths may be pure white, yet he is colored." Had Taliaferro known Wildermuth's position, he would have risked being drafted into World War II, against Mrs. Parham's advice, and attended another school. Today, Indiana University's intramural center is named in honor of Ora Wildermuth, but most students who pass through its doors probably know little about the man it was named after. If they did, public opinion may have demanded a name change.

Once he had decided to attend Indiana, word spread quickly throughout Gary Roosevelt. Apparently, the decision drew the concern of some of the school faculty, who worried that he would be more focused on football than academics at IU. They wanted his coaches to make sure that did not happen. So Taliaferro's principal, Mr. H. Theodore Tatum, football coach Bo Mallard, and track coach Leonard Douglas set up a meeting with IU president Herman B Wells. They impressed upon him the fact that they wanted Taliaferro to earn a college degree and that he was not to be "given" anything, no matter how important he was to the football team. Had the men known Herman B Wells and Coach Bo McMillin, they would have understood that such a visit was probably unnecessary.

That doesn't mean that their trip was unwarranted. In fact, it was probably brought about by Taliaferro himself, who had had some academic problems earlier in his high school career. In fact, he had almost dropped out of school. It was a spontaneous thing; he simply stayed home from school one day and told his parents that he planned to quit, that he was wasting time at school when he could be out earning money. He wanted to work in the steel mill like so many other men in Gary, to bring home a paycheck, to be a man. The US Steel Corporation and the US government had made a pact that during the war, because so many eligible workers were gone, high school seniors could work at the mill on weekends, even if they were not eighteen. Taliaferro worked there on weekends his senior year, in the mill where his father worked. He wanted to quit school and work there full-time to help his family. His father saw things differently, though.

"No way. Where are you going to live?" Robert Taliaferro asked. "There is no room for two men in this house, and *I* am the man in *this* house. You can take nothing with you. A man can provide for himself." Those few abrupt words had a big impact on Taliaferro, who wasn't quite ready to be that independent. His idea had been to earn a paycheck like a man but to continue to live at home, where his meals and laundry would be done for him, so he was easily convinced to remain in school. While that resolved the issue with his father, the issue still needed to be resolved at school.

Because he was accustomed to receiving praise following a football game and assumed it was more of the same when Coach Mallard called him to his office, Taliaferro quickly made his way there after class one day. That particular day, however, Mallard wasn't ready to praise. Instead, he looked Taliaferro square in the eye and said, "Son, you will not be playing football if you do not get your grades up."

"Nobody told me that," Taliaferro replied, but the conversation had shocked him more than his father's threat ever could have. He knew without a doubt that he could not give up football. That simply was not an option. He had been living for the sport ever since he and his friends had worked so hard to earn the money to buy that first football. Those sandlot games had created a passion in him. Taliaferro knew he had to start devoting himself to his studies.

It was this history that had prompted his principal and coaches to visit President Wells. Taliaferro, despite having been taught at an early age to value education, had not always been a model student, and college was going to require even more self-discipline academically, especially with the number of hours he would be devoting to football. His mentors simply wanted to ensure that he would achieve the same success academically as they were already confident he would attain in football.

So, despite a number of obstacles, Taliaferro's decision to play for Indiana University was finally made official, and the news quickly spread throughout his Gary neighborhood. He was the first person in his family to go to college, giving him the opportunity to get the education his parents wanted for him. They had told him nearly every day, "We love you. You must be educated." His father, who grew up in Tennessee in the early 1900s, had been denied the opportunity to get a formal education because he was black.

Taliaferro remembered telling his father once, "I want to be just like you."

"No way," his father had answered.

With no formal education, his father's only choice had been to make the most of his opportunity at the steel mill, and he had. He was never late, and he always put in a full day's work. But Taliaferro's father told him, "There is no reason for you to be like me because you will have more opportunity. Mine was the steel mill."

It wasn't long before Norman S. Werry, editor of the *Gary Post-Tribune* and the man who had so eloquently written about Taliaferro's accomplishments all season, contacted him. He wanted an interview with the IU-bound football star. Taliaferro agreed. Still conscious of his role as the local hero, Taliaferro dressed carefully for the interview. He decided on his black and gold Gary Roosevelt letterman sweater, which showed off all the letters he had earned, and black pants, so everyone would know that he was still "a dyed-in-the-wool Gary Roosevelt Panther." He was not nervous, and other than his attire, he did nothing to prepare for the interview because, he said, "The only thing I knew without a shadow of a doubt was that I was a good football player and given the chance, I could play with anyone." He had always been confident about his football ability.

His ability, however, would not be the focus of the interview. He showed up at the appointed time, and after the typical introductions, handshake, and small talk, the interview got under way. Taliaferro explained that he had decided to attend IU in the fall, where he would, of course, be a member of the Hurryin' Hoosiers football team under Coach Bo McMillin.

"How do you think you are going to make out at Indiana University?" Werry asked.

Taliaferro, sitting directly across from him, legs crossed, nonchalantly, and with a hint of the cockiness of a star football player, replied, "I should make out okay." He meant it, though. It wasn't bravado; he just knew he could play the game. Werry wasn't looking for that response, though. He restated the question.

"I mean, how do you think you are going to adjust to playing with white players?" he asked.

Because he had never considered his color a factor in his ability to play, Taliaferro was taken aback by the question at first. Still, it was a valid question as far as the people in Taliaferro's neighborhood were concerned, those who had discouraged him from attending Indiana in the first place. There were only a handful of black players at major universities. He was certain to face racism in some form—it was just a matter of how and when. How would he make out on Bloomington's segregated campus, they wondered. Once over his initial surprise at the question—he had thought he was going to be asked about his football ability—Taliaferro answered. His answer was an early indicator of the combination of confidence, humor, and optimism with which he would handle obstacles in football and in life. He was going to need all of them. "If they put their pants on one leg at a time, I'll do fine," he answered.

1945–46: ADJUSTING TO LIFE AT INDIANA UNIVERSITY

THE DRIVE FROM GARY TO Bloomington is a scenic one. Just outside of Gary are miles of flat acres with the occasional white farmhouse scattered amid the countless corn and soybean fields so often associated with Indiana. As soon as Taliaferro was south of Indianapolis, however, the scenery abruptly changed, much like his life was going to. He was in the middle of southern Indiana's rolling hills. In the fall people come from all over to see the vibrant autumn shades and the covered bridges tucked away in this hilly landscape. And because this is Indiana, it isn't difficult to find basketball hoops above the doors of century-old barns. Taliaferro was aware of the striking difference in the scenery, yet he was blissfully unaware of the many personal changes in store for him, which would begin with the upcoming football season.

This bus driver doesn't even know where Bloomington is, Taliaferro thought as he looked out the window at altogether unfamiliar scenery. In high school, he had played a game in Bloomington, but he didn't remember it looking anything like this. He was certain that the Greyhound driver's route was not the same. He looked around to see if other passengers were worried too. Since they all seemed content, he decided to keep quiet, even though he was sure they were going the wrong direction. He looked out the window again to pass the time. He didn't want to miss a thing, especially once they had gotten to those rolling hills. He had also come to Bloomington once on a recruiting trip, but it had been raining and he had been with other athletes and coaches, so he hadn't paid as much attention. This time, he couldn't take his eyes off the changing landscape, despite his worry that they were lost. "That's how naive I was," he said, remembering how surprised he had been to discover that the game he had played in Bloomington was in Illinois, not Indiana. That wasn't the only shock his arrival at Indiana University would bring.

The self-assurance he had displayed in his interview with Norman S. Werry was shaken when Taliaferro arrived in Bloomington in June 1945. The Greyhound bus finally came to a stop at Tenth and Walnut, where he disembarked and stretched his lean frame. Then he collected his things and got a taxi, not realizing that the home where he would be staying was just a few blocks away, at Eighth and Dunn. Taliaferro had graduated from Gary Roosevelt just a week earlier, on June 14. His early arrival in Bloomington was due to an invitation from Coach McMillin, who wanted to help ease the transition from high school to college for his young players. Arriving early gave the players the chance to learn, prior to the start of classes, the location on Indiana University's sprawling campus of the classroom buildings, practice fields, and dining areas. That way, they could devote their full attention to football when it was time to start the season. The transition to college life, however, would prove more difficult for McMillin's black players. For them, it was not just a matter of figuring out where their classes were. They also had to adjust to life on a segregated campus, to the invisible line that ran like a thick, ugly wall through Bloomington, cutting it in half, making much of it inaccessible to IU's black students. Taliaferro wouldn't take long to discover that he was in unfamiliar territory.

Soon after he arrived on campus, he reported to the football stadium, where he was ushered into a line of freshman players picking up football gear. To his surprise, he was the shortest and lightest person in the line of would-be players. Standing five foot eleven and weighing 195 pounds, he found himself in line in front of Pat Kane, who stood six foot three and weighed 210 pounds, and Tom Schwartz, a six-foot-five 215-pounder. Directly in front of Taliaferro was future football team captain John Goldsberry, who was six foot one and weighed 230 pounds. Their size difference, while apparent to everyone, seemed magnified to Taliaferro. Suddenly he wasn't the confident athlete he had been as one of Gary Roosevelt's stars. He couldn't even fake self-assurance. *Should I really be here?* he wondered. *They are taller and bigger than any football players I know. Will I fit in here?* He had to voice his doubts aloud.

"Are they all the same age as me?" he asked Coach McMillin. McMillin nodded in reply.

For the first time, the former Gary Roosevelt star wasn't the picture of cool confidence. "I am in the wrong place," he finally said to Coach McMillin. *All of them were right,* Taliaferro thought, reminding himself of the Gary fans who had doubted his decision to attend, who had vocalized doubts the moment they heard that Indiana was recruiting him. He remembered Werry's question too, and his confident reply that he would get along just fine.

It was to be the first of many times that Coach Bo McMillin would reassure Taliaferro, both on and off the football field.

"You were thoroughly scouted," he assured the shaken Taliaferro. "There *is* a place for you on Indiana University's football team." It wasn't just an empty statement to appease him. It reassured Taliaferro because he could hear the sincerity as McMillin told him that he looked forward to the role Taliaferro would play on his football team. There was a reason McMillin had dispatched Rooster Coffee to recruit him. McMillin knew football and had made it a point to pursue Taliaferro. He knew Taliaferro belonged on Indiana's football team. This reassurance wasn't enough to completely alleviate Taliaferro's anxiety, though.

Fig. 3.1 Indiana University football coach Alvin Nugent "Bo" McMillin works with his Hurryin' Hoosiers during football practice in July 1945. *Photo courtesy IU Archives.*

He had only been there one week when he asked McMillin, "When are we going to move into the dormitory?" McMillin explained that he wouldn't be moving into the dorm, that they weren't open to black students. Taliaferro, who understood that an education was more than reading books, became upset. He would be deprived of the experience of meeting people from all over the world and learning about their cultures because he wouldn't be living with them in the dorms. He called his father and told him he wanted to go home.

"Can you tell me why?" Robert Taliaferro asked.

Taliaferro explained. He couldn't go to the theater, swim in the pools, eat in the restaurants, live in the dorms, or sit in the front of the classrooms. He couldn't attend movies except on weekends, and at the commons, there was only one table, marked "colored," where he was permitted to sit. The table had ten spaces, so "if there were eleven blacks, one of them could not eat in that place," he explained.

His father asked, "Can I ask you one question? Is there another reason you are at Indiana University?" Then he hung up the phone. Robert Taliaferro, who smoked Chesterfield cigarettes or King Edward cigars and spoke very little, was his son's hero. He had raised five children on twenty-two dollars a week and was the first African American foreman at the steel mill because of his work ethic. Taliaferro thought that if anyone would have understood, it would have been his father. He cried for hours after his father hung up on him. It hurt more than anything he had experienced, Taliaferro explained, "because I thought of all the people on the planet Earth who would understand what it felt like to be discriminated against, it would be my father." Knowing that his father's life as an adolescent in Tennessee had been fraught with racism, he had been sure he would sympathize.

At some point Taliaferro must have finally fallen asleep. When he woke, he had more clarity regarding his situation. It was precisely because of the discrimination his father had faced that he was so insistent on Taliaferro remaining at Indiana. What his father had been trying to tell him, he realized, was that his football scholarship would enable him to get a college degree, something that would present opportunities for him later, keeping him from a life at the steel mill. "All I had to do was to apply myself and be educated," he decided. The rest, he would just have to deal with. At least for the moment.

While he may not have felt that he belonged on campus, any lingering doubts about whether he belonged on the football team were taken care of a short time later. At the first practice of the season, Taliaferro was asked to run one of McMillin's favorite plays. The T formation is just what it sounds like: a football formation that lines the players up in the shape of a T. At the bottom of the T is the quarterback, and three running backs are placed at

Fig. 3.2 Coach McMillin uses a chalkboard in the old trophy room of the men's gym to plan strategy. He enjoyed tricking opponents with creative plays like his Cockeyed T. Circa 1945. *Photo courtesy IU Archives.*

the top of the T: one on each end and one in the middle. This formation, Taliaferro said, had revolutionized football. It featured the use of a forward pass and put enormous pressure on the defense by spreading the offense's ability to use the entire field in a short amount of time. According to him, it also made the game more enjoyable to the fans, who could more easily follow the ball and who saw more scoring with the T formation.

Once everyone was doing the new T formation, Coach McMillin, known for his innovative style, had to change it to make it unique and interesting again. So he modified it. Instead of placing one running back on each end and one in the middle, McMillin would run a different version, his own Cockeyed T. For the Cockeyed T, he did not space the running backs evenly. Instead, he used an unbalanced line, shifting the quarterback right behind the guard and moving the right halfback to the outside end. The fullback was spotted behind the quarterback, and the left halfback was four yards behind the center. It seemed to work. "McMillin's Cockeyed T just baffled defenses," Taliaferro said.

Wanting to see what Taliaferro could do, McMillin put him in the formation. Taliaferro, who lined up as a tailback, handled the ball like the quarterback in the Cockeyed T. The ball was snapped to him, and he could pass it, hand it off, or run with it, depending on the play. The first time Taliaferro ran a play in the Cockeyed T, he kept the ball and ran with it, running eighty yards for a touchdown. McMillin called for the same play again, wanting to see if it was just a fluke. Again, Taliaferro ran eighty yards for a touchdown.

"Turn a little to the right, George," McMillin said after watching the two successive eighty-yard runs.

"But, Coach, how was it for distance?" Taliaferro replied, laughing. His execution of the play was, needless to say, a pleasant surprise for McMillin, and it promptly became McMillin's favorite play for him. "Let George do it," McMillin would yell when he called for the Cockeyed T. Despite his comparatively small stature, Taliaferro had earned a starting position for the Indiana Hurryin' Hoosiers, the Cream and Crimson.

While McMillin encouraged Taliaferro on the field, he also made a lasting impression on him in other ways. Coach McMillin's character affected Taliaferro, who noticed that his coach, among other things, refused to arrange class attendance, as other coaches were rumored to do. "My coach believed in winning, but never at all costs," Taliaferro said. McMillin's positive attitude also kept his players grounded. He pushed them on the football field, but he also pushed them to get an education. In fact, McMillin pushed Taliaferro harder in school than his own mother and father, his parents who said to him every day, "We love you. You must be educated," because they understood that education provided a way to avoid a long life of working in the steel mills. Taliaferro wondered if McMillin pushed so hard because the coach himself had left school without getting a degree, though he went back to finish it later. Or perhaps McMillin did not want people to perceive Taliaferro as just some "black dumb jock." Whatever his reason, the coach profoundly affected Taliaferro. "Bo McMillin changed my life," Taliaferro stated of the impact their relationship ultimately had on him.

There were many facets to Alvin "Bo" McMillin, a man who, biographer Bob Cook wrote, did not know his own age and had no birth certificate. The 175-pound McMillin was a fairly small man, in his forties, with a full head of gray hair. He had a button nose, big ears, and a Texas drawl. His childhood in Texas had been a struggle. His was a life of poverty, and he had to work hard at a young age to help his family. It may have been this childhood that forged in him a strong desire to champion the underdog—because, McMillin said, the underdog's "got something to fight for." As quarterback for Centre College in Danville, Kentucky, Bo McMillin was legendary. In 1921, his thirty-yard touchdown run was the only score of the game against a Harvard team that had been unbeaten for five years. The win by the Centre College Prayin' Colonels over Harvard is still considered one of the greatest upsets in college football, and McMillin's sole touchdown had earned him a ride on his team's shoulders. To sweeten the victory, McMillin, who didn't smoke or drink but who was known to gamble (the rumor was that he did it to help pay his college tuition), had even placed a winning bet on the upset. According to an article by Valarie Ziegler, his touchdown was the most famous one in Centre College football history, and during McMillin's entire five-year career at Centre, the team was only beaten three times.

His fame continued as a coach when he brought success to other underdogs. He had managed to bring winning seasons to Centenary College in Louisiana, Geneva College in Pennsylvania, and Kansas State University. A fourteen-year stint at Indiana University before he moved on to professional football would be no different. His first four seasons at Indiana also brought the first winning seasons the Hoosiers had seen in years. With success, though, McMillin also brought a strong sense of humor. Cook wrote that when the coach came to Indiana, knowing the state's fascination with basketball, he had said: "Oh, I love basketball too. I played it in high school. And I coached it. Like Bob Zuppke [Illinois coach] always said, 'It's a great recreational sport and something to do between the end of football and the beginning of spring practice.'" According to Taliaferro, McMillin could play any sport, including golf, pool, and even table tennis. The coach rarely cussed, but the players could tell if he was really upset when he would say, "Go piss in a lake!"

Each year his ability to keep the Old Oaken Bucket at Indiana University earned McMillin more respect from Hoosier fans. The Oaken Bucket game was created out of the high-spirited rivalry between two major Indiana universities, Indiana and Purdue. The two teams had been playing each other for more than thirty years, since 1891, when in 1925 a joint committee of the two schools decided to further the rivalry and excitement of the annual game. To do so, they decided that there should be a traditional trophy to go to the winner of the annual match between the two rival football teams. The committee decided on a well bucket as the trophy because it was something typically Hoosier, something everyone could associate with Indiana. Each year, possession of the wooden well bucket would go to the winner of the match. A link of either a block letter *I* or block letter *P* to represent the winning school would be attached to the trophy. The block letter links would easily enable the schools and their respective fans to determine who had held possession of the bucket most often, another way to sweeten the victory and intensify the rivalry. The first Oaken Bucket game was played at the dedication of the original Memorial Stadium on Indiana University's Bloomington campus. It ended in a 0–0 tie. Until McMillin came along, Purdue had managed to add more block letters to the trophy than Indiana. With McMillin at the helm, though, the Hoosiers began to catch up. Under McMillin's tutelage, the "po li'l boys," as McMillin called his team, earned more *I*s for the bucket than Purdue did *P*s. It was even rumored that his contract was ripped up after each Oaken Bucket game win and a new contract offering him more money would be signed. In jest, McMillin even began referring to the Old Oaken Bucket as his "meal ticket," according to Cook.

The football field was not the only place McMillin was assertive. McMillin was also ahead of his time when it came to civil rights. At a time when Big Ten basketball had a gentleman's agreement not to recruit black players, and while some other Big Ten football teams were without black players altogether, McMillin was not afraid to be different. It was not just black players he was willing to defend but anyone McMillin saw treated unfairly. In the McMillin biography, Cook recounts one incident involving Indiana's head trainer, Dwayne "Spike" Dixon, who had a noticeable limp. Dixon's first time on the field during a football game later brought complaints from a fan who called to voice his opinion about having a "crippled" trainer. Cook wrote that the assistant coaches took the phone away from McMillin after he yelled into the phone, "You object to what? His limp? I hadn't noticed it, does he limp? Look asshole, that limp is a result of a bout with Polio . . ."

And even when most schools, like other major Indiana universities Purdue and Notre Dame, did not have black players on the roster, "Bo didn't just accept them. Early on, he sought them just as actively as he did other prospects," Cook wrote. McMillin's pursuit of George Taliaferro was just one example. Cook also recounted an incident at an away game in Kentucky, in which McMillin changed the team's hotel because his black players were not permitted to stay there. This was often the case when teams from the North played teams in the South. Most of the time, the team ended up staying in two different hotels, one for the black

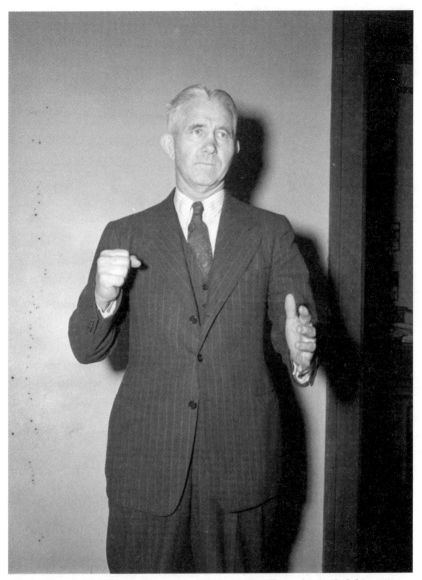

Fig. 3.3 Coach McMillin on January 15, 1945. McMillin, who hailed from Texas, was sometimes able to move his players to tears with his locker-room talks. *Photo courtesy IU Archives.*

players and one for the other members of the team, or the black players would stay in private residences. Although many people just accepted it as the way things were, McMillin wasn't like most people. He used his position to facilitate change, to fight for his players. When he was told that his black players couldn't stay in the hotel, he responded, "Then forget them. Find a hotel that wants us. That's a thing of the past," Cook recounted. Taliaferro recalled that he and his IU teammates, unlike most teams, were never split into different hotels on road trips. That would not be the case later in his career, when he would play for the army, and even later in professional football.

Despite McMillin's unfailing support of his black players, Taliaferro still had to face the color barriers that were drawn across Bloomington, Indiana, in the 1940s. After living in Gary, he experienced quite a culture shock. Racial tension was prevalent, even on his own football team. Taliaferro remembered a conversation he had with one teammate, an All-State football player out of Muncie, who asked him if he was All-State as well. When Taliaferro told him that he wasn't, the player wanted to know how he had managed to get a scholarship without that honor. During the conversation, the teammate had also made it clear that he wasn't accustomed to working with black players. Taliaferro decided not to argue but to let his ability speak for him. He just looked at his teammate and said, "I'll see you on the field." So, while no one called Taliaferro "nigger" and there were no fistfights, there were some players who, Taliaferro said, "just didn't want to be bothered with me. They treated me like I was nobody, nobody." There was one player who was more vocal than others about his attitude toward the black players, Taliaferro said, but for the most part, the racism involved pretending that the black players simply did not exist. To Taliaferro, that was worse.

A racial etiquette that reinforced the idea that African Americans were second-class citizens continued to exist into the 1940s. This informal set of rules included things like refusing to shake hands, a symbol of equality, with a black person. Although it was different from the legal discrimination that existed with segregation, it could be just as devastating if not more so. It was this code of behavior that affected Taliaferro the most. The idea of being treated as if he didn't exist at all was worse to him than the more deliberate racism that included racial slurs and "separate but equal" facilities, because with those, at least he existed. It was for this reason that it was so notable when Carl Biesecker had crossed the football field to shake his hand after that high school game—it made him feel like he was somebody.

Although the subtle forms of racism were difficult, the blatant forms of racism were hard on Taliaferro and his teammates too. The black players on the team, Taliaferro said, knew one assistant coach as the coach who would not recommend them for positions on the team. They understood that no matter how talented they were or how hard they worked, they would never do well enough to please him. His apparent prejudice was evident when classes started at Indiana University in August 1945, just a couple of weeks after the United States dropped atomic bombs on the Japanese cities of Hiroshima and Nagasaki. The first day that Taliaferro had to juggle his class schedule with football practice, he was twenty minutes late to the football field. A required class was only available at a time that conflicted with football. It ended at three o'clock, the same time practice started. Although Taliaferro had tried to get into a different section, they were all closed. He had no choice but to be late to practice, as his education was his main priority. When Taliaferro showed up at 3:20 p.m., he was reprimanded by this particular assistant coach. Taliaferro tried to explain why he was late, but the coach would not listen. "He just kept yelling," Taliaferro said.

Hearing about the dispute, McMillin came over to see what was going on, and unlike the assistant coach, McMillin actually listened. Taliaferro said, "I explained the situation, and McMillin looked at the assistant coach and told him to get me registered in

a different section of the class and to get on with practice." Taliaferro was somehow transferred into a different section of the class
that he had been told was closed. With the incident behind him,
Taliaferro decided to move on. He knew that dwelling on the
matter wouldn't do him any good. The assistant coach continued
to say and do things to try to get to Taliaferro and his black teammates, but Taliaferro ignored them. He was determined not to let
the assistant coach bother him, not to give him the satisfaction of
having accomplished that. "I learned [football] from the guy, and
that was, after all, why I was there," Taliaferro said.

Incidents like that became motivation for him. Every time
something like that happened, he resolved to succeed. He wanted
to be the best athlete he could be. As an athlete, he had the opportunity to do what he couldn't do anywhere else. It was his chance
"to go against the white guy," he said. It was the only way he could
physically demonstrate his anger against discrimination without
getting in trouble. Taliaferro fought racism the only way he could:
with his performance on the athletic field. At Indiana University,
he experienced both forms of racism, the form that existed in the
unwritten etiquette that prevailed in race relations, and the system of segregation that existed in Bloomington, Indiana, at the
time. The optimistic outlook with which Taliaferro approached
life was evident in his reaction to racism in whatever form. "This
was a problem they had, not a problem I had," he said. "We have
more things in common than we do not," Taliaferro continued.
"Fingers, toes, we wear clothes," he said, demonstrating the fact
that, when it comes down to it, we're all just members of the human race.

While those like the one assistant coach made life more difficult for black players, there were also people who made going
to Indiana University worthwhile for Taliaferro. One such person, of course, was Coach McMillin. "Bo McMillin's interest in
my welfare motivated me to stay despite all the crap," Taliaferro
explained. His support system went beyond the coach, though.

Fig. 3.4 The coaching staff of the 1945 Hoosiers. *From left to right*: Charles McDaniel, John Kovatch, Alvin "Bo" McMillin, Paul "Pooch" Harrell, and Gordon Fisher. Harrell was also the head baseball coach at Indiana University from 1939 to 1947. *Photo courtesy IU Archives.*

A number of people influenced his life and motivated him to stay at Indiana University, despite the racism. Another member of this support system was another assistant coach, John Kovatch. Kovatch, a former Northwestern football player, was aware of the difficulty Taliaferro was experiencing adjusting to life at IU, so he became a source of constant and steady support.

This network of support and Taliaferro's desire to make racism his motivation for success helped. Despite this, though, there were hard days, days when he couldn't shake the effects of racism on his psyche. In those moments, Kovatch would remind Talia-ferro that he was there because he was capable of contributing to the team and that he should make the best of his experience. Teammate Howard Brown played an important role, as well. On days when he noticed that Taliaferro was having a harder time than usual, he would reassure him. It didn't take much from Brown, just a simple "Everything's going to be all right," to keep Taliaferro going.

The African American students on campus also formed a support system. Whether undergraduate or graduate students, they all stuck together. Lehman Adams, a graduate student and friend of Taliaferro, explained how these relationships formed: "How do you become friends when you're a few black students among thousands? You become friends—you're forced to!" Being a member of Kappa Alpha Psi fraternity also provided support for Taliaferro during these times. Founded in 1911 at Indiana University, the fraternity was intended to help the few black students who not only were rejected by the white majority on campus and in town but were also dissuaded from remaining there. Kappa Alpha Psi's mission was to provide the support needed for black male students on campus to remain there and become successful, despite the many obstacles put in their way. More than three decades after its founding, this fraternity continued to help black students on campus, students like George Taliaferro who, like their predecessors, continued to face racism and segregation. About sixty years later, San Francisco 49ers quarterback Colin Kaepernick would become a fraternity brother.

The Kappa Alpha Psi fraternity house was nothing more than a kitchen and dining area, but fraternity brothers who lived in the house actually lived in those areas because everyone ate at the home of John and Ruth Mays, the unofficial union building for black students. While Taliaferro never resided in the fraternity house, he was an active member of the organization. He needed reassurance, and he needed friends, not just because of what he was going through with teammates but also because of what he was experiencing while living in a segregated Bloomington. The town of Bloomington was seemingly divided in half. The east side of town, the "gown" side, was the university half of the town. The "town" side was just that, the town side. The line

drawn between the two also marked the color line in Bloomington, with African Americans limited to the town side. There was
a covenant in Bloomington at the time, Taliaferro said, that no
black people could live on the east side of town.

All of the black football players, including Taliaferro, lived at
418 East Eighth Street, the home of John and Ruth Mays. That is
where Taliaferro was sitting on the steps on August 15, the day
Japan surrendered to the Allies, marking the end of World War II.
The Mayses' home, just off campus, was considered to be on the
gown side of town. Because black students were not housed on
campus, homes off campus, like the Mayses' home and the Lincoln House, in which black female students lived, were authorized
by IU president Wells as university facilities. They had the same
rules as the dorms on campus, and black students on scholarship,
like Taliaferro, were given a monthly stipend to pay for their room
and board, since they weren't permitted to live in the on-campus
housing. The room and board of the white students on scholarship
went through the bursar's office, like the money for tuition and
books. Taliaferro's stipend for room and board was fifty-two dollars a month. He paid around forty dollars to Mr. and Mrs. Mays.
This left him plenty of money for his other expenses, he said.

A family home that had been converted, the Mayses' home
was home to single, black male students. The diminutive house
held anywhere from twelve to sixteen people, with three or four
people in each small room, which could really only comfortably
fit two people. It was also rumored that there were a couple of
ghosts living in the basement, although Taliaferro never made
the trip down the dank basement steps to verify their existence.
Also, because black students were not welcome at restaurants
on campus, the Mayses' home had become the unofficial union,
serving as both hangout and cafeteria, meaning that even more
people were often crowded into the already-small space.

Making the living situation more interesting was Mr. Mays
himself. "He was always angry, and he drank anything he could

get his hands on, and he was always going to put somebody out. He'd say, 'I'll put you out of here!'" Taliaferro said. Mrs. Mays, the reverse of her husband, "was an angel," he said. She would just shake her head when her husband started yelling. Taliaferro and the other football players learned to pay Mr. Mays little attention. "He was so much smaller than most of us anyway," he explained. The threats never amounted to any more than that. Despite the cramped quarters and occasional drama, Taliaferro considered himself lucky to have a room at the Mayses' home. Black men who did not get a spot there had to live on the west side of Bloomington, the town side, even farther from campus than the Mayses' home. Lehman Adams was one of the unlucky ones who did not get a spot at the Mayses' home.

Adams arrived on campus before classes started so he could find a place to live. Although he tried everywhere, he could not find an available room anywhere in the segregated town. Desperate, having already registered for classes, he went to an adviser to ask for help, which got him nowhere. The adviser explained that there were no options, since he wasn't permitted to live on campus. If there were no places on the town side for Adams to rent, he was told, he might just have to go back home. The adviser, who didn't seem too concerned with Adams's problem, said there was nothing he could do. Although angry, disappointed, and frustrated, Adams was not deterred. He was determined to attend IU and to get an education, so he spent the night at a different friend's house each night until he finally found a room to rent in the private home of an African American couple. While he was happy to have found living arrangements, living on the west side, the town side, was difficult for students like Adams. He had to walk about four miles from the 900 block on the west side of town to the 800 block on the east side of town every day, rain or snow, to get to his classes.

Equally difficult for black students at Indiana University was finding a place to eat. It was especially difficult for those who did not live in the Lincoln House or the Mayses' home. For meals, they had to either leave campus and go back to the west side of town or eat at the Mayses' home. There was no restaurant on the east side of town, the gown side, that welcomed black customers. The Mayses' home was closer than the west side of town, but it was still a couple of miles from campus. Every meal was a hassle for Indiana University's black students. Taliaferro understood that his was a more fortunate situation than most. Still, it bothered him that he had been actively recruited by a university where he was not permitted to live in the university dorms and where he had a hard time getting his meals. It just wasn't right. He knew it, and it gnawed at him every time he ate a meal in Bloomington.

Every day at lunch, for example, Taliaferro would have to walk a couple of miles from his class at University School, across the extensive campus, to the Mayses' home, where he would have to scarf down his food. He didn't have time to talk. He barely had time to sit down. Although he shoved the food in his mouth as quickly as he could, he still had to sprint the two miles back to campus to make it to his next class on time.

Getting a haircut was no easier. The barbershop was located next to the segregated Princess Theater. Although it was owned by Mr. Shawntee, a black man, and was just a few blocks from the Mayses' home, Taliaferro was not permitted inside because it was located on the gown side of Bloomington. Instead, Taliaferro had to make an appointment to go to Mr. Shawntee's home. But his home was located on the opposite side of town from the Mayses' home, so getting a haircut meant a three-mile walk instead of the three-block walk to the barbershop.

"That was my world. Small world. Very small," Taliaferro said. But to him, these were just inconveniences he had to put up with in order to get an education. In order to deal with his frustration so that it wouldn't consume him, he had to find something positive in the experience. Dealing with the racism and segregation that existed in Bloomington may have actually kept the black

Fig. 3.5 The studious side of George Taliaferro in December 1945. Having attended Indiana University on a football scholarship, he said racism was "a small price to pay" for the education he received. *Photo courtesy IU Archives.*

students from flunking out of the university, he decided. "We didn't have any place to go or anything to do, and therefore we studied," he explained. The black students would get together, sometimes having dances and parties at one of the private homes they lived in, but they were so confined by space and location that they simply could not do too much socializing. They could not overindulge in an activity that had been detrimental to many of the white students. "I cannot remember a black student failing at Indiana University when I was at school. Being discriminated against in Bloomington, Indiana, was a small price for me to pay to get a quality education. It has prepared me for the world," Taliaferro explained. In an article by Bob Hammel, Taliaferro says, "There were things I couldn't do and places I couldn't go. But I didn't let anything stand between me and playing football. I made up my mind, 'If I can't go there, I can go to class.'"

Although Bloomington was segregated and Taliaferro was not able to live in the dorm with his white teammates, in many ways Indiana University seemed to be ahead of other major Indiana schools. Neither Purdue nor Notre Dame had black players in their football programs in 1945. At Indiana University, however, there had been black football players since Preston Eagleson became the first to play both football and baseball for the Hoosiers in 1890. Eagleson started what Herman B Wells, George Taliaferro, and Bo McMillin would continue. On a trip to another Indiana college, Eagleson was denied accommodations in a hotel because of his race. He filed suit against the hotel and received damages, setting a precedent in Indiana. He set another precedent by becoming the first black man to receive a degree from Indiana University when he received a master of arts degree in philosophy. Like Taliaferro, Eagleson understood that education was the means to his self-determination.

According to a book by Frances V. Halsell Gilliam, the Eagleson family continued to fight social injustice when Eagleson's younger brother attended IU in 1921. Halston Eagleson Jr. didn't play football but played in the band instead. Probably to prevent him from earning his letter sweater, he was kidnapped on his way to Lafayette, Indiana, for the 1922 game at Purdue. He was taken to Spencer, Indiana, and jailed. The kidnapping managed to keep Eagleson from getting to Lafayette for the game, and thus from earning his letter sweater, an honor the kidnappers apparently did not want bestowed on a black man. It wasn't until 1982 that a retired Halston Eagleson was finally awarded his sweater.

Aside from Preston Eagleson, there were other early black football players for IU. Jesse Babb, a halfback, and Fitzhugh Lyons, an end, both played for the Crimson from 1931 to 1933. This tradition continued at IU, and in 1945, under Coach McMillin, George

Taliaferro and Mel Groomes were starting for the Hoosiers, and other black players were on the roster—including Bill Buckner, whose son Quinn was to be a Hall of Fame basketball player and a two-year football starter at IU.

While Taliaferro was learning how to navigate, both physically and emotionally, segregated Bloomington, some students in Gary, Indiana, were having a difficult time adjusting as well. Gary Froebel High School was in the largest integrated neighborhood in the city, "an area called 'The Patch'" in what was "the rougher part of the city," according to Yolanda Perdomo. Approximately one-third of Froebel's students were black. However, black students could not swim in the pool or take part in extracurricular activities. Principal Richard A. Nuzum decided it was time to fully integrate. In *Time* magazine, Eliza Berman reported that Nuzum started by integrating extracurricular activities like the orchestra and the student government. His "pro-Negro policies," according to David Lehman, included allowing 270 black students to participate in student government and to "use the school's swimming pool one day a week." Perdomo reported that the new pro-Negro policies angered a group of white students, led by Leonard Lavenda, who organized a protest. *Life* magazine pointed out that the reason for the protests may have been parents "goading on these childish grievances" and that they were motivated by a fear of "competition for their steel-mill jobs from Gary's increasing Negro population," like Robert Taliaferro. On September 18, a group of white students walked out, demanding that the black students leave and that the principal be fired. According to Belle Beth Cooper, the walkout ended on October 1, when the school board investigated Nuzum. However, three weeks later when the investigation ended and Nuzum was not relieved of his position, the walkout recommenced.

It was the second walkout that garnered national attention. Having failed at ending the student strike themselves, the administration sought celebrity help. Initially, they invited Joe Louis to visit, but he was unable to attend, Cooper noted. At around the same time, however, Frank Sinatra was getting a reputation for his outspoken views on integration. According to Scott Simon with NPR, Sinatra "had always insisted on playing with integrated orchestras. He was the best and wanted to play with the finest: Count Basie and Duke Ellington. Sinatra wanted to sing with Ella Fitzgerald." Berman wrote that Sinatra refused to play segregated nightclubs. He had also appeared in *The House I Live In*, a short film about acceptance of others. In short, he used his platform as a popular artist and teenage heartthrob to fight against systematic segregation. So in lieu of Joe Louis, the administration invited Frank Sinatra to come to Gary to convince the students to attend class again.

According to Cooper, Sinatra canceled a lucrative $10,000 gig to speak at Froebel. On November 1, thousands of students packed Memorial Auditorium to hear Sinatra, who sang "The House I Live In," a song about tolerance. In fact, David Lehman wrote, "Anyone doubting the depth of Sinatra's liberal convictions should listen to the soundtrack of *The House I Live In*." Lehman described the movie, in which Sinatra stops a group of teens from beating up a Jewish boy "by saying that bigotry makes no sense to 'A Nazi or somebody as stupid.'" At Froebel High School, Sinatra followed the song with a speech, the theme of which, *Life* magazine stated, was that "no kid is by nature intolerant. It is one of the few forms of ignorance which has to be cultivated." According to NPR's Scott Simon, a *Chicago Daily Defender* article from November 5, 1945, described Sinatra's appearance: "Sinatra, blue-suit and red bow tie, five feet ten inches tall and 138 pounds, the heavyweight in the hearts of teenagers, stepped to the stage amid weeping, some fainting, much crying, and said, 'You should be proud of Gary, but you can't stay proud by pulling this sort of strike.'" According to Simon, Sinatra told them, "You have a wonderful war production record. Don't spoil it by pulling a strike. Go on back to school, kids." Despite the enthusiastic reception, applause, and national headlines, including a spread in *Life*, the visit did not lead to an immediate end of the protest. In fact, it wasn't until a couple of days after the event, Perdomo wrote, that the protest ended when the school board threatened to expel the striking students. Still, Sinatra made an impact. Perdomo reports that resident William Hill said, "The Sinatra concert sparked a lifelong interest in Civil Rights."

The rest of the country weighed in too. Letters to *Life* magazine editors on December 3, 1945, after the story on Sinatra and Gary Froebel ran, illustrate the racial tension of the times. Arlie Wharton, of Texas, for example, wrote, "Sirs: How anyone can agree with the birdbrain who wrote this is beyond me. . . . When negroes are put to white folks' equal, I quit! May *LIFE* never publish another article like this to louse up their excellent magazine." Others supported Sinatra. Robert Baidukiewicz simply asked, "Am I living in Nazi Germany?" Another, Walter Duncan, wrote, "Frank Sinatra is to be commended. . . . Thanks to *LIFE* for reporting his activities in behalf of racial tolerance. It should be a challenge to all of us to join in this fight to recapture the spirit of democracy."

Not contested is the fact that Sinatra risked fame and career in speaking out publicly against intolerance and hatred. His political support of Franklin Delano Roosevelt had even drawn the ire of his own mother, who, Lehman wrote, "bawled him out for being so pro-FDR." According to *Jet* magazine, Sinatra "developed relationships with Blacks that made him renowned for rallying behind causes to advance racial tolerance." In 1986, *Jet* recalled how Sinatra had used the magazine in July 1958 to make a statement about race: "A friend to me has no race, no class, and belongs to no minority. My friendships were formed out of affection, mutual respect and a feeling of having something strong in common. These are eternal values that cannot be racially classified," Sinatra stated. Still, these outspoken beliefs marked the "beginning of a downward spiral for Sinatra's career due to his strong (and unpopular) political views, particularly on equality and racial integration," wrote Cooper. Sinatra was not the first, nor would he be the last, to put his values of equality over career. In fact, decades later, numerous NFL players would face the same dilemma.

FOUR

1945–46: INDIANA UNIVERSITY FOOTBALL

IN GARY AND IN COLLEGE football, 1945 was a volatile time. Although World War II veterans were often on the roster, college teams everywhere lost players to the wartime draft. Similar problems plagued the National Football League. Attendance at NFL games dropped during the war, and there was a shortage of players. According to Robert W. Peterson's *Pigskin: The Early Years of Pro Football*, 638 active NFL players had gone into the armed forces by the war's end. *The NFL's Official Encyclopedic History of Professional Football* cites that of these players/soldiers, 355 were officers, 66 were decorated, and 21 were killed. Because of the loss of players and coaches (even George Halas was called up for navy duty in the middle of the 1942 season), the team limit was cut from 33 to 25, and an unlimited substitutions rule was implemented. These regulations were not enough, however, and many teams did not have enough players to field a team. In 1943, for example, the Cleveland Rams suspended operations for the season because of the shortage. Some teams avoided shutting down by merging with another team in order to have enough players. This is how the Phil-Pitt Steagles were born in 1943, a hybrid of the Philadelphia Eagles and the Pittsburgh Steelers, who merged for one season to survive the shortage. Two years later, the Brooklyn Tigers and Boston Yanks merged for the 1945 season. Nothing, it seems, was certain for football, and college football in 1945 was no exception.

Even with the constant changes, it is fair to say that many college football fans were not expecting a season like the one Indiana University ended up having. The night before their first game of the season, Coach McMillin held a team dinner. Unfortunately, key players were noticeably absent. Pete Pihos, the fullback who would go on to be a Professional Football Hall of Famer, would not return from military service until late September. Howard Brown and Charlie Armstrong were also still in the service. Among those present, however, were Ben Raimondi, the quarterback; and Mel Groomes, a halfback. The ends were Bob Ravensberg and Ted Kluszewski. Altogether, despite missing some key players, McMillin's "po li'l boys" were a talented group of individuals.

According to Hammel and Klingelhoffer in *Glory of Old IU*, Ravensberg was the only consensus All-American selection on the team. Ben Raimondi, however, was a strong quarterback. Years later when he was rated using the NCAA grading system, his pass rating was a high 145.1. And Ted Kluszewski's skills weren't limited to football. Kluszewski, who also played baseball for the Hurryin' Hoosiers, was noticed by scouts for the Cincinnati Reds when the two baseball teams shared practice facilities after wartime restrictions forced the Reds to Bloomington from 1943 to 1945 for their spring practice. Despite having only played sandlot ball until that point, Kluszewski maintained a .443 batting average at IU. Taliaferro said, remembering, "And he didn't just hit the ball—he crushed it!" The Reds, Taliaferro said, witnessed one of Kluszewski's power hits. Standing about where the little Beck Chapel now stands, next to Indiana Memorial Union, Kluszewski hit the ball past what today is the Wildermuth Intramural Center, for an easy home run. "They signed him the next day," Taliaferro recalled. Kluszewski, the "quiet man," as his teammates referred to him, stood six foot three and weighed about 235 pounds. Taliaferro said, "His biceps were the size of most people's thighs, and he could just as successfully have played professional football as pro baseball." If that is the case, he would have been an impressive tight end in the NFL, because his statistics with the Reds are impressive. He played for fifteen seasons, three times hitting at least forty home runs and three times hitting more home runs than he had strikeouts. In fact, he was so successful that in 1998 the Cincinnati Reds retired his jersey, number 18, and when they built a new stadium, a statue of "Big Klu" went up outside. But before he would become one of Cincinnati's most beloved baseball players, he still had one more football season to play for Indiana.

Linemen John Goldsberry and Russ Deal; Bob Meyer, center; and tackle Joe Sowinski were also at the team dinner the night before the first game, as part of the talent pool McMillin had accumulated. The team had been preparing for the game all week, so the dinner was more of a bonding experience than game preparation. McMillin used the opportunity to discuss an idea with Taliaferro.

"Are you a superstitious person?" McMillin asked him, his Texas drawl conspicuous.

"Not really," Taliaferro replied. McMillin was, however, and he told Taliaferro that he wanted to change his jersey number from 43 to 44.

Billy Hillenbrand and Vern Huffman had previously worn the number 44 jersey, McMillin explained. Huffman was the 1936 Big Ten MVP. He was also the only IU athlete to win All-American honors in two sports, football and basketball. Billy Hillenbrand was IU's all-time punt return leader and also an All-American. Taliaferro figured McMillin wanted him to wear the same number because he saw something special in Taliaferro as well; maybe he thought Taliaferro, too, would become an All-American.

"That's fine with me," Taliaferro said. In fact, he would consider it an honor. After his initial doubts about becoming part of the team, to be asked to wear the number of two of Indiana's All-Americans was a compliment Taliaferro took seriously. He felt that a certain responsibility came with the honor, and he planned on living up to the expectations.

The next day, September 22, 1945, Taliaferro was ready to wear his new number in his first college football game. The first challenge of the game was just in getting there. Having no team bus, the team had to borrow gas-rationing stamps and travel the day before in about thirty cars to Ann Arbor, Michigan. In the visitors' locker room the next day, Taliaferro geared up for the game. He put on his jersey and listened to McMillin's locker-room talk. Known for his fiery inspirational speeches, McMillin had managed to bring his players to tears on several occasions. Nobody cried after his talk that day, but the Cream and Crimson were fired up and ready to play. When it was finally game time, Taliaferro ran onto the field and looked up to see the tallest, widest stadium he had ever seen. It was packed full of loud Michigan Wolverine fans, an intimidating experience for the eighteen-year-old freshman. To add to the pressure, he was one of the starting eleven—a freshman starting as a tailback and halfback was something that wouldn't happen again at IU for forty-nine years. Taliaferro worried that he would let the team down.

But being young and inexperienced wasn't a factor once Taliaferro received his first hit, his initiation into college football. "Once you get hit, you forget about everything else," he said. After that, his desire to play was all that mattered. "Nobody ever enjoyed playing football any more than I did. I lived to play football. It was that much fun," he said. Still, this was the first game of the season, and it would prove to be a challenge for the young Hoosiers. Michigan Stadium was a place where "historically visiting teams' hopes of unbeaten seasons have died," Hammel and Klingelhoffer wrote. To make matters worse, they added, the Indiana University Hoosiers had actually defeated Michigan at Michigan Stadium the previous year, 20–0, so Michigan was seeking revenge. It wasn't the Oaken Bucket, but it was a serious conference rivalry.

In the first quarter Taliaferro ran for fourteen yards to put Indiana on Michigan's thirty-nine-yard line. He then passed fourteen yards to end Ted Kluszewski to put Indiana on the Michigan twenty-five. On the next play, Taliaferro ran through Michigan's line for a thirteen-yard gain and then managed to make it into the end zone "shaking off tacklers," according to Jack Overmyer, the Hoosiers' press director. This first touchdown, wrote Hammel in a *Bloomington Herald-Times* article, came on a fifty-six-yard drive in the first quarter that "introduced the Wolverines to Taliaferro." As spectacular as it was, a holding penalty cost the Hoosiers the touchdown and put them back on the fifteen. This setback didn't deter Taliaferro, who subsequently threw a screen pass to Dick Deranek to perfectly set up the next play; quarterback Ben Raimondi threw a pass to Kluszewski, who took it into the Wolverine end zone. The second Hoosier touchdown came on an eighty-one-yard drive by Nick Sebek, Mel Groomes, and Ben Raimondi, giving the Hoosiers an early 13–0 lead.

Despite a valiant effort by the Wolverines, their only score came on an Indiana blunder. In the third quarter, Michigan capitalized on a short punt by Taliaferro to the Hoosiers' own 49, making the score 13–7. The Bomen, as Bo McMillin's team was sometimes called, managed to hold on to its lead until there were only two minutes to go. Michigan had the ball on the Hoosier eight-yard line, along with the opportunity to take the lead from its visitors. Hammel described what happened next: "Two running plays advanced the ball to the four. A third try didn't advance it. . . . On fourth down, the Wolverines took too much time getting a play set and backed up to the nine. There, with fifty-five seconds left, they lined up in field-goal formation. It was a fake. Indiana played for it and stuffed the play, killing the threat and clinching victory." When the game was over, Indiana had won

13–7 and had set in motion what would be a memorable season, for several reasons.

In his debut, and despite his initial qualms, Taliaferro did not disappoint McMillin, who had entrusted him with a starting position and lucky jersey number. Of Taliaferro's introductory performance, Hammel wrote for *Bloomington Herald-Times*, "Taliaferro didn't score but did everything else in as spectacular and crucial a debut as an eighteen-year old ever had." It was after this Michigan game that Taliaferro began to realize he was establishing himself as a starter. "When I played football against the University of Michigan and won, I said, 'This is different. In the history of Indiana University, this is different.'" Perhaps that was because Taliaferro ran for ninety-five yards in twenty carries and completed three of three passes for twenty-three yards. He would have debuted with a hundred-yard game if he hadn't taken a loss to run out the clock on the last play. Taliaferro's impressive initiation into college football was not perfect, however. Hammel noted that he had botched a couple of punts and that when McMillin asked what happened, Taliaferro replied, "I was too scared to know."

The next game on the schedule came against Northwestern on September 29. Pete Pihos and Howard Brown, who had been in the service for two years, were back and ready to play. According to Hammel and Klingelhoffer, the two were on a sixty-day leave, having come back from impressive stints in the military. "Pihos won a battlefield promotion to Lieutenant with General Patton's 35th Infantry Division in bloody fighting during World War II. Brown won three purple hearts in the same war theater," they wrote. Pihos and Brown only had a couple of practices with the Hoosiers before the Northwestern game, but rusty or not, their skills were needed. Despite the strong season opener against Michigan without two of their key players, the Hoosiers were going to have a hard time battling Northwestern. Hoosier center

Fig. 4.1 The 1945 Hoosier starting backs. In the front row is Ben Raimondi; in the back row (*from left*) are Mel Groomes, Pete Pihos, and George Taliaferro. *Photo courtesy IU Archives.*

Bob Meyer had broken his leg during the Michigan game, so John Cannady, who hoped to be a linebacker, was stepping in for him. According to Hammel and Klingelhoffer, Cannady said, "It rained. I had never snapped the ball in the rain. The morning of the game at our hotel, Bo took me upstairs with the backs. He put six footballs in the bathtub. A coach would hand one to me, I'd snap it to the quarterback, and they ran plays right there in the room." Taliaferro said Cannady was a natural at the position, though, and he continued at center for the Hoosiers on offense; on defense, he remained a linebacker.

After the impressive debut at Michigan, Taliaferro's performance was a bit disappointing. Northwestern outplayed the Hoosiers for the first three quarters and had scored the only touchdown, which came from a blocked Taliaferro punt. And although Taliaferro had carried nineteen times for seventy-seven yards, he had also lost twenty-one yards, for a net of only fifty-six. In the fourth quarter, passes to Groomes and Ravensberg advanced the Bomen to the Northwestern fifteen-yard line. McMillin put in Pihos and Brown. On the next play, Raimondi passed to Pihos, who caught the ball at the five and powered through three Northwestern defenders, whom he dragged with him into the end zone. Charlie Armstrong's place kick tied the game. Just back from the war, Armstrong had been a bomber pilot who, according to Hammel and Klingelhoffer, was decorated with the Distinguished Flying Cross. Armstrong had been intent on quitting football and getting a commercial pilot's license. Luckily for the Hoosiers, he changed his mind and decided to play another season of football. His kick, right on target, saved the Cream and Crimson from near defeat, ending the game in a frustrating tie, which McMillin likened to "getting a kiss from your sister." It wasn't a win, but it wasn't a loss either, a fact that would become more important as the season wore on. Although they had beaten Michigan without them, Taliaferro noted the addition of Pihos and Brown to the Hoosier lineup. It was an important game for that reason too. The team would be that much stronger.

The Hoosiers faced the Fighting Illini in the October 6 game. Despite two completions into the end zone in the second quarter, the Hoosiers had failed to score. For the first, Raimondi had thrown to Kluszewski in the end zone, but the play was called back when the Illini band's mascot, a dog, trotted onto the field. The same play a second time yielded the same results when officials ruled that Kluszewski had stepped out of bounds. Taliaferro was held in check until the fourth quarter, which the Hoosiers started by taking the ball on a penalty at the Illinois forty-two.

A couple of Taliaferro running plays and some complete passes put the Hoosiers on the ten. This time, the Raimondi pass to Kluszewski in the end zone wasn't called back, and the Hoosiers had the winning touchdown.

Twenty-two thousand people showed up at Indiana's Memorial Stadium for the October 13 homecoming game against Nebraska. The Bomen donned their red home jerseys with white numbers for the game. Although the school colors are cream and crimson, they wore black pants with a white stripe down the side and black helmets, made of padded leather and created well before the addition of the face mask. It was Taliaferro's first game at Indiana's horseshoe-shaped Tenth Street Stadium. Once considered one of the premier college playing fields, the stadium was the setting of the movie *Breaking Away*, about Indiana's famous Little 500 bicycle race. The stadium, which has since been torn down, was the setting of many Little 500 races and memorable Indiana football games. One such game was the 1945 game against Nebraska. By halftime, Taliaferro had helped his team to a 27–0 lead. Hoosier halfback Bob Miller ran a ninety-five-yard kickoff return to end the second half with another touchdown. Reserves finished the game, giving everyone the opportunity to play, and the Cream and Crimson came away with a 54–14 victory. The Nebraska Cornhuskers, on the other hand, had only managed to cross the fifty-yard line twice during the entire second half of the game.

The Hoosiers racked up more points against Iowa the following week. Taliaferro, the "Gary Flash," contributed with some big touchdown runs, one for sixty-three yards and again later down the sideline for seventy-four yards. By the third quarter, substitutes were in again, but the Hoosiers still managed to score a whopping fifty-two points in their third Big Ten victory of the season. The Hawkeyes had managed to score twenty points, but it wasn't enough to overcome the offensive might of the Hurryin' Hoosiers.

Fig. 4.2 George Taliaferro, number 44, carries the ball during the Indiana-Tulsa game on October 27, 1945. Both teams were undefeated going into the game, but Indiana came out with a 7–2 win. During this game, some of Tulsa's players made it clear that they did not appreciate playing against black players. They lost their captain early in the game for roughing up Taliaferro. *Photo courtesy IU Archives.*

After the two amazing runs against Iowa, the Tulsa game was even more memorable for Taliaferro. Before the game, Indiana had had two consecutive fifty-point wins. But Tulsa, also undefeated, would be a contest between two of the best college teams of 1945. The game, Taliaferro said, was "what college football is about: blocking, tackling, defense, and teamwork." After several punts, the first score of the game came in the second quarter. It started with a Mel Groomes pass to Taliaferro for a considerable gain. On the next play, Indiana's end, Bob Ravensberg, on a pass from fullback Pete Pihos, got into the end zone. Tulsa then managed to score two points when a tackle of Taliaferro in his own end zone led to a safety. Strong defense from both teams left the remaining action scoreless, though not without nail biting, and the game ended with a hard-earned Indiana win, 7–2.

"That was one of my best games," Taliaferro said, notwithstanding the safety. The Tulsa game, however, was memorable for another reason as well. In *Hoosier Autumn*, a book about the 1945 Hoosier football team, Robert D. Arnold wrote, "After a few plays, it was obvious that the Tulsa players didn't appreciate playing against blacks." Tulsa, Arnold wrote, actually lost their captain, C. B. Stanley, early in the game for roughing up Taliaferro. Mel Groomes, another black player, was also targeted, but Taliaferro seemed to receive the bulk of Tulsa's antics.

With much less drama, the Hoosiers beat Cornell on November 3 at Indiana's Memorial Stadium, 46–6. The fact that Coach McMillin was absent to scout the Minnesota Golden Gophers and that starters rested much of the game to avoid injury mattered little. Although he didn't play as much as he usually did, Taliaferro still managed to contribute a touchdown to the win.

As the season progressed, Taliaferro played an increasingly larger role in the Hoosiers' wins. His triple-threat skills, which would, in time, propel him into professional football, were a key contribution to the Bomen's success. Taliaferro, who played tailback for the Hoosiers and had secured his star position on the team when he ran two consecutive eighty-yard touchdown runs in practice, was not a disappointment to McMillin, and his skills were noticed on campus as well, with his popularity on campus increasing with every game. Even at a time of prevalent racism, he was often asked for his autograph while walking around campus between classes. His easy nature and charm made him approachable, and he would happily oblige the autograph seekers. It became clear that McMillin had not overstated Taliaferro's place on the team when he reassured him on that first day.

McMillin was actually one of his biggest fans, as Sam Banks, a writer for *Our Sports* magazine, illustrated in an article about Taliaferro. Apparently, Coach McMillin was having his usual coffee break one morning when Taliaferro and a couple of other players stopped by to see him. It wasn't out of the ordinary for them to stop in. They respected McMillin, whose conduct as both a coach and a person had encouraged and inspired them, and they considered him not only a coach but also a friend and mentor. During the visit, however, the players had started to mess with each other. "As kids will do, they were wrestling on the stairs and George slipped and fell flat on his back," Banks wrote. McMillin rolled his eyes up as if in prayer and then ran to Taliaferro's side. As soon as the coach got to him, Taliaferro rolled over laughing and jumped up to his feet. McMillin didn't find it quite as humorous. "Boy, don't you ever do that to me again. Why you're my bread and butter," he told Taliaferro.

Although McMillin seemed to be joking, there was some truth to his statement. At the end of the season, Taliaferro would make All-Big Ten as a freshman at Indiana, and he would lead the Hoosiers in rushing, with 719 yards (he averaged 4.5 yards a carry and had six touchdowns). He would also lead the Hoosiers in punting, with 1,315 yards, averaging almost 33 yards a punt. He was the only Big Ten back to average more than 100 yards a game running and passing. While statistics may give some indication as to ability, however, to see him in action was more thrilling, and there were plenty of people on hand to witness his football aptitude at the memorable game against Minnesota.

On the way to the game, Coach McMillin noticed a white horse in a field. Known for being superstitious, he immediately licked his finger and stamped it in his hand for good luck. Indiana was going to need it. The Hoosiers had only won two of its last fifty games against Minnesota, and the frigid temperature was going to make for a game the Hoosiers wouldn't soon forget. At home, Minnesota could usually count on the weather to play a factor in the game's outcome. Other teams simply were not used to playing in the extreme weather found there during football season, an obvious advantage for the Gophers. Stan Sutton wrote

Fig. 4.3 Bo McMillin, who saw talent, not color, rests his hand on George Taliaferro's knee. McMillin, who recruited, played, and started black players, refused to stay in hotels that did not welcome his black players. *From left*: Pete Pihos, Coach Alvin "Bo" McMillin, George Taliaferro, and Bob Harbison. *Photo courtesy IU Archives.*

that the Minnesota weather "would keep a postman from finishing his route" and that "Minneapolis winters were cold enough to make penguins shiver."

Although back in Indiana the weather on that November day hovered around sixty degrees, Minnesota was a different story, according to Taliaferro. A large snowstorm and freezing temperatures met the Hoosiers, whose uniforms and coats provided little relief from the bitter cold. It was exactly the kind of weather that put Minnesota at a serious advantage, earning it the title of "twelfth man." Before the game even started, Taliaferro was jumping around, trying to keep his muscles warm. It wasn't working, though, and he could feel his muscles freezing as he stood and looked out over the field. *It is going to be a very long game,* he thought. It may have surprised the Gophers to hear that Taliaferro was having a problem coping with the weather, though, since he started the game with a ninety-seven-yard kickoff return to the Minnesota three. His fumble on the next play, recovered by Minnesota, may have been more along the lines of what they were expecting, or at least hoping for. The play was supposed to be a snap to Taliaferro, but it went too far left, and Taliaferro lost it. Mistakes like that one were rare, though, as Taliaferro and company continued to astonish the Gopher defense despite the subzero-degree weather.

The bone-chilling temperatures didn't keep Taliaferro from scoring three touchdowns and making a ninety-yard interception return. McMillin took him out, to Taliaferro's delight, to give him a break after the third touchdown. By the time the game had ended, the Hoosiers hadn't just beaten the Golden Gophers but had handed Minnesota, a team that had won five national championships between 1934 and 1941, a 49–0 thumping, in their home stadium in weather conditions only they could truly appreciate. The Gophers, for their part, had contributed to the Hoosier win by throwing six interceptions. A combination of coaching and playing talent had earned the Hoosiers an impressive victory. Coach McMillin's gamble to miss the November 3 game against Cornell in order to scout the Gophers had been rewarded. Even in his absence, the Cornell game had turned out well, and he brought back a scouting report that took the Minnesota weather out of the game for the Hurryin' Hoosiers, validating McMillin's confidence in his team and his coaching staff.

The Bomen continued their season with another shutout against Pittsburgh on November 17, winning 19–0. This left the Hurryin' Hoosiers with only one more obstacle on their way to an undefeated season: archrival Purdue. The Cream and Crimson topped off the season on November 24, 1945, at the forty-eighth Old Oaken Bucket game against the Purdue Boilermakers.

Fig. 4.4 An aerial view of Tenth Street Stadium on November 24, 1945, during the last game of the season against Purdue. Approximately twenty-seven thousand fans watched the Hoosiers beat Purdue and earn the coveted Old Oaken Bucket trophy, an undefeated season, and the first undisputed Big Ten championship in the school's history. *Photo courtesy IU Archives.*

On hand to watch the historic match were about twenty-seven thousand zealous fans. Unlike other Oaken Bucket games, however, this one was missing a crucial element, the Battle of the Bands. This traditional halftime feature, a battle between the rival marching bands, had to be canceled because Indiana's nationally acclaimed band, the Marching Hundred, was missing too many members because of the war. The Hoosiers had been fortunate to keep their band together as long as they had. Other universities had been forced to give up altogether on having their bands, they had such a shortage of members.

Despite the lack of halftime entertainment, at least the game was being played. In true rival fashion, the teams battled through the first half, with serious attempts to score from both sides, neither finding success. At halftime, the players went to the locker rooms evenly matched at zero. By the time the third quarter was under way, however, it was clear the Black and Gold had little left

Fig. 4.5 Captain John Goldsberry and George Taliaferro count the *Is* on the Old Oaken Bucket after the historic win against Purdue that clinched an undefeated season and Big Ten championship. *Photo courtesy IU Archives.*

to give to the effort and were no match for the Hoosier might. The Hoosiers, on the other hand, had more fight left to exert. Their first score started when Taliaferro, Pihos, and Groomes helped get the ball to the Purdue thirty-one. Then Raimondi passed to Taliaferro, who made it to the one-yard line. Pihos finished the drive, making it into the end zone on his second attempt for the first IU touchdown of the game. A Kluszewski interception led to another Pihos score before the third quarter ended. The Hoosiers weren't finished, though. Two more Raimondi touchdown passes, to Kluszewski and Louis Mihajlovich, added another thirteen points in the fourth. The Hoosiers, as had so often been the case during that 1945 season, had dominated their opponent. The victory over rival Purdue meant that the Hoosiers had managed not just a win

Fig. 4.6 Members of the 1945 championship team admire the Old Oaken Bucket trophy after beating rival Purdue. *From left*: Coach Bo McMillin, Pete Pihos, Russell Deal, Mel Groomes, and George Taliaferro. *Photo courtesy IU Archives.*

but an undisputed Big Ten championship, an undefeated season, and the Old Oaken Bucket trophy. The tie against Northwestern had been the only glitch in an otherwise perfect season.

An *Indianapolis Star* program honoring the unbeaten team described the end of the game: "As the final shot ended the game, hundreds of fans rushed onto the field, caught Bo in an avalanche, and hurried him off to the Hoosiers quarters." It went on to describe the scene in the locker room: "And the dressing room was busier than a well-stocked cigarette counter during the war shortage, all was confusion, but everyone knew that Indiana beat Purdue." Many fans remained in the locker room, still cheering their Cream and Crimson heroes. Among those, the program indicated, was McMillin's own mentor from his grammar school days in Texas, Robert Myers, McMillin's first football coach. Myers asked McMillin which underdog win had been more thrilling for him, the time he led Centre to beat Harvard or Indiana's defeat of Purdue that day. McMillin's reply, that the Indiana game was the more thrilling, came without hesitation. To sweeten the victory, President Wells, also in the locker room, canceled classes the following Monday and scheduled a convocation for later in the week for a student-body celebration.

In a ceremony after the game, another *I* was added to the Oaken Bucket to celebrate Indiana's 26–0 shutout victory over Purdue. A poem written by Carl Lewis explains the bucket's glory: "I'm called the 'old' oaken bucket, but I can never be old. I live with youth and will as long as there are young men to vie for my favor one November day each year." The Hoosiers could not have scripted a better ending to their perfect season than earning the coveted trophy. After the game, Russell "Mutt" Deal's Indiana teammates voted the decorated World War II veteran the permanent captain of the team. It was Deal's fourth game against Purdue and fourth victory over this rival.

So, under the leadership of Coach McMillin and Russell Deal, in 1945, Indiana University, with a record of 9–0–1, had an undefeated football season for the first and only time in the school's history. The football team also won an undisputed Big Ten championship for the first time, though this powerful conference was actually called the Western Conference or "Big Nine" at the time. The University of Chicago had been part of the conference but had dropped out, thus earning the conference its new nickname. Although it remained the Big Nine the entire time Taliaferro played for Indiana, many people still referred to the conference as the "Big Ten." Later, when Michigan State joined the conference, it became the Big Ten again anyway. So Indiana had won an undisputed Big Ten championship. Today, there are fourteen teams in the Big Ten Conference.

"It can happen. A football team wallowing in the muck of mediocrity suddenly takes off and soars, higher than it has ever

Fig. 4.7 *From left*: John Goldsberry, Russell Deal, Bob Ravensberg, and George Taliaferro read *Hail the Champs*, on January 10, 1946. The *Indianapolis Star* sponsored the brochure, which celebrated Indiana University's conference championship and undefeated season. An emotionally overwhelmed Bo McMillin appears on the cover. On the back is a list of Indiana Hoosier football players and former players who served in World War II. *Photo courtesy IU Archives.*

flown before. And then almost as abruptly it descends, never to repeat its journey," Mark Montieth wrote in a 1995 *Indianapolis Star* article about that 1945 football season. "Call it kismet, karma, destiny, or anything you like. It's what happens when talent, effort and good fortune merge for one brief shining moment to produce something that borders on perfection," he continued. Yet some critics, who apparently did not believe in kismet, karma, or destiny, credited World War II with Indiana's perfect season. Coach McMillin did not take kindly to such suggestions. He was rather insulted at the idea, believing his "po li'l boys" simply had the determination and the talent to make it happen. The fact that five of his starters had earned postseason honors supported McMillin's position. Bob Ravensberg was named All-American first team, second team, and All-Big Ten second team. Pete Pihos was named All-American second team and All-Big Ten first team. Ted Kluszewski was named All-Big Ten first team, and John Goldsberry was named All-Big Ten second team. Freshman George Taliaferro also racked up the honors. On top of this, the Indiana University football program earned, along with a conference championship, a fourth-place ranking in the Associated Press football poll. In first, second, and third place were Army, Navy, and Alabama's Crimson Tide. The Hoosiers were in good company. Adding to the accolades was Bo McMillin, who was named Coach of the Year.

McMillin would have liked IU to get a chance to play number-one-ranked Army, and there had actually been talk of a postseason game between the two greats. Hammel and Klingelhoffer explained that Big Ten rules prohibited postseason play for its teams but that there was a movement for a bowl matchup between Army and Indiana at Soldier Field for war relief. As many as 125,000 people were expected to attend what was sure to be a battle. Apparently General Eisenhower denied permission, citing that the cadets had to study for their midterm exams. However, McMillin was confident his Hoosiers could have taken the popular Army team. According to Hammel and Klingelhoffer, McMillin said in a speech at his Coach of the Year dinner, "I haven't seen Blanchard but until I do, I'll settle for Pete Pihos any time. . . . I've heard a lot about DeWitt Coulter, Army's wonderful left tackle. I never saw Coulter play, but until I have, I'll take John Goldsberry, our 230-pound left tackle and the fastest man on our line." He continued, "Maybe you've never heard of Ted Kluszewski and Bob Ravensberg, our ends. They were the best ends Fritz Crisler of Michigan saw all season, by his own quotes. . . . Our line was probably the best in the Big Ten in ten years, the real secret of our unbeaten season and Big Ten Championship. That line allowed only one touchdown all season, and that was by Michigan in the first game, before Brown, Cannady and Pihos were in the lineup." McMillin didn't stop there. "It was a hell of a line. . . . It's too bad Army had a full schedule. We'd have loved to meet them," he said.

Although the two teams never got a chance to play, that didn't keep people from debating who would have won. Hammel and Klingelhoffer pointed to the Michigan games, which were the only true comparisons that could be made of the two football teams. Indiana had beaten the Wolverines 13–7, while Army had beaten the Wolverines by a slightly larger margin, 28–7. Still, that wasn't a true comparison because the Indiana-Michigan game, the first of the season, was before the return of two of Indiana's key players, Pete Pihos and Howard Brown. Who would have won a contest between the two is anybody's guess. Hoosier fans, no doubt, believed the Bomen could have taken a tough Army team. The only thing that wasn't up for debate was that it would have been a hell of a game to watch.

The end of the 1945 college football season signaled a new beginning for professional football. At the same time that IU was winning the Big Ten championship, the National Football League was emerging as a force in professional sports. Robert Peterson, author of *Pigskin: The Early Years of Pro Football*, wrote that by the end of the 1945 season, pro players, like their college counterparts, were starting to return to their teams after having served in World War II. NFL fans were also beginning to return. In 1942, attendance had dropped to about 900,000. In 1945, however, an attendance record was set with 1,918,631 fans enjoying professional football, an average of 28,636 for the season's sixty-eight games and a big boost from 1942. Things were beginning to look up for the war-scarred league.

The league was evolving because of the war, and it was bringing with it a new tradition for the same reason. A pregame event that had started as a show of patriotism during the war became a permanent part of NFL and athletic competition tradition. Peterson wrote, "During the war, playing the national anthem had become a ceremonial prelude to NFL games." Even though the war was over, the commissioner felt that the anthem should continue to be played before each game. Peterson quoted Commissioner Elmer Layden's announcement: "It should be as much a part of every game as the kickoff. We must not drop it simply because the war is over. We should never forget what it stands for." The NFL, responsible for starting the tradition, would be the source of a controversy surrounding it more than seventy years later, when dozens of its players would kneel and link arms during the playing of the national anthem to protest racial inequality. However, the anthem protests, as they came to be known, were not the first time football was used as a platform through which to promote social change.

Peterson wrote that a 1945 *Newsweek* article also predicted positive changes for professional football. He quoted *Newsweek* columnist John Lardner, who wrote, "The end of the war may be the event which will build the sport into national proportions both geographically and commercially, just as the end of the last war gave pro players their original impetus and made them begin to think of organization and responsibility." The war was over, bringing changes to the world and to professional football. Lardner was right. There were big changes in store for professional football, and George Taliaferro would eventually be a significant part of those changes.

Taliaferro was a varsity letter recipient his freshman year. He was a major contributor to Indiana's football glory, and he was named the league's best all-around offensive player, Associated Press first team Big Ten, and second team All-American by the *Sporting News*. He was also the only Big Ten back to average more than a hundred yards a game, running and passing. His role as a star player at a major university widened his influence on African American boys, moving it beyond the confines of Gary,

Fig. 4.8 In the 1940s, posed pictures were common, including this one of George Taliaferro carrying the ball in 1945. The helmets were leather, and there were no face masks. *Photo courtesy IU Archives.*

Indiana. Later, William Wiggins, as an IU professor, would describe Taliaferro's influence on writer Ryan Whirty: "Whenever guys played football in the backyard, everybody wanted to be George Taliaferro." Professional football, which would further Taliaferro's influence, was in his future, but he still had a couple of years before it would significantly change his life. Although 1945 was a good football year for both Taliaferro and the NFL, each still had obstacles to overcome before their destinies would become intertwined. Taliaferro had color barriers to fight, and a new professional football league, the All-America Football Conference, was about to challenge the dominance of the National Football League.

During the 1945 season, Taliaferro had encountered some racism on the football field and in Bloomington. But the racism that hit Taliaferro the hardest occurred right after the Big Ten championship. A wall-sized picture of the 1945 championship team, which ran as an ad in the Indiana University football game programs, was hung on a wall at the Gables restaurant, a restaurant on the gown side, the campus side, of Bloomington. The restaurant "was just down the street from where Hoagy Carmichael wrote 'Stardust,'" Taliaferro said. Segregation prevented Taliaferro and the other black members of the football team from entering the popular restaurant, thus also preventing them from seeing the hand-tinted photograph that featured the eleven starters. Taliaferro was in the second row, just to the right of center. Occasionally, he would try to see the picture, managing to get just a glimpse. Since the picture hung on the far-left wall, he would go to the far-right window of the Gables, cup his hands around his face, and press his forehead against the glass. After several attempts turning his head this way and that, he discovered just the right angle to see some of the championship picture. He couldn't see the left side of the picture at all, no matter how he turned his head, but he "could see the most important person on that picture, which was me," he joked. It would be another two years

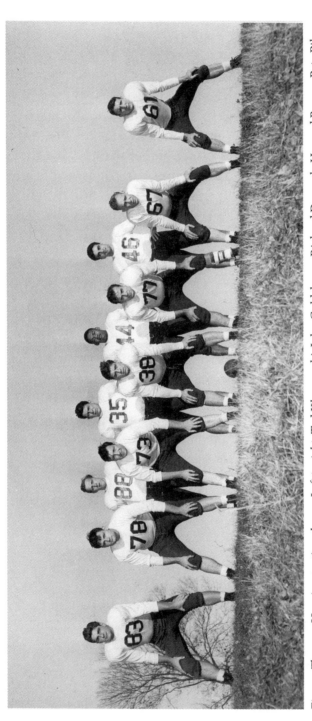

Fig. 4.9 The 1945 Hoosier starting eleven. *Left to right:* Ted Kluszewski, John Goldsberry, Richard Deranek, Howard Brown, Pete Pihos, John Cannady, George Taliaferro, Joe Sowinski, Ben Raimondi, Russell Deal, and Bob Ravensberg. This hand-tinted picture hung in the Gables restaurant to celebrate the undefeated season. Because the restaurant was only open to white patrons, Taliaferro could only peek through a window to catch a glimpse of part of the picture. *Photo courtesy IU Archives.*

before Taliaferro actually had the opportunity to see the picture in its entirety.

In November, the Nuremberg trials began. Twenty-two German officers were put on trial in Nuremberg, Germany, for war crimes. The judges were from France, Great Britain, Russia, and the United States. When the trials were over, twelve men were sentenced to death by hanging, seven were given jail terms, and three were set free. While the trials signaled that the war was ostensibly over, the draft was not. Before he had a chance to finish his freshman year, Taliaferro received a letter from Uncle Sam demanding that he serve his country. He wouldn't be back at Indiana University in the fall to play for McMillin. Instead, like so many black servicemen, he would spend his time in the army fighting racism, a more visible enemy than any others he would encounter as an American soldier.

FIVE

1946–47: ARMY DAYS

ALTHOUGH SHE HAD MEANT WELL, Mrs. Parham's advice, despite a rule that deferred state college students from the draft, ultimately had not kept Taliaferro from being drafted into the US Army. In fact, he would later learn that his decision to play football for Indiana may have been the impetus that got him drafted. Although the notice was not welcome, he would eventually appreciate the significant impact his time in the army had on the course of his life. But when he received his draft notice on February 4, 1946, he was only aware that it meant he would be leaving Indiana football and his education behind. Shortly after he received the letter, he departed for his induction in Indianapolis, from where he headed to Camp Atterbury in Edinburgh, Indiana, to be processed. That took only two days, and then it was time for him to leave again, this time for basic training. At Camp Lee, an army post in Petersburg, Virginia, Taliaferro would experience the basic training required of all soldiers, but unlike some of the other soldiers, he would also deal with racism and fall in love.

During basic, Taliaferro and the other new recruits were confined to the post for two months, at which time they received instruction in weapons, drills, and tactics, while enduring seemingly endless hours of physical training. Although they were free to leave the post in the evenings and on weekends, they were required to report for roll call each morning. Under those circumstances, and having spent countless hours with each other in just a short period of time, the inductees quickly became acquainted. Among Taliaferro's fellow trainees were some University of Michigan football players, the same ones he had played against a few months before in IU's season opener. Conversations among them often consisted of their shared Big Ten football experiences. Most of the time, these conversations were just small talk, a way to kill time in order to avoid the boredom that comes with the daily routine. During one such exchange, however, Taliaferro made an interesting discovery. There was a rumor, it seemed, that the political connections of one of the Michigan football coaches may have actually landed Taliaferro in the service. The Michigan players told Taliaferro that at the end of the season their coach had practically guaranteed the team that they would not have to worry about playing against freshman phenom George Taliaferro the following season. Taliaferro laughed at first, assuming that they were kidding, but the serious looks on their faces revealed that they weren't.

"Well, how could he know such a thing?" Taliaferro asked, still not quite believing their story. It didn't seem possible, as far as he was concerned.

"All I can tell you is that's what he said," a Michigan player responded, not really offering any more in the way of explanation.

This information frustrated Taliaferro. In Gary, he had been a star athlete in an integrated neighborhood. He was accepted for who he was, and he was seemingly in control of his life. In the last year, however, he had begun to encounter more incidents of racism and segregation. Now, the idea that Michigan coach Fritz Crisler could have had that kind of impact on his life solidified for Taliaferro the thought that he was no longer in control of it. The realization that so many others could affect what he could do settled like a heavy weight in his stomach. It was a lesson he would never forget.

Fig. 5.1 Despite the fact that World War II had already ended, after his freshman year Taliaferro was drafted into the army. He was stationed at Camp Lee in Petersburg, Virginia. Circa 1946. *Photo courtesy George Taliaferro.*

Taliaferro could not confirm whether it truly had been Crisler who had gotten him drafted. However, it was true that the Michigan Wolverines would not have to play against him in 1946, and the 1946 Indiana and Michigan game had been anticipated to be a real duel between Michigan's halfback, Walt Teninga, and Indiana's George Taliaferro. Ironically, neither would end up playing in the Big Ten in 1946. Teninga was in the same basic training at Camp Lee and was among those telling Taliaferro about the supposed conspiracy to keep him from playing Michigan. Not only was there to be no duel between Teninga and Taliaferro, two of the Big Ten's biggest talents, but they ended up teammates in the army—along with two other Michigan players, Al Wahl and George Chimes.

Taliaferro's contribution to IU's championship football team had not gone unnoticed, netting him a position on the football team and other advantages during his time in the service. For a soldier who had just completed basic training, Taliaferro was somewhat privileged. He was in the quartermaster division, the supply people for the military. Taliaferro, however, was put into the special services, a position that he said allowed him to choose his own assignment. He decided to do what he had done in high school; he played football, basketball, and baseball, and he trained boxers. These assignments, the result of his recognized athletic prowess, were designed to keep Taliaferro in the entertainment aspect of the service. They even kept him from going to Japan with the rest of his outfit. In fact, he never left the United States the entire sixteen months that he was in the service.

His athleticism could only take him so far, though. Despite some preferential treatment due to his athletic ability, Taliaferro could not quell the racism that existed in every facet of his life, even when he was serving his country. Disadvantages, he was realizing, always came with his skin color, no matter how exceptional his athletic skills. He wasn't the only one. On his army football team, there were five other black football players—all,

Fig. 5.2 During what should have been his sophomore year at Indiana, Taliaferro (*front row, third from the left*) played for the Camp Lee football team, seen here circa 1946. *Photo courtesy George Taliaferro.*

Fig. 5.3 Even as a soldier, Taliaferro was recognized for his pigskin prowess. Circa 1946. *Photo courtesy George Taliaferro.*

like him, serving their country in the United States military and all experiencing the spoils of athleticism and the frustration of racism.

In one incident, Taliaferro recalled, his football team had been traveling to a game. From their base in Petersburg, Virginia, they had taken a couple of army buses to Aberdeen Proving Ground in Maryland to play against another military installation's football team. It was not this particular game itself, but the return trip home, that was notable to Taliaferro. After the game, Sam Francis, the head coach, made a last-minute decision to stay in Washington, DC, for the weekend. He left Taliaferro, his team captain, in charge. Francis gave Taliaferro some government vouchers and instructed him to use them on the way back to base to pay for the team's dinner at a restaurant. Having given those few instructions, Francis headed to DC, and the team boarded the bus for Virginia.

Wanting to wait until they were closer to base before they stopped, they decided to eat somewhere in Virginia. So they drove through Maryland and stopped when they came upon a rustic restaurant in Alexandria, Virginia. By that time, they were famished. The entire team climbed off the buses and walked into the restaurant, where they stood under chandeliers made of old wagon wheels. The place didn't look fancy, but as long as it had food, they would be content. Taliaferro walked ahead of the others, government vouchers ready in his hand, but before he could say anything, the manager approached him.

"Hey! Hey! Hey! What are you doing? What are you doing?" the manager barked. He hadn't even reached them yet; he was yelling as he ran toward them, his arms pumping at his sides as if he were running a race.

Taliaferro waited until the man was in front of him, so as not to shout, and began to explain. "Well, we are the football team from Camp Lee in Petersburg, Virginia, and we want to eat. We have a government voucher," he said, not understanding the intent behind the question.

"You can't eat in here," the manager replied abruptly, cutting Taliaferro off, offering neither explanation nor apology.

"What do you mean we can't eat in here?" Taliaferro asked.

"*You* can't," the man said, pointing to Taliaferro, the emphasis on the word providing Taliaferro all the explanation he needed. Suddenly it was clear exactly what the man meant.

"You mean because I'm colored?" Taliaferro asked him, trying to control his voice, but the waver in it indicated his growing resentment.

"That's right. *You* can't eat in here." The man said it again, in the same tone, with the same emphasis on the word *you*.

Noticeably upset, Taliaferro did not want trouble, and he was getting used to being barred from places. So he simply turned to his teammates and said, "Guys, let's go," signaling for them to leave.

Taliaferro and his black teammates turned and began to walk away.

Jerry Tuttle, a fullback from Ohio State, said, "George, you guys go ahead and get on the bus. We'll be right out."

Taliaferro nodded. He didn't dwell on it; it had happened before. He and the other black members of the team would wait on the bus while their white teammates ate in the restaurant. They walked out to the buses as their white teammates remained inside.

They had only been waiting for a few minutes, though, when Tuttle; Teninga; Tony Gator, a player from North Carolina; and the other white players came running out of the restaurant. They didn't stop until they were back on the bus.

"Let's go! Let's go! Let's go! And don't go down the main highway!" one of them yelled to the bus driver.

"Well, what's the matter?" Taliaferro asked.

"We just tore that place up!" Tuttle said.

"Oh my God, here we go. Now we're going to be court-martialed and shot before a firing squad," Taliaferro said, not really worried at all. In fact, the only emotion he felt at the time was pride. Recalling the whole experience decades later, a huge grin spread across his face. "Us Big Ten guys stuck together," he said.

They may have gained some satisfaction from the impromptu protest in the restaurant, but their stomachs were less than satisfied. When they finally got back to Petersburg, Virginia, they were ravenous. Taliaferro thought of a place where they could all eat, where he had connections. His position on Indiana's championship team and his All-American honors had earned him recognition even in the South. One such admirer owned a restaurant, the Green Lantern, in Petersburg. "It's on Halifax Street. I know we can eat there," Taliaferro assured his teammates. So they drove to Halifax Street and found a place to park near the Green Lantern. For the second time that day, they all got off the bus and filed together into the entrance of a restaurant.

This time when they entered, they were relieved to find that the greeting from the owner was a friendly one. "Hey, George!" he said, as he walked up to Taliaferro. There was a short pause as the man looked around at the army football team in front of him. "Wait a minute, wait a minute. What are you doin'?" he asked, seemingly confused. Taliaferro again explained the situation. They were on their way back from a football game; their coach had stayed in DC, "and we have a voucher that we need to spend. We want to get something to eat," Taliaferro finished.

The reply was unexpected. The owner was Taliaferro's friend, had greeted them in a friendly manner, yet the man said, "You can't eat in here." It was the same sentence they had heard earlier.

"Come on. What do you mean?" Taliaferro asked, his frustration increasing with every minute the conversation continued, with every ridiculous explanation of a system that made no sense.

"Black people and white people can't eat in the same dining room in the state of Virginia," the man explained. The army football team, used to eating together on base, had been unaware of this.

No matter how many times Taliaferro experienced the injustice of racism, it left him in shock and disbelief. He said, "Well, in other words the guy in Alexandria was Jim Crow, so this is Joe Crow."

That was the typical treatment that he and the other black servicemen received, even though they were in the United States military. They were fighting for a country that didn't accept them, that saw them as second-class citizens, that sometimes acted as if they didn't exist. "Even being dressed properly in our uniforms did not make any difference," Taliaferro said. They left the Green Lantern, still hungry and with only one option left. They returned to base to eat in the mess tent, the only place the entire team was free to eat together, the unspent vouchers untouched in Taliaferro's pocket.

There was very little talking when they finally got to eat dinner. "We ate like butchers' hounds, we were so hungry," Taliaferro said. The short amount of time it took him to eat his meal was the only time he wasn't thinking about what they had gone through that night in order to eat. His stomach was finally full, but Taliaferro felt empty. It was disheartening to wear the uniform of the Army of the United States of America, to hear talk about defending the rights and freedoms of this free country, and then to be denied those rights himself. He was in uniform to defend a country that did not want him, that treated him as if he were nothing. He wasn't the only black soldier to wrestle with that reality.

Segregated restaurants were only one small part of the racism that Taliaferro encountered during his stint in the military. It was part of the experience of the black soldier, and he was no exception. Even though it was common, that did not mean that Taliaferro had to accept it, though. There were times, as in those two restaurants, when he just walked away. Other times, it got to him so much that he couldn't keep the anger and frustration inside any longer. One of those times happened at an away football game. His football team took a Greyhound bus from Petersburg, Virginia, to Fort Benning, Georgia, for a game. Once they arrived, Coach Francis was told that his black players could not stay in the same facility on the base as the white players. It was, after all, the segregated South.

During a phone call with his mother, Taliaferro had mentioned the Georgia game. This prompted Virnater Taliaferro to worry. She did not want her son to go to a southern state, where the racism was known for being more pronounced and for taking a more violent, more physical form. She was so worried about her son going to Georgia that she called Coach Francis to discuss the situation. She was worried that something would happen to her son in the racially charged state, she told Coach Francis, who calmed her down and allayed her fears. Her son, he explained, was in the US military, so he would have behind him the full protection

Fig. 5.4 Taliaferro with two of his Camp Lee teammates: Mel Lewis of Howard University (*far left*) and Robert Alexander of UCLA (*right*). Circa 1946. *Photo courtesy George Taliaferro.*

of the US Army. Coach Francis would see to that personally, he assured her. Although she had her doubts, his words had calmed her down enough to let the matter go.

The full protection of the army, it seems, was still no match for the Jim Crow laws of the South, laws that were embedded in its very culture. Once they arrived on base, Taliaferro and the other black members of his team were immediately segregated from the white players. The black players were sent to Sand Town, an area of the post where all of the black troops lived, while their white teammates were in a large brick dormitory. The brick barracks, unlike the simple wooden ones of Sand Town, had standard amenities.

Even the food in Sand Town was of inferior quality. The meal prepared for them at breakfast was re-served to them for lunch.

The eggs were hard, and they stuck stubbornly to the metal trays on which they were served. Taliaferro, who had often ignored racism when faced with it, simply refused to eat the food. This time, he was too frustrated to overlook the racism. He called Coach Francis and told him that he and the other players needed some real food to eat, that the leftover egg paste was not going to be sufficient. "And I have no intention of playing in that game tomorrow," he informed his coach, anger etched into every syllable.

In an act of solidarity, the other five black players, following Taliaferro's lead, also refused to eat the food or play in the game. Not wanting them to get in trouble too, Taliaferro told them, "Hey, you don't have to be a part of this. This happens to be the way that I feel, and I feel this way because of the promise that Colonel Francis made to my mother indicating that I would not be discriminated against in any way, shape, form, or fashion, and since it has not happened, I am not in any way obligated to play the game." This was his fight; they did not have to stand with him, he said. His teammates felt the same frustration and anger he did, though. Why should they play in the game if they were treated as inferior to the white players? They would continue to protest right alongside him. Their protests prompted Colonel Francis to address the issue with the commanding officer at Fort Benning, who then called for an audience with Taliaferro and Francis.

Taliaferro remembered walking into the room. Fort Benning's commanding officer, wasting no time, looked him in the eye and threatened, "Soldier, you can be dishonorably discharged."

Refusing to be intimidated, Taliaferro stood firm. "Sir, I mean no disrespect, but you better start doing it, 'cause I won't play," he replied.

Until he and his teammates were housed in the same barracks, given the same food, and treated with the same respect as their white teammates, Taliaferro said, they would simply refuse to play the game. The protest was risky, a fact that he and the other players considered, but they could not ignore the blatant racism.

It worked. Opting not to pursue the dishonorable discharge, the commanding officer sent a weapons carrier, similar to today's Humvee, large enough for all six of the black players. They climbed aboard with what little luggage they had, and the weapons carrier took them back to the brick barracks with the rest of the team. They would be playing in the game after all.

The game itself, according to the Sand Town cook, also signified a change in Fort Benning, Georgia. Taliaferro had struck up a conversation with the man when he first arrived in Sand Town. During a friendly exchange, the cook, a black man, had asked Taliaferro, "Whom are you going to play football against?"

"We are going to play the Doughboys," Taliaferro replied.

"No, you're not going to play the Doughboys," the cook corrected, chuckling a little. He went on to explain, "We have two football teams. We have a black football team, and we have a white football team. And if you're going to play anybody, you are going to play the black football team."

"No, we are going to play the Doughboys," Taliaferro insisted. He hadn't realized that Fort Benning had two teams, but he and his teammates had already been told that they were competing against the Doughboys, so he assumed that was still the case.

"I tell you what. I have two three-day passes in my pocket. I am going to give these passes away because I want to see you play the Doughboys in Fort Benning, Georgia. That's going to be history. It's going to be the first time that blacks and whites ever competed against each other in the state of Georgia," the cook said.

Taliaferro and his teammates did play the Doughboys, Fort Benning's aptly named all-white football team. A huge Georgia audience came to watch. The Doughboys, led by Captain John Green, a College Football Hall of Fame inductee, had a tremendous reputation. In total, five players from the United States Military Academy's 1945 championship team were on the Doughboys. There was a huge OCS (officer training) attachment at Fort Benning, and many of the players had been transferred there from

Fig. 5.5 George Taliaferro runs the ball for his Camp Lee football team. Circa 1946.
Photo courtesy George Taliaferro.

West Point. Taliaferro and his teammates were going to be battling a tough opponent.

The talent level would have been difficult by itself, but the Doughboys also had the weather on their side. They were used to the stifling southern heat and humidity, but Taliaferro and many of his teammates had never played in temperatures that high before. They fought hard, in spite of the temperature, but so did the Doughboys. Both defenses were resolute, so there was no score for the first three and a half quarters. The last eight minutes of the game told a different story altogether, though. The Doughboys' offense kicked in and scored several times in just eight short minutes. Not only did they win, but they dominated, beating Taliaferro's team 26–0. The Doughboys had capitalized on their dominant stamina in the oppressive heat. "I wondered if

I almost had a heat stroke, and here it was October. But October in Georgia is still plenty hot," Taliaferro said. "We just got tired," he continued. Still, in some ways they had achieved victory. They had kept the talented team scoreless for most of the game, but more importantly, they had used football as a vehicle to begin breaking down the barriers of segregation. It wouldn't be an immediate change, but it was a start.

Despite some incidents of racism and segregation, being in the service was not all bad. Taliaferro was able to play the sports he loved. And he met the girl of his dreams, Viola Jones. Virginia State College for Negroes was located in Ettrick, Virginia. It was just outside Petersburg, about five miles from Camp Lee, his base. On his first weekend pass, having nothing better to do, Taliaferro had an idea to pass the time. He rode the bus from Camp Lee to Petersburg, got directions in town, and walked to campus to watch the Virginia State Trojan football team in its spring workout. Upon finding the stadium, he climbed about halfway up the empty stands and took a seat to watch, thinking about what he would be doing at Indiana University if he were there. McMillin was probably working on versions of the Cockeyed T with Taliaferro's teammates, he thought. Although he missed Indiana University, he knew he couldn't complain; he was fortunate to get to continue playing football while in the army.

Shortly after he took his seat, another person climbed the same set of bleachers and sat near him. Taliaferro, lost in his reverie and in the action on the field, was unaware of the presence until someone asked, "Are you George Taliaferro?" A little surprised that someone there would know him, Taliaferro affirmed his identity. The man introduced himself. "Milton Purvis," he said, offering his hand. He recognized Taliaferro, who was in civilian attire, by his colorful jacket, the one given to members of the 1945 Indiana University football team to commemorate its undefeated season and undisputed Big Ten championship.

Milton Purvis was the sports editor of the Virginia State campus newspaper, so he was familiar with Taliaferro's football prowess. Purvis also explained that there had been several articles announcing that the popular athlete would be playing football at Camp Lee. The All-American, one article had indicated, would be seen in the area in the fall. So it hadn't taken Purvis long to identify him. The two conversed for a while, about football and the army, until Purvis excused himself and left the stands. Taliaferro watched him as he made his way down the bleachers and onto the practice field. There, Purvis began talking to Virginia's Coach Jefferson. It didn't take long for Taliaferro to realize that they were talking about him. Purvis motioned to the stands, clearly pointing him out, then beckoned for Taliaferro to join them on the field. Purvis made introductions. They talked briefly, and then Coach Jefferson asked Taliaferro to tell the team about his experiences playing football for Indiana University and in the army. Taken aback at first, because many of the players on the team were older than he was, Taliaferro reluctantly agreed. Coach Jefferson gathered his team and the other coaches around, and Taliaferro launched into an impromptu speech. When it was over, he couldn't even remember what he had said, he had been so nervous. But, despite his initial qualms, the applause and gratitude he received indicated he must have done okay. When the Trojans resumed practice, Taliaferro accompanied Purvis back to the stands, relieved that the experience was over.

The two continued their conversation until practice ended. Though they had not known each other long, Purvis had been impressed by Taliaferro and had devised a plan to take him to dinner on campus, where he could introduce him to his "play sister." Historically black colleges used a program of inviting freshmen men and women to pair off as "play brothers and sisters," in order to give them someone they could relate to and turn to as they adjusted to college life. Purvis invited Taliaferro to be his guest for dinner. Taliaferro acquiesced and followed Purvis out of the stands, the two talking the entire walk to the dining hall on campus. There, they got in line, picked up trays, and made their food choices. With a full tray balanced in his hand, Taliaferro followed Purvis, who was scanning the dining room. Finding what he was looking for, Purvis made his way to a table on the other side of the cafeteria, where three young women were sitting. Purvis was focused on one in particular. "George Taliaferro, I want you to meet my play sister, Viola Jones," he said.

When he saw her, Taliaferro absolutely could not believe his eyes. The well-built beauty with dark hair that just brushed her shoulders had rendered him speechless. His mouth opened, but no sound escaped his stunned lips. "The lights went out when Milton introduced us," he later said of the encounter. Beyond that, he could not remember much of the meeting, just that he could not get over the beautiful Viola Jones. "I was completely out of my mind and didn't want to make an ass out of myself," Taliaferro said. He was pretty sure they exchanged the usual small talk about hometowns, the army, college majors, and football, but that was the extent of it. Although he could tell that she was incredibly bright, she was clearly not a loquacious person.

At the end of dinner, as they were saying good-bye, Taliaferro could only nod at the other two women, whose names escaped him. And while he was relatively sure he had eaten, because he had returned an empty tray to the wash area, he couldn't recall actually doing so. The only recollection he had of the entire experience was being so smitten with Viola Jones that everything else had left him. Once they were safely out of the dining hall, he began pumping Purvis for more information about her. He wanted to know about the play brother/play sister program and the length of time that Purvis had been Jones's play brother. Purvis humored him, patiently answering his every inquiry. They had met as freshmen, he explained, and were on their third year as play siblings. Understanding what Taliaferro was really digging for, Purvis finally just asked what Taliaferro was too shy to admit: "Do you want to see her again?" Taliaferro could not hide his eagerness. Of course he wanted to see her again. He hadn't been able to think of anything else since he had met her. Purvis told him where she lived and offered to find out what her dorm's visiting hours were so that Taliaferro could see her again.

The idea that he might get to see her again encouraged Taliaferro. But it wasn't enough to satiate his appetite for information on Viola Jones. Purvis continued patiently answering each new request for information. Jones worked as Coach Jefferson's secretary, Purvis told Taliaferro, and she was pursuing a degree in business education. The conversation went on like that for a while. Taliaferro did not want to leave campus that night, but eventually he had to go back to base. He did not hesitate to contact her, though, and a short time later he had made plans for their first date.

Dating off campus was not permitted for the Virginia State students, so his first date with Jones took place on campus. The information from Purvis combined with his conversation with Jones was revealing. Despite her quiet demeanor and modesty, she was actually one of the most popular girls on campus, he noticed. She was a cheerleader, a princess in the homecoming activities, and she was involved in several clubs. She also played tennis and volleyball and loved to dance. Their first date did not disappoint Taliaferro. He asked her out again, and many more dates followed, always on campus. They went to movies and to concerts and out to eat. They even took in some football games. After a few weeks of dating, Taliaferro even brought a couple of his army buddies to meet the young woman he had been constantly jabbering about. When it was time to introduce them, he was too nervous to remember her last name. Instead, he just introduced her as his girlfriend. He noticed happily that she didn't deny it. She might have been trying to spare him the embarrassment, he thought, but she also might have agreed that their relationship had moved to the next level. Taliaferro preferred to believe the latter, and the fact that their dating continued into basketball season was a good sign. They took in some basketball games and even attended church together on occasion. They continued to go to dances together and sometimes just strolled the campus talking. Taliaferro enjoyed her company, especially their conversations. As they learned more about each other with every date, Taliaferro began to wonder if she was the woman with whom he would spend the rest of his life. He certainly hoped so.

As he headed to her dorm one afternoon, Taliaferro walked by a scale, one of the full-sized machines that tell one's weight and fortune. Shrugging his shoulders and thinking, *why not*, he stopped, stepped on its base, and inserted a nickel. The arrow moved around the face of the scale, finally landing on 195, the same weight he had been for years, and a small fortune card came out. He had told Coach Bo McMillin that he wasn't a superstitious person, but he had to wonder when he took the card from the slot and read the words: *You will meet the campus queen.* Looking around to see if anyone else had witnessed the event, then realizing that he was alone, he said aloud, "I've already met her." Smiling, he couldn't help but wonder if maybe the fortune was more than a coincidence. *It must be fate*, he decided. It made him think again about his chance meeting with Milton Purvis that day in the football stadium and the way Purvis had introduced him to the slim beauty whom he now couldn't stomach leaving. Since that meeting, Taliaferro had spent all of his weekends on campus with her. Regrettably, school was closing for the summer, and Viola Jones was packing to go back home. The thought of their separation stole the smile from his face as he made his way to her dorm for one of their last dates before she left.

He couldn't just let her go, especially if they were destined to be together. Taliaferro was prompted to take action. After only a few short months of dating, he did the only thing he could think to do. He simply asked her, completely out of the blue, "Viola, will you marry me?" He could read no emotion on her face, but he wouldn't have had time to anyway. She did not hesitate. Her response was an abrupt and resounding no. She was only seventeen, she told him. She had graduated early from high school and had promptly enrolled in college. She had too many plans for her future. She wanted to graduate from college, get a job, and return home to help her parents financially. And even if that weren't the case, she explained further, she really did not know him or his background well enough to marry him. She had plenty of reasons to justify her answer, but all Taliaferro heard was the *no*. He wasn't sure why he had expected her to say yes, but he had. He knew he was in love with her. Apparently, she just didn't feel the same way. Crushed and dejected, Taliaferro headed back to his post. Usually he would arrive there in high spirits after one of their dates, but not this time. Instead, he went straight to his bunk and took off all of his clothes. Then he walked into the latrine, stood in front of the full-length mirror, and asked himself aloud, "How could she say no to perfection?"

There was some hope, at least, in the fact that her refusal of his impromptu proposal had not completely ended the relationship. The two continued to correspond by mail over the summer. Taliaferro's position had not changed. He was still completely smitten with her. On a two-week furlough home to Gary, he could think or talk about nothing but her. He was miserably in love, and to make matters worse, his high school girlfriend was getting married, a painful reminder of his own rejection.

At the end of the summer, Taliaferro's furlough was over and Jones was headed back to school. Both returned to Virginia, where their relationship continued where it had left off. There was, however, no more talk of marriage. Taliaferro held on to the hope that dating would provide the opportunity for her to get to know him well enough to finally agree to marry him. They certainly enjoyed being around each other when the opportunity presented itself. However, they were both busy, and Taliaferro, playing football for the post, was away at football games on alternate Saturdays. When they were together, he made his intentions to marry her clear, even though he never came right out and said it, afraid of both scaring her off and being rejected again. Still, he wanted his feelings to be clear. His strategy seemed to be working, as if he was finally making some progress in their relationship, when she invited him, after the last football game on the post, to visit her family in Evington, Virginia.

In Evington, he was introduced to her mother and father and her two brothers, both recently discharged from military service. Her father, a farmer and practical joker, challenged the "city slicker" Taliaferro to strength, agility, and shooting contests, as well as other contests involving farming. Taliaferro wanted to make a good impression, but he was too competitive to just let her father win. The honest thing to do, he thought, was to try his hardest. The outcome was that he either equaled or beat her father in every contest. Jones's mother enjoyed that immensely and cheered on her daughter's boyfriend during the contests.

Finally, Jones's father had seen enough, and Taliaferro had apparently proved himself. Her father suggested they all go inside for the large dinner spread. They ate and talked about Taliaferro and his plans for football and college. The conversation continued after dinner as well. Taliaferro talked with Jones's brothers late into the night, discussing their military experiences and his experiences playing football at IU and in the service. Although Taliaferro did not drink, he accompanied her brothers to a local bar, where they visited with some of the local men to catch up on the latest sports news. For Taliaferro, the family visit had been a huge success. Her family seemed to like him, and his relationship with the beautiful undergrad seemed to progress at a new level after the visit. She was introducing him to her background and her family, something dear to her. Taliaferro was hopeful about what that meant.

The couple continued seeing each other weekly until she graduated in June 1947. Upon graduating, however, she took a job at the Tuskegee Institute in Alabama, the home of World War II's first black fighter pilots, the successful Tuskegee Airmen, whose 332nd Fighter Group had never lost a bomber to enemy action. Like so many African Americans of the time, the Tuskegee Airmen had fought both for their country and against the racism they experienced while doing so. Their fight against oppression in the US Army Air Corps led the way to Executive Order #9981, desegregating the armed forces, which would be signed by President Truman in July 1948.

Jones's move to Tuskegee meant a separation for the couple, but it would have happened soon anyway. Taliaferro didn't know it at the time, but he was soon going to be discharged from the army. The couple managed the separation by corresponding via mail, but it wasn't the same. Taliaferro had grown accustomed to seeing her often, which had meant that he always had something to look forward to. Not seeing her was going to be difficult. At least seeing his family in Gary would help ease the loneliness. Taliaferro couldn't be sure how it happened that he was getting out of the army early, but he knew it started when he received a call from his Indiana University football coach, Bo McMillin, who told him that a man named Frank Summers would be calling him. Summers was one of Taliaferro's fraternity brothers, but the two had never actually met. McMillin gave no other information. Taliaferro had no idea what the call would be about, just that Summers would be calling. The call offered little more information. Summers simply asked a series of questions and then requested the name of a contact person on base. Taliaferro was unsure what the purpose of the call had been. He had given the information as requested, because McMillin had told him to, but he still didn't understand why. Assuming that McMillin would eventually explain, Taliaferro dismissed it.

Within four days, the reason became clear, though he still hadn't heard back from McMillin himself. Taliaferro found out that his entire outfit would be shipped out to Japan as part of the postwar occupation. The day they were all to leave, however, Taliaferro was called in by the first sergeant, the "top kick." The top kick was the guy who did seemingly everything for the administration. "If the commander wanted to communicate with you, in any way, they never lowered themselves to speak with you; the top kick did it all," he said. So Taliaferro went to see the top kick, wondering why he had been summoned. It was good news. The man handed Taliaferro two three-day passes and told him, "I'll see you when you get back." Taliaferro was confused; his outfit was leaving, and he was being handed passes. He wondered what it could mean.

"Well, I didn't request anything," he said, fishing for information.

"Just go. You got six days. I'll see you when you get back," the first sergeant replied, not offering any further information, simultaneously handing him the passes and dismissing him.

Taliaferro knew better than to argue, so he took the offered passes. Jones was no longer in Virginia, so he couldn't go see her. Instead, he decided to go to New Jersey to visit his Indiana University teammate Mel Groomes. Although Taliaferro had made arrangements to stay at the YMCA, Groomes insisted he stay with him instead. The two spent the time catching up. Groomes filled Taliaferro in on the 1946 Indiana football season, while Taliaferro told him about playing football for Camp Lee and falling in love with Viola Jones. Although the visit was a pleasant one, it pained Taliaferro to talk about two of the things he missed so much. It was a reminder that they were both gone. Feeling more homesick than he had in a while, he left Groomes and headed back to base. He arrived to discover that his outfit had departed for Japan, leaving him behind. That is when he was told that he had been honorably discharged. His formal discharge on June 23, 1947, was just sixteen months after he went into the army. Of this odd situation he just said, "The same way they got me in, I got out. I didn't ask any questions." Apparently, Big Ten coaches had some political clout, at least when it came to the draft.

1947: A VOLATILE TIME FOR PROFESSIONAL FOOTBALL

WHILE TALIAFERRO WAS IN THE service, professional football had continued to evolve. With the formation of the All-America Football Conference (the AAFC), the NFL would no longer have a monopoly on professional football. NFL commissioner Elmer Layden was so unhappy about the formation of the new league that he decided not to acknowledge its existence. However, the AAFC, described by Peterson as the "first serious challenge to the supremacy of the NFL," planned to begin sanctioning games in the 1946 season, whether Layden acknowledged its existence or not. Despite Layden's attempt, the AAFC could not be ignored for long, and the subsequent feud between the two leagues made a lasting impact on the sport.

The new league had eight franchises, four teams in the East division and four teams in the West division. The East division consisted of the New York Yankees, the Brooklyn Dodgers, the Buffalo Bisons, and the Miami Seahawks. In the West division were the Cleveland Browns, San Francisco 49ers, Los Angeles Dons, and Chicago Rockets. This new league was, in general, competition to the NFL. However, in three cities—New York, Chicago, and Los Angeles—the new league was in direct competition with established NFL teams, making the rivalry fiercer.

Because they would be vying for some of the same players and for some of the same fans, the AAFC's leaders wanted to have a preseason meeting with their NFL counterparts to discuss player contracts and territory rights. Still trying to ignore the new competitor, Commissioner Layden simply disregarded the request to meet. According to an article in the *Chicago Daily Tribune*, Layden said, "Tell them to get a football first." According to Peterson, Layden's curt reply was, "Let them get a football and play a game, and then maybe we'll have something to talk about." Interestingly, the AAFC's commissioner and president, Jim Crowley, and NFL commissioner Layden had been teammates, both a part of Notre Dame's legendary Four Horsemen.

Notre Dame's website tells the story of the famous quartet who earned their name in a game against Army. Sportswriter Grantland Rice wrote, "Outlined against a blue, gray October sky the Four Horsemen rode again. In dramatic lore they are known as famine, pestilence, destruction, and death. These are only aliases. Their real names are: Stuhldreher, Miller, Crowley, and Layden." Harry Stuhldreher was the quarterback; Crowley was the left halfback; Don Miller, the right halfback; and Layden, the fullback. The quartet, made up of only sophomores, was running all over defenses under the leadership of Knute Rockne. It was 1924, and Notre Dame was three games into a perfect season and eyeing a Rose Bowl championship when Rice coined the famous passage, which was then used by George Strickler, a Notre Dame publicity aide, to create the unforgettable image of the four men on horseback.

Despite their illustrious history, Layden and Crowley, who would both eventually be elected to the National Football Foundation Hall of Fame, were no longer playing for the same side. Crowley responded to Layden's attempt to ignore the new league with a warning to the NFL. According to Peterson, Crowley said, "We originally resolved not to tamper with National League players, but since the NFL snubbed us we see no reason why we can't hire their players." This statement's impact on professional football became immediately clear. The feud led to trouble for both leagues as they competed for players. The subsequent salary war inflated player compensation, causing financial ramifications for both the NFL and the AAFC.

Sportswriter Hugh Fullerton Jr. noted that teams of both leagues reported losses because of the rivalry and the bidding up of salaries in order to compete for players. Although the inflated salaries were causing both leagues to suffer, the AAFC seemed to be winning the battle for players. According to Peterson, forty-four of the sixty players on the 1946 All-Star team went to the AAFC. That small success wasn't enough to keep the AAFC out of financial difficulty, though. Edward Prell of the *Chicago Daily Tribune* wrote, "There has been a growing awareness of late that professional football's battle of dollars is taking its toll." Part of the problem, he explained, was the exorbitant player salaries. "Twenty-five years ago, the annual club salary perhaps was no more than $25,000. Now it is $250,000! A maximum of $175,000 would strike an average of $5,000 for the 35 players on the squad," he suggested. Both leagues were suffering, and it was soon clear that both would be in trouble if the war between them did not end.

Some thought the only way to resolve the issue was for the two leagues to merge. Prell, however, felt otherwise. He said, "There should be no swallowing up of one league by the other, for professional football then would revert to its dark ages—with lopsided schedules and the owner again holding too much of a whip hand over the player." Instead, he suggested following baseball's example by having sixteen teams covering all metropolitan areas and ending the season with a final series between the two conferences. That wouldn't happen, however, until the two leagues began to communicate, and it didn't look as if that would happen any time soon.

While the AAFC had difficulty initially, it managed to achieve minor success. Many key players were lured to the league, and the

franchises completed their schedules. Despite this, financial difficulties plagued many of the AAFC teams. The Miami Seahawks
were just one example. They had numerous unpaid hotel bills
that they didn't have the funds to pay, and sparse home-game
crowds furthered their financial difficulties, leaving the league
to pay the players' salaries. By 1947 the league had taken back the
troubled franchise. Fortunately, a group of investors from Baltimore stepped in and bought the beleaguered team, and soon the
Miami Seahawks had become the Baltimore Colts.

Although the changes in professional football did not affect
Taliaferro in 1946, they would be significant to him in a couple
of years. And although the war between the two leagues was significant, of even greater interest to professional football was its
reintegration. Unlike pro baseball, which had always been an
exclusively white sport, professional football had employed black
players from its outset. The first black professional football player
was Charles W. Follis, who played from 1902 through 1906 with
the Shelby Athletic Club. Robert W. Marshall, the second black
professional football player, played for twenty years, from 1905 to
1925, for the Akron Indians. Other black players include Henry
McDonald and Gideon Smith, who also played professional football in the early 1900s. McDonald played from 1911–17 for the
Rochester Jeffersons, and "Charlie" Smith played one game for
the Canton Bulldogs in 1915. Between 1920 and 1932, many more
African American football players were playing professionally.
Frederick "Fritz" Pollard played for several teams between 1919
and 1925; Paul Robeson played from 1921 to 1922; and Sol Butler
played from 1923 to 1926, to name just a few. Through 1932 there
were at least fifteen African Americans who either were playing
or had played professional football. This all changed, however, in
1933. By then, professional football, like professional baseball, was
an exclusively white sport.

Many factors produced this color line. Peterson wrote that the
same justifications for the color line in major league baseball also

applied to professional football. The first justification was that many white football players simply would not take the field with a black player. The fact that black players could not travel with the club because hotels and restaurants would not accommodate them was given as another justification. Training, which often took place in the South, where it was illegal for blacks and whites to compete together, was another reason for the color line. Finally, the actual ability and mental capacity of the black players were questioned. They were simply not good enough or smart enough, according to some critics, to play professional football. Taliaferro thought it more likely that the same critics who worried that blacks weren't good enough actually worried that black players would be better at the sport than their white counterpoints. Either way, these justifications were used by both professional football and professional baseball to draw a color line in their respective sports.

Professional football added one more reason to the already long list. Because football is a contact sport, there would be more opportunity for racism among players on the field. This was accurate. Players did use the close contact for this purpose, and incidents of racism were not uncommon. According to Peterson, Fritz Pollard, the first black star in the NFL, said, "The white players were always trying to hurt me, and I had to be able to protect myself if I was going to stay in the game." Whether or not the other justifications were true, there were other possible and more plausible reasons for professional football's color line. Sportswriter Stuart McIver was one of many journalists and historians who credited Redskins owner George Preston Marshall with professional football's racial barrier. According to Peterson, historian Thomas G. Smith said, "To avoid offending Marshall and southern players and fans, NFL owners may have tacitly agreed to shun black athletes. Marshall himself once publicly avowed that he would never employ minority athletes. Indeed, the Redskins were the last NFL team to desegregate, holding out until 1962." George Taliaferro had no trouble believing that Marshall was responsible. Later, he would have his own run-in with the man. The Redskins signed its first black player, Bobby Mitchell, in 1962, long after other teams had integrated. According to Jeff Brown in the *Daily Mississippian*, even this event occurred only because the federal government had pressured the team, threatening to restrict the use of their new stadium if they did not integrate. Ironically, according to Brown, the Redskins had their most successful season in five years, just one year after finally integrating the team.

Football historians speculate that the economic impact of the Depression may initially have had something to do with the widespread discrimination in pro football. Peterson wrote that during the Depression, football teams had to cut from thirty-three players to a meager twenty-two in order to save money. (Today, teams have forty-five players because the positions have become so specialized.) The African American players were, of course, among the first to be cut. By 1932, Joe Lillard was the only black man still playing in the NFL. During this time, black players were forced to play for all-black professional teams or go to minor league teams instead.

Of the all-black pro teams, the most notable was the New York Brown Bombers, who were coached by Frederick "Fritz" Pollard. Pollard had an interesting professional football career. He played for the Akron Indians in 1919. Then he went on to play for teams in the American Professional Football Association and in the NFL from 1920 to 1926. Pollard coached for some NFL teams as well—including Akron, Milwaukee, and Hammond—making him the first black coach in the NFL before the league managed to oust its African American players. (Pollard would use his position to help empower the black community by establishing the first black investment firm and the first black-owned newspaper, the *New York Independent News*, according to Cooper, Macaulay, and Rodriguez.) Pollard and other black players experienced racism in the league even before the color lines were drawn. For example, according to the Professional Football Researchers Association, in 1926 the New York Giants were forbidden to take the field against the Canton Bulldogs until the African American quarterback for Canton voluntarily withdrew from the game. At that time, there were only five black players left in the NFL.

Of Pollard's all-black New York Brown Bombers, based in Harlem, there is very little information. According to an article by professional football researcher John M. Carroll, this was because white papers did not cover the all-black team, and black papers, which generally came out on Thursday, would have been reporting on a game that had happened four days prior. While little is known, then, about the team, it is said that the Brown Bombers provided a means for Pollard to fight racism in the league. He put together a talented team to play against the league's all-white teams. The Brown Bombers began their career with five straight wins, and they did not lose until the final game of the season. Pollard organized the Brown Bombers, and later the Chicago Black Hawks, to fight the color line in the NFL. Although Pollard made his point, that his black players were talented and deserved to play, he did not accomplish everything he set out to do. Some white teams, including both New York teams, the Dodgers and the Giants, refused to play Pollard's Bombers, and the Brown Bombers struggled financially.

Still, Pollard's all-black teams were one option for African American football players during the 1930s and 1940s before professional football was reintegrated, and these teams continued opening doors for black players in the league. The minor league teams provided another option for these players. Of the minor leagues, the Pacific Coast Football League (PCFL) was more receptive to black players than the American Professional Football Association. In 1946, thirteen years after the color ban in the NFL, two of the Pacific Coast Football League's players reintegrated the NFL. Kenny Washington, the first black player in the league since 1933, and Woody Strode were both signed by the Los Angeles Rams that year, officially reintegrating the league. The Los Angeles Rams were formerly the Cleveland Rams, but the team had relocated to Los Angeles in 1945. Washington and Strode had Los Angeles connections as well. Both men had attended UCLA at the same time as baseball's Jackie Robinson, and both, like Robinson, had been popular athletes there. It wasn't until they were both in their thirties, however, that they ended up with the Rams.

Later in that 1946 season, two other black men, Marion Motley and Bill Willis, crossed the color line into professional football by playing for the Cleveland Browns of the All-America Football Conference. Motley and Willis, both eventual Professional Football Hall of Famers, constantly encountered racism on the field. According to Peterson, players would purposely step on Motley's hands with their cleats on, even when a play had already ended. In one game, Peterson wrote, referee Tommy Hughitt finally managed to put an end to it. Noticing what was going on, he began penalizing these teams fifteen yards each time an incident occurred. Other referees took note, and they too started to protect the league's black players from this blatant racism.

Motley, according to Peterson, said, "Of course, the opposing players called us nigger and all kinds of names like that. That went on for about two or three years, until they found out that Willis and I was ball players. Then they stopped that shit. They found out that while they were calling us names, I was running by 'em and Willis was knocking the shit out of them. So they stopped calling us names and started trying to catch up with us."

Willis and Motley also had Jim Crow laws with which to contend. While the Fourteenth Amendment prohibited state governments from discriminating on the basis of race, it did not restrict private organizations or people from doing so. Therefore, businesses like restaurants, hotels, and even movie theaters could discriminate, and the system of segregation became widespread.

This system of segregation carried over to professional football. When the Browns played Miami, for example, Willis and Motley stayed home in Cleveland. While it was widely accepted, though, not everyone agreed with the South's system of segregation. According to Peterson, a Cleveland columnist wrote after the Miami game, "It seems that a majority of the law-makers down in Florida don't know yet that the Civil War is over."

Black players like Washington, Strode, Motley, and Willis were a promising sign, but segregation dominated professional football. In the NFL in 1946 and 1947, only the Los Angeles Rams had black players. By this time, Taliaferro had finished his military service and returned to Indiana. He, like Willis and Motley, was also experiencing racism and segregation. He, like Willis and Motley, was also going to make professional football history in just a couple of years. First, though, he had to go back to Indiana University, where he still had a couple of years of college football to play. Perhaps more importantly, he would also continue to use football as a means for prompting social change.

SEVEN

1947–49: BACK AT INDIANA UNIVERSITY

TALIAFERRO NO LONGER LIVED AT the Mayses' home when he returned to Indiana University in the summer of 1947. It was the summer that Jackie Robinson broke major league baseball's color barrier, despite taunting by players and fans, by starting at first base for the Brooklyn Dodgers. Robinson fought through discrimination all season to earn Rookie of the Year honors in the National League. He went on to play for ten years, helping the Dodgers to six pennants and a World Series championship. Robinson, like Taliaferro, was breaking down barriers, but society was slow and resistant to change.

Not a lot had changed at Indiana University in Taliaferro's absence. He still was not permitted to live on campus, so he got a job cleaning the office of a female pediatrician in town and rented a room in the small building that attached to the back of the office. This was a novel idea for the time, and other black students wanted to know how Taliaferro had managed to get a room to himself. At the Mayses' home, they were still packed in with three or four people to each diminutive room. Upon his return, he planned to finish his health, physical education, and recreation (HPER) degree and prepare for the 1947 football season. He also continued to write and phone Viola Jones. Despite his absence for the 1946 football season, Taliaferro's return to campus was met with a warm welcome. He was still earning respect on the football field.

His prominence as an athlete did not help his circumstances when it came to segregation, at least not yet. He still had to cut across campus to go to the Mayses' home to eat because places like the Gables restaurant and the Book Nook on campus continued to prohibit entrance to African American customers. Taliaferro had finally reached a point where he could no longer accept this blatant racism. His experience in fighting discrimination in Fort Benning, Georgia, had given back to Taliaferro some of the self-assurance he'd had in high school. Now, fueled by frustration, he decided he could no longer be complacent. He would begin by trying to end segregation in restaurants on IU's campus. To do this, he would first have to meet with Indiana University president Herman Wells about the situation. He had no way of knowing what a strong ally he would find in Wells.

"Describe Santa Claus and you got Herman Wells," Taliaferro said of the man whose term as Indiana University president was marked by his focus on campus integration and on the controversial Kinsey Report. The Kinsey Report came out a few years after Taliaferro left Indiana, but he had been a participant. Kinsey, he said, was "some kind of a human being." Of Wells's ability to justify the study to a conservative public, Taliaferro explained, "He handled it with the aplomb of a magician." Wells had managed to convince the many doubters that Indiana was at the forefront of researching every area of human behavior and that Kinsey's research on sexual behavior was an important aspect of the entire picture.

Wells's demeanor may have also helped him convince the skeptics. Known for his jolly nature, Wells would walk the campus every day at lunch to meet as many of the ten thousand students on IU's campus as he could. It was this focus on the students and his commitment to integrating campus to which Taliaferro would appeal.

"What can I do for you?" Wells's secretary asked.

"My name is George Taliaferro. I'd like to see Dr. Wells," Taliaferro replied, but by the time he had finished, Wells's substantial body had filled the doorway.

"Did I just hear the name George Taliaferro?" he asked.

"Yes, sir," Taliaferro replied.

"Come right in. What can I do for you?"

Taliaferro launched into his explanation. He was not permitted in the restaurants on campus (many on the town side were also off limits to him) because of his skin color, but because of his class schedule, his need to eat elsewhere caused problems for him every single day. He was teaching at the University School and had to run from there to the Mayses' home for lunch and then back to University School in the short amount of time he was allotted between classes, he explained. He could not eat at the restaurants that were located right next to his classes. "I have a dollar and twenty-five cents in my pocket, and I have to go all the way to Mr. and Mrs. Mays's house to eat," he told Wells, frustration etched into every syllable. He continued. The proximity of the restaurants on Kirkwood Avenue would enable him to eat between classes if he were permitted to enter them. One such restaurant, he said, was the Gables, which stood almost directly across from Wells's office on Fifth and Indiana. Taliaferro did not mention the 1945 Big Ten championship football team picture that still hung there, which he had never seen in its entirety.

Wells listened patiently, allowing Taliaferro to explain the situation without interruption. When he was finished, Taliaferro was unsure how Wells would react to his plea for help—he just knew he had to try something. As was typical of the man who had convinced J. C. Coffee to integrate the pool simply by jumping into it, Wells took action. He picked up the phone and called Gables owner Peter Poolitsan. After a brief exchange of pleasantries, Wells got directly to his point, asking Poolitsan whether "Negro" students were permitted to eat at his restaurant. Poolitsan replied negatively, explaining that he was in business to earn a living and that allowing "the colored kids" to dine in his restaurant might deter the white students from frequenting it, causing him to lose the majority of his business.

"Well, maybe I'll have to make all of the restaurants on Kirkwood off limits to *all* of the students," Wells replied. Taliaferro would never forget that response. Losing Indiana University students would mean certain failure for the restaurants. Poolitsan had no choice but to make a deal with Wells. By the time the conversation had ended, the two had devised a plan to integrate the Gables. They would capitalize on Taliaferro's popularity on campus. He would eat at the restaurant for one week with any black friend of his choosing. If, when the week was over, there were no complaints, Taliaferro could add two more friends. For another week, the four of them would dine at the restaurant. If there were no complaints at the end of the second week, Poolitsan would allow total integration permanently. The success of the plan, a compromise between Wells and Poolitsan, hinged on Taliaferro's status as a football player.

Taliaferro and teammate Mel Groomes, who still lived at the Mayses' home, ate lunch at the restaurant for a week. This was Taliaferro's opportunity to finally see in its entirety the 1945 championship picture that had been hanging inside the restaurant for the last two years. That was the first thing he and Groomes did upon entering the restaurant. For a while, Taliaferro couldn't stop staring at it. Eventually the two sat down to lunch, where they encountered no complaints about their presence. This continued for a week, and every time they walked in, they looked at the picture and sat down for lunch, again not encountering any complaints. When the week was over, Groomes and Taliaferro arranged to add two guests the following week. Each would bring a date, they decided. Taliaferro's date was Betty Guess, a friend who later ended up marrying Bill Garrett, the Indiana University basketball player who would integrate Big Ten basketball in 1948.

Of course, Taliaferro and Groomes pointed out the championship picture to their guests. This time four of them sat down to eat, meeting no resistance or disagreement from the other patrons. Even a poll taken on campus about the experiment supported the integration of the restaurants. President Wells had helped Taliaferro, Groomes, and their dates to successfully integrate the Gables restaurant. This set a precedent that other restaurants, like the Book Nook, which was just a couple of doors down, would soon follow.

That was just one of President Wells's attempts to desegregate the campus. According to a Wells biography, he would later receive the NAACP (National Association for the Advancement of Colored People) Brotherhood Award for 1961–62 for such attempts as these. It was Wells who fully desegregated the union building on campus by simply having the placards that read "colored" removed from the tables there. His effect on the Bloomington campus was evident in the citation for the award, which read in part, "Both Indiana University and Bloomington are far better places, in terms of race relations, than they were a quarter-century ago." Taliaferro's experience with Wells was one of the many attempts the president made during his tenure to eliminate discrimination on the Indiana University campus.

Many years later, a man named Clayton Puckett bought the Gables restaurant that Taliaferro had helped integrate and where the championship picture, so large it took up nearly the entire south wall, was hung. Shortly after, Taliaferro offered to buy the enormous picture from him. Puckett, who had changed the name of the restaurant to Garcia's, agreed. It was a new restaurant, and he had no plans for keeping the picture on the wall. Soon after, Puckett and his wife went to Champaign, Illinois, on a private plane to watch Indiana University play Michigan to see who would be competing in the NCAA basketball championship. On the way home, fog rolled in. The Pucketts' plane made it to Bloomington but hit a tree as it was approaching the runway, killing both of them. Taliaferro donated the picture to Indiana University's Assembly Hall in the names of Clayton and Evelyn Puckett.

Taliaferro's success at integrating the restaurants prompted him to do more. The movie theaters were his next project, but not at his suggestion. One of the most popular pastimes for Indiana students, the theaters were also among the most obvious in their discrimination. Their "colored" patrons were only permitted on Fridays, Saturdays, and Sundays, and then only in the balcony seating. When the manager approached Taliaferro to help integrate the Indiana Theater, which stood just around the corner from the Gables, he agreed without hesitation. The plan, similar to one Wells had devised to integrate the pool and restaurants, relied on Taliaferro's status as a popular football player. The manager wanted Taliaferro to come to the theater any weekday, a day its "colored" patrons were not permitted, and to sit in the downstairs section typically off limits to them. The manager presumed that Taliaferro's presence would be accepted because of his popularity on campus. As it had before, the plan succeeded. Few people even seemed to take notice, and Taliaferro's acceptance there encouraged other black students to do the same, successfully integrating the Indiana Theater.

Emboldened by his successes, Taliaferro continued his campaign. At the Princess Movie Theater, located just down the street from the Indiana Theater, he took a screwdriver and removed from the wall the blue sign with the word *colored* on it in bold white letters. Then, he sat in the whites-only section, achieving the same result as he had at the Indiana Theater. He was again joined by some of his peers. Taliaferro, who still has the sign, and others who were brave enough to challenge the status quo managed to quickly and quietly integrate Bloomington's movie theaters. As the first black student teacher from IU at University High School, Taliaferro continued to capitalize on his influence to make gains in race relations in Bloomington. The fact that he did not face resistance to the changes suggests a couple of things: one, that Bloomington was a town ready for change, and two, that football could be a powerful tool in the fight for social justice.

While he was busy advocating for social change, Taliaferro was also continuing his football success, and it was to be the year of "The Run." In the 1947 Dad's Day game against Pittsburgh, Taliaferro ran for a play neither the Pittsburgh nor the Indiana spectators will ever forget. In an *Indiana Daily Student* article, David Hackett wrote, "It is simply called The Run. To those who saw it, no other explanation is needed; it may be the most exciting play in IU football history." If one looks only at the numbers, The Run is actually not all that impressive. Starting at the fifty and ending at the eleven, it was a gain of only thirty-nine yards, a decent gain but not memorable for that alone. "I sure felt like I ran a mile though," Taliaferro said, according to Hackett. And that is why The Run was so remarkable that it is still a topic of discussion among Indiana football fans today. Hackett described why it was so memorable: "Taliaferro zig-zagged from sideline to sideline, breaking twelve tackles in all. Every Pittsburgh player hit him but failed to bring him down. One poor fellow failed twice. Finally, he was gang-tackled at the eleven." Taliaferro was never able to see his famous run. In an article by Hammel years later, Taliaferro explained why: "They filmed the games then, but it happened that the Indiana photographer ran out of film just before that punt. He was changing his film." Taliaferro checked with Pittsburgh too, but they didn't have the film in their files either, they said. He wondered if maybe that was for the better. "If I had seen it, I don't know if it would have had the same mystique to me. It's funny, but I never go into the stadium that my mind isn't drawn to that spot where it started: on the north sidelines at the forty-five," he said.

After the game, Taliaferro ran through the gauntlet, a line of fans waiting to congratulate the players. "They slapped me on the back saying, 'How great thou art,'" Taliaferro said. The gauntlet was so long that it took Taliaferro from the stadium to the May-ses' house, where a number of black players and their families were having a reception. There, Taliaferro's father was waiting for him. Although he didn't understand football and had only been to a couple of his son's games, Robert Taliaferro had taken a train from Gary to attend the Dad's Day game. At the reception, Taliaferro overheard a conversation that he would never forget and that would soon take on more meaning.

"Is your son on the football team?" a man with a fat cigar hanging from his mouth asked Robert Taliaferro.

"That's my boy," Robert answered, pointing to Taliaferro.

To Taliaferro, who was accustomed to being written about in articles and to walking a gauntlet of adoring fans, it was the best compliment he had ever been paid. Those three words were more significant, he said, "because my dad owned me." The satisfaction he felt at that moment he wouldn't feel again until later in life when each of his four daughters would also "own" him in some way, pointing him out and saying, "That's my dad," with the same reverence his father had shown when acknowledging him after the Dad's Day game.

With the exception of The Run and the acknowledgment of his father's pride, the 1947 football season was not as successful as that first, undefeated season Taliaferro played for the Hoosiers. The Hoosiers ended the season with a 5–3–1 record, tying for sixth place in the Big Ten Conference. The team had at least eked out a win over archrival Purdue, 16–14, allowing them to retain custody of the Old Oaken Bucket. The Battle of the Bands also made a return in 1947, but in a slightly different format. This time the battle was held in the University Men's Gymnasium at IU, with two bands at either end, during Sigma Delta Chi's Annual Blanket Hop. The fraternity gave out *I* blankets to outstanding graduating senior athletes at the dance. Not yet a senior, Taliaferro did not receive a blanket, but he still received plenty of recognition.

Fig. 7.1 George Taliaferro (*left*) and Mel Groomes (*right*) walk with Hoosier fans after the game against Pittsburgh on October 18, 1947. *Photo courtesy IU Archives.*

He was named second-team All-American again in 1947. He had rushed for 339 yards, averaging almost four yards a carry. He scored four touchdowns and punted an average of thirty-five yards per kick. But the accolades didn't end there. In December, Taliaferro was also named one of the sixty-five outstanding college football players, which garnered him an invitation for a weekend and dinner at the Waldorf Astoria in New York City. The event provided him the opportunity to reconnect with Viola Jones, who agreed to be his date for the evening. Having two brothers and two sisters in the city meant she could take the opportunity to visit them while she was in New York as well. She planned to stay with her sister, Anna, even though she already had a room reserved at the hotel.

Taliaferro and Jones, along with four football players from other schools and their dates, attended the ball at the Waldorf

GEORGE TALIAFERRO

20---GEORGE TALIAFERRO
Halfback — Indiana

Weight—195 lbs.   Age—20
Height—6'   Year—junior

Paced Indiana to 1945 Big Ten title with his running and passing. Gained 719 yards and completed 10 out of 19 pass-attempts. Voted all-Big Ten as freshman. Excellent broken field runner. Good pass receiver, too. Hails from Gary. Played under Bo McMillin, now coach of Detroit Lions.

ALL-STAR FOOTBALL GUM
Collect this series of Gridiron Greats.

Send 5 All Star Wrappers and 10c for big 12″ x 6″ felt pennant of any team listed on any All Star card.

N. Y. Giants	Navy
Michigan	No. Carolina
Stanford	Chicago Cards

Send Wrappers and Coin to
LEAF GUM CO., Box 5907   CHICAGO 80, ILL.
Copyright 1948

Figs. 7.2a and 7.2b A 1948 Leaf football card of George Taliaferro.

together. Although she was no longer the "campus queen," Jones still loved to dance, and she was on the floor for every tune, her vitality reminding Taliaferro why he had fallen in love with her in the first place. She managed to wear him out on the dance floor until finally, exhausted and hungry, Taliaferro had to sit one out to look for food. Earl Banks, a friend, joined him, and the ladies kept dancing. Taliaferro and Banks each decided on a salad and sat down at the table, only to discover that they were surrounded by forks. Neither was sure which to choose. In fact, they couldn't even be sure which forks belonged to which table setting. After some discussion of the matter, Taliaferro decided that since they were both right handed, they should eat with the fork on their respective right. Having reached that conclusion, they shrugged, picked up their forks, and began eating.

Their lack of proper table etiquette was discovered when Jones and the others returned to the table. Taliaferro happened to be eating his salad with the fork of the woman sitting next to him. In an unrelenting campaign to embarrass the men, rather than finding another fork, she made a show of informing them of the proper place settings. Etiquette required that they use the fork on the left, not on the right, she explained, rather snootily, Talia-ferro thought. Jones tried to appease her by offering one of her own forks to the woman, but she refused. This pushed Taliaferro beyond his patience. He finally said, "I am right handed. I am eating my salad with this fork, and she better accept Vi's offer or she will have to go without a salad." This abruptly resolved the fork issue, but the episode was a valuable lesson for a man who would be attending many more important dinners over the years. He wondered, too, if he would have already learned the lesson had he not been ostracized from the formal dinners that white athletes were often invited to on the campus of Indiana University.

The entire evening solidified for Taliaferro his feelings for Jones. He had been confident in them before but was wholly convinced of them now. He could see himself spending the rest of his life with her. After the ball that night, instead of going to her sister's house, Jones spent the night at the Waldorf with him. The next morning, when he had to say good-bye once again to the beautiful, classy woman who had won his heart, he realized that the weekend had been too short. Jones returned to Alabama, and Taliaferro returned to Bloomington.

There was much to celebrate: his relationship with Jones and the fact that he was tearing up the football field. He was blissfully unaware of the tragedy he would soon face. He returned home to Gary over the winter break to visit his family, something he had been looking forward to doing. On Christmas Eve he gave his parents a present and told them he would see them early the next morning. They were going to a Christmas party with the neighbors, the DeMents, and he was going to a party with an old high school friend, Adam McCullough. McCullough was playing football for Wilberforce University, one of the black universities that had been recruiting Taliaferro just a couple of years earlier. McCullough and his girlfriend wanted to introduce Taliaferro to a girl who was a friend of theirs. Although Taliaferro wasn't interested in her, he was a twenty-year-old college student, so he was interested in attending the party and spending time with friends. Taliaferro and McCullough went to East Chicago, near Gary and still in "the region," to McCullough's girlfriend's house. They weren't there for very long before Taliaferro felt an urgent need to leave. "I have to go home," he told McCullough. He didn't know why; he just had a feeling that something had happened, that he needed to get home immediately.

When he arrived home, his mother and the DeMents were walking out the front door and getting into a car. "You're celebrating Christmas really early," Taliaferro joked. Knowing that they would have just returned from the party, he asked, "Where are you going now?" He was trying to maintain a sense of normalcy, to push down the persistent feeling that something wasn't right.

Something told him he didn't want to hear whatever his mother was about to tell him.

"We're going to the hospital," she answered, ignoring his attempt at humor. Her tone forced him to feel the fear he had been trying to stop. Then he heard the rest of her sentence, and a heavy wall came down. Everything he heard and saw after that was muffled, as if from the end of a dark tunnel or from under water. It couldn't be real. His mother and the DeMents were going to the hospital because his father had been shot. He knew, without being told, exactly when it had happened; it was the same time he had felt that sudden, uncontrollable urge to leave the party.

Taliaferro's uncle Walter had been at the Christmas party with his parents. When they left the party, the DeMents and Taliaferros stopped by Walter's apartment to visit a while longer before going home. While they were there, Walter decided to show Robert Taliaferro a Christmas present he had received, a new shotgun. Robert Taliaferro walked out onto the balcony to examine it. A hunter, he had to aim at something to get a feel for the gun, so he pointed it up at the stars. Apparently satisfied, he walked backed into the apartment nodding his approval. Uncle Walter wanted to point out one more feature. "Let me show you something," he said. Robert turned the butt of the gun to his brother to hand it to him, but as they made the exchange, it went off, blowing away much of the left side of Robert Taliaferro's body. Neither had realized that the powerful shotgun was loaded.

Seconds felt like hours as Taliaferro accompanied his mother to the hospital. When the DeMents finally pulled the car up to the entrance, Taliaferro wasted no time jumping from his seat and running inside. Even though it was early in the morning by that time, someone was manning the information desk. He frantically asked for his father's room number.

"Room two hundred three," the woman said, and before she could give further direction, he was gone.

He moved quickly to the second floor and located his father's room. It was dark when he pushed open the door, the only light coming from the dimly lit hallway. Even though there was no way his father, whose bed was around the corner, could see him, Taliaferro heard him ask, "Junior?" Although Taliaferro had a younger brother who shared his father's name, the nickname Junior had always been his alone. His father knew he was standing there. In the mere seconds it took Taliaferro to round the corner and get to the bed, however, his father had died. That his father had seemed to recognize his presence and that his nickname had been the last word his father ever spoke brought little comfort to Taliaferro. He hadn't been able to say good-bye. It was Christmas morning.

The untimely death of Robert Taliaferro, who was only forty-two years old, sent his loved ones reeling. The man Taliaferro described as a "quiet disciplinarian" was small by most standards, at five foot seven and 155 pounds. Not small, however, was his impact on his son. During his childhood, Taliaferro had always thought that to be like his father would be "the greatest thing that could happen to a person." Despite having just a fourth-grade education, Robert Taliaferro was an intelligent man who could talk shrewdly about any subject and accomplish any manual task. The only thing Robert Taliaferro could not do was work with electricity. He just didn't understand it, Taliaferro said. But he did everything else, including carpentry, masonry, and plumbing. He also had a keen sense of what was important, and he had instilled in his son a set of values that would carry him through life, values that included the importance of education, honesty, and a strong work ethic.

Had his father not offered him the choice of quitting and supporting himself or staying in school and being permitted to remain at home, Taliaferro would have quit high school to work in the steel mill like his father. Instead, his father's tough love kept him in school, where his football ability led to a college education and the possibility of a better life. Two years after Taliaferro's near withdrawal from high school, when he was leaving for his first semester at Indiana University, Robert Taliaferro pulled out a worn, brown wallet and laid out a five-dollar bill and five ones, "all the money he had in the world," Taliaferro said. He told Taliaferro he was going to split it with him because he was proud of him for finishing high school and getting a football scholarship. He asked which half Taliaferro wanted.

"I'll take the ones," Taliaferro said. "It'll look like I have more money that way." Then he told his dad that he would never ask him for anything again. Taliaferro had kept his word; he had never asked his father for anything since accepting those dollar bills. He didn't want to have to ask. Not because his father wouldn't be willing to—quite the contrary. He knew his father would help, even though it would be a struggle financially for him to do it. Taliaferro remembered standing in line for eggs and powdered milk to keep enough food on the table. The food-relief lines, Taliaferro said, were part of President Roosevelt's New Deal. Families could get a certain amount of free food based on the number of people in the family. His father, too proud to accept what he didn't work for, refused to go. His mother, however, said, "My children are going to eat," and she went anyway. Taliaferro's life was going to change without his father's steady presence in it.

Taliaferro struggled to quell the torrent of emotions that came with his father's abrupt and violent death. The grief was so intense that it seemed to inhabit every cell of his body, but there was also a tremendous sense of worry. His mother, he knew, would be struggling both emotionally and financially. He wanted to leave Indiana University to get a job and help ease some of her burden, remembering that he had promised her as a young boy that he would take care of her someday. He didn't want her to become a maid, to have to leave her own home in order to take care of someone else's, especially since she still had children at home.

He would have sacrificed his college education and football for her without hesitation, except for one thing. He had promised both his mother and father that he would get a college degree, and he knew his mother would hold him to that promise. He decided to finish the school year and make his decision over the summer, when he would have more time to think about it.

When the school year ended, Taliaferro went to work in the same steel mill that had employed his father. In fact, he was in the Tin Mill, his father's section, working with the same group of men Robert Taliaferro had supervised. The first day he dwelled on just that—he touched what his father had touched, walked where his father had walked—and it was a painful reminder of his loss. Soon, the pain was replaced by a keen sense of comfort. He could feel his father's presence there. Not only that, but it helped Taliaferro work through the internal conflict that had plagued him for months. He mentioned to the crew that he was considering quitting school to work there permanently in order to help his family. Their response was unexpected. They had worked closely with Robert Taliaferro, had known him well, and they knew without question that he had wanted his son to get a college degree. Moreover, he had not wanted Taliaferro to work in the steel mill his entire life as they all had. It was a difficult life from which there was little escape. It was as if they were speaking his own father's words. He had his answer. He had to return to IU.

His mind finally made up, he headed back to Bloomington at the end of the summer. At first, he was comfortable with the decision, confident that it had been his father's wish. Worry for mother's well-being, however, continued to haunt him. Although he had promised his father that he would get an education, he had also promised to take care of his mother if anything ever happened to his father. He remembered how he had dug a garden by lantern light after his father's lesson that a man is only as good as his word, but he would have to break one of his promises in order to fulfill the other. It would be difficult to focus on school with his thoughts on his family. Taliaferro returned to Indiana University in 1948, but his future there was uncertain.

Taliaferro would lose another significant male figure in his life, making the return even more difficult. Bo McMillin resigned from his coaching position at Indiana to become the head coach and general manager of the Detroit Lions. Although coaching professionally was a good opportunity for McMillin, it was obvious during a farewell banquet held in his honor that he felt strong ties to Indiana University. According to an *Indiana Daily Student* article, McMillin said during his farewell speech, "I never could repay Indiana in 50 years for what it's done for me in 14 years." Then, crying, he hugged Vern Huffman, the All-American whose jersey number Taliaferro had inherited. McMillin's abrupt departure was difficult for Taliaferro, especially on the heels of his father's death. Feeling lost and alone, he became something of a recluse.

That began to change when he met Clyde Smith, Bo McMillin's replacement. Smith was such a kind person that Taliaferro, despite having just met him, couldn't help but open up. Like McMillin, Smith was a fairly small man, at five foot seven. Since Smith had been a line coach under McMillin, he was familiar with the way McMillin had run the program. Getting the program going and playing one of the toughest schedules in the NCAA would present numerous challenges, however, especially since the majority of the starters from that magical 1945 season were gone. All-American Pete Pihos was coming back during spring training as an assistant coach under Clyde Smith, but it was going to be a difficult transition year for the Cream and Crimson.

Football kept Taliaferro busy for the first few months of the school year, but it didn't stop the incessant worry. Playing professional football would allow him to ease his mother's financial burden and, per his father's wishes, keep him out of the steel mill. Although he was seriously considering it, he didn't tell anyone. He had to be sure first. When he answered letters from Viola

Fig. 7.3 Indiana University president Herman B. Wells and his mother, Anna Bernice Harting Wells, attend the October 16, 1948, homecoming game against Ohio State. Like McMillin, Wells was ahead of his time in race relations, and he fought to desegregate Indiana University's campus. *Photo courtesy IU Archives.*

Jones, the only bright spots to those dark days, he left out any references to what he was contemplating. The situation would be difficult enough to explain to Virnater Taliaferro, let alone to the woman he planned to spend the rest of his life with. Jones, in the meantime, had taken a job at Howard University in Washington, DC, as an assistant to the dean of the medical school.

With his older brother, who had a family of his own, in the navy, Taliaferro felt that the responsibility to take care of his mother and younger siblings rested solely with him. Like his father's, his mother's education was limited, and although she was an intelligent person, she had only a sixth-grade education. Like so many women, she worked during World War II making ammunition, but for the most part, she had stayed home to raise her family. Now, without her husband's support, her financial situation had become difficult.

Taliaferro pondered the situation, eventually sharing his concerns with the athletic director, who, in turn, urged him to speak with President Wells. He did, and Wells listened intently. At the end, though, the president said it was not his decision to make. The best he could offer was his assurance that he would be there for Taliaferro regardless of his decision.

"Do whatever you have to do," he told Taliaferro.

Taliaferro knew what he had to do, but convincing his mother of it would not be easy. She would just have to accept it, he thought, but it was not that simple. Virnater Taliaferro knew all about Taliaferro's friend, Buddy Young, who had quit the University of Illinois his sophomore year and had not returned to get his degree. She was adamant that Taliaferro stay in school. Her understanding was that once you quit, you broke all ties with the university and could not return. It wasn't until after the 1948 Oaken Bucket game against Purdue that Taliaferro began to convince her otherwise. Virnater Taliaferro traveled to West Lafayette, Indiana, with Taliaferro's aunt to watch the game. It was a brutal game that ended with Taliaferro being taken from the field on a stretcher.

"I was not hurt," he said, "just tired—because I was the only person on that team Purdue had to worry about carrying the ball—and they buried me in the ground." Indiana had been shut out, 39–0, payback for some of the humiliation they had handed Purdue in recent years. Taliaferro felt the beating personally, in every fiber of muscle. After he recovered enough from his fatigue, he again broached the subject of quitting school with his mother. He indicated his exhaustion and pointed out his battle wounds to the woman who had insisted on thorough examinations before allowing him to play in high school.

"The difference between getting pummeled on the field in college versus getting pummeled on the field in professional football

Fig. 7.4 A cartoon depicting George Taliaferro during the 1948 season, his last football season at Indiana University before going pro. *Photo courtesy George Taliaferro.*

is that I'd get paid. I could also take care of you, Claude, and Ernestine," he told her.

"Remember your promise to your father," she reminded him, still not convinced. He did not need reminding of that at all. Numerous people, including himself, had been reminding him of it since his father's death, and he had struggled with the decision for almost a year. Taliaferro had finally come up with a solution that would allow him to fulfill both promises—to take care of his mother and get a college degree.

"Mom, I will get it. I will have it put into my professional contract that I must return to Indiana University to get my degree." He could play professionally and get an education, he insisted. He would not be breaking ties with the university at all and

Fig. 7.5 George Taliaferro striking another pose, this one in October 1948, his last year with the Hoosiers. A triple threat, Taliaferro could run, pass, and kick, and he played both offense and defense. *Photo courtesy IU Archives.*

could continue to take classes there. With that, she was finally convinced.

When the 1948 season ended, the Hoosiers, under new coach Clyde Smith, had fared only a little better than they had the previous year, tying for fifth place in the Big Ten Conference. The Hoosiers had an inexperienced team and a new coach, difficult obstacles to overcome in such a tough conference. While understandable, the team's performance disappointed Hoosier fans, who still remembered the elation of the 1945 season. Under Smith, the team started strong, with two consecutive wins, but they could not sustain the momentum. Taliaferro had a solid season, though, lettering again and beating his previous season's punting record with an average of 41 yards. He rushed for 262 yards in ninety-eight attempts, for an average of fewer than three yards per carry, and he scored four touchdowns. As a triple threat, Taliaferro passed for 550 yards. He was the team MVP and was named All-Big Ten. He was also named first-team All-American again, making him the only Indiana University football player to be named to All-American teams in three different seasons. Had he not spent a season in the army, it likely would have been four.

IU football may not have lived up to everyone's expectations in 1948, but sports history was still being made at Indiana. Bill Garrett, a forward for the Hoosiers' basketball team, became the first African American to play Big Ten basketball. Unlike Big Ten football, which had some black players, Big Ten basketball had not had a single black player until Garrett came along. According to Tom Graham and Rachel Graham Cody in Getting Open, there had been some speculation that Indiana's Mr. Basketball of 1946, Johnny Wilson, a black player for state champion Anderson High School, would play for IU and take that honor. Of course, President Wells had been open to the idea, but the gentleman's agreement that existed among Big Ten coaches had kept Wilson from playing for the Hoosiers. Similar circumstances happened the following year with Bill Garrett, who had led Shelbyville to

Fig. 7.6 The 1948 Hoosier starters. *Front row from left*: Joe Bartkiewicz, Walter C. Bartkiewicz, John Goldsberry, Casimir Witucki, Joe Polce, Jerry Morrical, and Frank Hoppe. *Back row from left*: Del Russell, Harry "Chick" Jagade, Nick Sebek, and George Taliaferro. *Photo courtesy IU Archives.*

a state championship and was Indiana's Mr. Basketball of 1947. Rumors circulated that he would be the one to break the color barrier in Big Ten basketball, but for a while it looked as if history was to repeat itself, as no Big Ten basketball coaches were present at Shelbyville's April 2 celebration. In typical fashion, Indiana football coach Bo McMillin had attended, however, and was even the keynote speaker, once again championing the underdog. With pressure from several sources, including McMillin and Wells, IU basketball coach Branch McCracken challenged the status quo and recruited Bill Garrett, finally breaking the gentleman's agreement that had persisted in the Big Ten.

Also significant that year were the strides Taliaferro was making in his personal life. In December, while she was in Cleveland to see an aunt, Taliaferro visited Viola Jones. Trying his luck again, he proposed to her in his aunt's living room, with both the engagement and wedding ring, and this time, to his utter delight, she accepted. Jones, however, was not as convinced as Taliaferro about his decision to leave school. Although she felt it was her fiancé's decision to make, she did not understand how anyone could give up the opportunity to get an education. Like Taliaferro's parents, hers had instilled in her the value of education. They regularly attended Parent-Teacher Association (PTA) meetings, and her father had even been its president at one time. Not confident that he would actually return to college, Jones could not support his decision to quit.

Taliaferro finished out the 1948–49 school year. He had attended Indiana University for three years and had made a lasting impression. He had not only endured the racism and segregation that existed in Bloomington, Indiana, but also fought against it and helped integrate restaurants and movie theaters. Taliaferro had also helped his team achieve an undefeated season and Big Ten championship in 1945. Few would forget The Run in 1947. He was a letter winner all three seasons, and in 1949 he had been selected for the College All-Star game in Chicago against the Philadelphia Eagles.

1949–55: INTEGRATING PROFESSIONAL FOOTBALL

TO APPEASE COLLEGE COACHES WHO were tired of losing players to the professional leagues, Joe Carr, NFL president from 1921 to 1939, passed a rule forbidding any professional team from signing a player before his class graduated. This meant that Taliaferro had to wait until the class he started with in college graduated before he would be eligible to play professional football. Because of his stint in the army, he was not graduating in 1949. But the class he started college with in 1945 was graduating, making him eligible to play professional football.

Although it was not time for him to graduate, it *was* time for him to make history. The morning of the NFL draft, Taliaferro, who had since moved back to Gary, had been working out in Chicago with friends Buddy Young, Earl Banks, and Sherman Howard. Their shared love of football and similar experiences in the Big Ten had solidified a tight bond among them. One of those Big Ten games had pitted Indiana against Iowa, for whom Banks played. Taliaferro remembered the game that day, how he had crossed the field to greet Banks when the opportunity presented itself. The response had surprised him.

"Shut up and play," Banks growled. Before Taliaferro could respond, the game resumed. As soon as it ended, however, he crossed the field again.

"Why are you in such a bad mood?" Taliaferro asked, half laughing, trying to get a smile out of his friend.

"Why won't they let me sleep in the hotel?" Banks replied. His team, which had come to Bloomington the night before the game, had stayed in a whites-only hotel. Banks had been forced to spend the night in Indianapolis, an hour-and-a-half drive from IU's campus. He had had to wake up early that morning to make the drive.

Taliaferro had understood. It was shared experiences like these that had bonded them. After college, they had all gone to live in the Chicago area and often worked out together. To Taliaferro, workouts were also a learning opportunity because Banks, Howard, and Young were already playing pro ball. Occasionally they worked out together in Gary, but that day they happened to be in Chicago. Their workout, which commenced at nine o'clock that morning, was over around eleven. Afterward, they decided to go out for a quick lunch. Howard, Young, and Taliaferro were going to shower and change at the gym. Banks decided to run home to shower and change. He would meet them at the restaurant.

The last to arrive, Banks walked up to the table where the other three were already sitting. "Guess who was drafted by the Bears?" he asked, a smirk playing at the corner of his mouth. The others didn't notice, but he was trying to keep from smiling, trying to keep the secret from leaping out before he could tease them with it. They all began to guess, throwing out the names of players they thought were possible candidates. They were all white players, of course. Banks kept shaking his head, smiling. Finally, unable to contain it any longer, he unfolded a copy of the newspaper, the *Chicago Defender*, he had hidden behind his back. According to PBS, the *Chicago Defender*, established in 1905 by Robert S. Abbott, was a vital part of the black press, the first with a circulation over a hundred thousand. On its cover that day, in three-inch block letters, were the history-making words "George Taliaferro Is 'Drafted' by Chicago Bears."

Taliaferro's mouth was agape, but no sound escaped it. *This has to be a joke,* he thought, alternately looking from the headline to his friends. The Chicago Bears, just two years after Jackie Robinson broke the color barrier in baseball, broke an unwritten NFL rule and picked Taliaferro in the thirteenth round of the 1949 draft, making him the first black man to be drafted by a National Football League team. Until 1949, the black players in the NFL were present only through tryouts.

Before the draft, Bo McMillin, who was still coaching the Detroit Lions, had also been hoping to sign Taliaferro. According to Harry Warren, "Halas and Coach A.N. McMillin engaged in a lively battle for George Taliaferro, Negro halfback from Indiana University. . . . McMillin was anxious to get the Gary speedster because he had coached him at Indiana." Unable to acquire Taliaferro, McMillin was at least able to get another of his former Hoosier stars, Mel Groomes.

Ironically, George "Papa Bear" Halas, who had played, coached, and owned the Bears since the club's inception, had possibly played an influential role in segregating the NFL in the 1930s. African American coach Fritz Pollard blamed Halas for keeping him out of the league in the 1930s and 1940s. An article in the *Chicago Defender* hinted that drafting Taliaferro was a different experience for the Bears: "Not since the days of Duke Slater, former All-American tackle at the University of Iowa . . . and Joe Lillard, have any negroes played on any Chicago teams in the National Pro League." It continued, "The negro stars, for some reason or other, never 'made' the Bears' teams."

Like Taliaferro, Halas had also been a Big Ten football player, leading the University of Illinois to a Big Ten title in 1918. Also like Taliaferro, he spent time during his college career in the military, serving in the navy during World War I. Aside from playing football for Illinois coach Bob Zuppke, Halas also played baseball and basketball for the Illini, going on to play semipro baseball. It was his association with a starch manufacturer, A. E. Staley, however, that would lead to his vital role in the NFL. As a player and coach of the company's football team, Halas elected to use the blue and orange colors of his college alma mater for the team uniforms. In 1920, he represented the company at a meeting in Canton, Ohio, which led to the formation of the National Football League. Staley's starch company was awarded a franchise, and they chose the name "Decatur Staleys."

The Staleys did well that first season, going 10–2–1, but it was a difficult season financially. The Staleys moved to Chicago and won the NFL championship in 1921, then changed the name to the Bears in honor of the Chicago Cubs, who had allowed them to play their games at Wrigley Field. Halas became a permanent and influential fixture in the NFL. His career with the Bears lasted decades.

For Taliaferro, who grew up just outside of Chicago, to play for the Bears would fulfill a childhood dream. When the Bears drafted him, however, Taliaferro had already verbally committed to play for the Los Angeles Dons in the All-America Football Conference. Now he had a decision to make. He could fulfill his dream of playing for the Bears or honor his word. Torn, he decided to talk to his mother about his dilemma. She had been his best friend growing up, the one person he could talk to about anything. Neither her lack of formal education nor her mildness had kept her from being the family doctor, lawyer, and cook and, while Taliaferro was in high school, the occasional moderator between him and his father. Still relying on her for advice, he called her and explained the situation. He had agreed to play with the Dons, he said, but that was before he had been drafted by the Bears, something that hadn't even been a possibility to consider when he entered into the agreement. The proximity to Chicago meant Gary residents were typically Bears fans. He remembered telling his sandlot team that someday he would play for the Bears. They had all thought he was crazy. So when the impossible happened and the Bears drafted him, Taliaferro was tempted to sign.

She listened as he explained everything, and then she reminded him of the lessons she and his father had instilled in him about honesty and integrity.

"A man's word is his bond," she said, repeating the words his father had spoken to him throughout his youth, such as when he neglected to dig out the garden. Convinced, Taliaferro gave up his childhood dream on principle, although it didn't hurt that the Dons' salary offer was a little higher. "The announcement did not disclose the price, but the consensus was that the Negro star did all right because there has been a financial tug-of-war between the Dons and the Chicago Bears for his services," a *Chicago Daily Tribune* article stated. Taliaferro's situation was typical of the NFL and AAFC war. Harry Sheer, of the *Chicago Daily News,* wrote, "Reports trickling in from the football marts indicate that the All-America has taken the offensive in grabbing off all the talent it can lay its hands on . . . big names or not." He continued to list the players, including Taliaferro, who were snatched up by the AAFC. Seymour Shub, of the *Chicago Sun Times,* however, reported that Halas wasn't too upset with Taliaferro's decision. He'd planned to wait to sign Taliaferro until 1950 anyway because he knew Taliaferro still had one year left of college eligibility. While Taliaferro retained the honor of being the first African American drafted *by* an NFL team, when he declined the Bears' offer, Wally Triplett, a halfback from Penn State who was picked in the nineteenth round of the 1949 draft, became the first African American to be drafted *into* the NFL. Triplett was drafted by none other than Coach Bo McMillin.

Triplett's and Taliaferro's lives paralleled in numerous ways when it came to football and race. In high school, Triplett was recruited by the University of Miami. According to an ESPN 30 for 30 story, he wrote back, indicating in what he said was a caustic way that there must have been some mistake because he was black. Miami rescinded the scholarship offer with a note from Edward Dunn that read, "Do not be bitter against a group

Fig. 8.1 In 1949, George Taliaferro made history by becoming the first black man drafted by an NFL team. He chose to play instead for the Los Angeles Dons of the All-America Football Conference. *Photo courtesy George Taliaferro.*

of people that have nothing to do with present conditions." Triplett was also recruited by Penn State, where he ended up playing on a scholarship instead, one of only two black players on the team. There were only twenty-five or thirty black students in the entire school. As Taliaferro experienced at Indiana and in the army, Triplett's teammates also rallied behind him.

At the end of the 1946 season, the Penn State Nittany Lions were scheduled to play an away game against Miami. According to the ESPN story, the game would only be played if the black players stayed home. The team held a players-only meeting to discuss their options: play without two of their players or boycott the game. Team captain Steve Suhey made his opinion clear. According to ESPN, he said, "We are Penn State—All or none." The team voted unanimously—they would not play in Miami. Suhey's statement, which became a rally cry for the Nittany Lions, was also a powerful testament to the power of football. The following year, Penn State would end its season with a bid to the Cotton Bowl. Played in segregated Dallas, the game pitted Penn State against Southern Methodist University. The Nittany Lions had to make arrangements to stay at a nearby air base because the hotels would not host Triplett, who would end up scoring the touchdown that ended the game in a 13–13 tie. Now, Triplett would be playing for Taliaferro's former coach Bo McMillin, who would support Triplett the way he had Taliaferro.

Whether Taliaferro played for the Bears or the Dons was irrelevant to Indiana University fans, who either way mourned the fact that he would not be playing another year for the Hoosiers. An article in the *Chicago Defender* on January 8, 1949, probably sums it up best: "Gloom weighs like a ton on Bloomington. Big George is gone. Not that the University of Indiana [Indiana University] expected to field a championship football team next fall, they just hoped to hold their own. But Big George Taliaferro of Gary was their team." Taliaferro had scored two-thirds of Indiana's total points and had played forty minutes of each game of the 1948 season. Indiana University was losing its key player on both offense and defense.

To Taliaferro, the $7,000 contract and $4,000 signing bonus from the Dons gave him "all the money in the world." As a very young boy, he had often told his mother that she would never

Fig. 8.2 Taliaferro poses in 1949, his first season of professional football with the Los Angeles Dons of the All-America Football Conference. *Photo courtesy George Taliaferro.*

have to worry about anything. He had quit school to fulfill that promise, and now it was happening. He was going to take care of the woman who had always taken care of him, and he began by buying her a house. George Taliaferro was now a professional football player, but he did not forget the promise he had made to his mother after the Purdue game. His contract with the Dons included a statement that he would return to Indiana University to finish his degree.

Another bonus to signing with the Dons was a brand-new 1949 Chevy. So on a Saturday, Taliaferro caught a train and went to Chicago to pick it up. From there, he drove the car to Gary, where he would spend the night before heading back to Bloomington the next day. He was talking to his mom when his older brother, James, who also went by Jack, came home from work.

"Let me have the car," he asked. Taliaferro agreed, but only if James would have it back before eight in the morning, when he planned to leave. The next day Taliaferro was up early. He took a quick glance at the other twin bed in the back bedroom he and James shared. It was empty. Taliaferro cleaned up a little in the restroom and then walked to the kitchen, where from the window he could look out and see the car. The front end was dented in. He woke his mom and asked her to get Jack.

"If I get close to him, I'm gonna kill him," he told her.

"I'm so sorry," she said.

The car, still drivable, had a dented front end. Taliaferro's Bloomington friends teased him when they saw it, telling him he needed to learn to drive. Unlike Taliaferro, James, he said, "was a disaster." At eighteen James had joined the navy, but he came home after three years when the war ended. Despite having an athletic scholarship to North Carolina A&T University—he was also a talented athlete—he didn't go. Instead, he went to work in the steel mill. He had already started drinking and smoking when he was fourteen. He just "wanted to be grown, to come and go as he saw fit," Taliaferro said. The drinking and smoking continued into adulthood. Eventually, James would become the number one riveter for the US Bridge Works, where at soaring heights he would catch white-hot steel in his glove. But by Friday and Saturday, he "couldn't tell you where he was standing, he was so drunk," Taliaferro explained. For whatever reason, Taliaferro's response to his parents' lessons was much different from that of his brother. James would be the first of his siblings to die, at a young age, of an apparent heart attack, while Taliaferro was still playing professional football.

Being the first black man drafted by an NFL team was not the only trailblazing Taliaferro was doing in 1949. He also continued to erase the color lines that crisscrossed nearly every aspect of his life. In his starting position for the Dons, a team that played a wing-T formation, he continued to play in the quarterback/tailback position, making him the first black quarterback to play professional football. Professional football, however, was notoriously slow to change, and although the two significant strides made by Taliaferro did not quickly integrate the league, they did help to open the door for other black players who would follow.

Before starting his professional football career, Taliaferro had one more collegiate task, to play in that College All-Star game in Chicago in August 1949. The College All-Stars were to play against the Philadelphia Eagles, and, proud of his accomplishment, he called Viola Jones to ask her to come. Because she was still working in Washington, DC, however, she said she wouldn't be able to attend. This started an argument, with Taliaferro not understanding why she wouldn't make the trip to support him and Jones not understanding why it was such a big deal. By the time they hung up, despite a heated exchange, neither had changed position on the matter. Still upset, Taliaferro penned a letter, further indicating his displeasure with the situation. This served only to make matters worse. In response, Jones simply sent him back his engagement ring. Although her response to his second marriage proposal had been positive, the results were the same. George Taliaferro was not going to marry Viola Jones.

The College All-Star game was a contest between the best graduated college seniors and the defending NFL champions. Sponsored by *Chicago Tribune* sports editor Arch Ward, the All-Star game was a charity fundraiser. At the 1949 game, 93,780 spectators watched the Eagles stuff the All-Stars 38–0. Viola Jones was not one of them. Playing for the Eagles was Taliaferro's former teammate Pete Pihos. Two years earlier, friend Buddy Young from Illinois had been the game MVP. While fan interest obviously was not a problem, the players' fear of injury and the almost-guaranteed win by the NFL team would eventually bring an end to the annual tradition. After the last one was played, in 1976, the NFL had clearly dominated the series, with a 31–9–2 record.

With the College All-Star game officially ending his college football career, it was time for Taliaferro to test his athletic prowess in the professional football arena. He was finally ready to pursue a professional career to help his mother. Disheartened by his broken engagement, Taliaferro kept himself distracted by working. Because professional football players in the 1940s did not sign multimillion-dollar contracts or lucrative endorsement deals, most of the players had second jobs during the off-season. Taliaferro and another pro football player from Gary, John Brown, worked together in construction for a man named Jeter Means, who expected more work and better results from his two football players than from the rest of his employees. They were, after all, supposed to be stronger and faster than the other men, he had decided. One day Taliaferro and Brown worked even harder than usual filling up the boards for the bricklayers. Brown would bring the bricks and put them on the hod, a V-shaped apparatus for carrying bricks. When it was full, they would walk up the ladder, take the bricks off the hod, and put them on a board by the bricklayer, who would never have to stop laying to find a brick. It was hot, exhausting work, and it must have shown on their faces one day. Means called out to the two, "Taliaferro and Big John, give out—don't give up, because all sickness ain't death!" Taliaferro would adopt this phrase as a personal mantra, writing a shortened version of it on a board in Ballantine Hall at Indiana University decades later.

The time went by quickly despite the grunt work, and it was soon time for Taliaferro to join the Los Angeles Dons for his rookie year. One of his first games was against New York. Although the Dons lost 17–16, Taliaferro had given an impressive debut performance. The next day an article in the *Chicago Tribune* read, "Los Angeles almost tied the score in the final thirty seconds when George Taliaferro, ex-Indiana Star, returned a punt 52 yards for a touchdown." Unfortunately, the extra point that would have tied the game was blocked. Earlier in the game, Taliaferro also had a forty-four-yard run and some successful passing plays. It looked as if the Dons would be getting their money's worth. After New York, the Dons traveled to Hershey, Pennsylvania, to prepare for their next game against the Cleveland Browns. Taliaferro and Jones, meanwhile, had made amends. While he was in Hershey, they tried to set a date for him to go to Washington, DC, so they could get married. But there was just no way to get it done. There was not enough time, it was too far away, and there was a clause in his contract that forbade marriage during the rookie season. Taliaferro was starting to wonder if he would ever marry Viola Jones.

Taliaferro continued playing football, something that remained a constant in his life even when other aspects of it were not going well. It had always provided comfort and distraction. About midway through the season, Taliaferro had an especially impressive game against the Baltimore Colts. Before the game, his teammates had warned him about the Baltimore fans. "If you have to run out of bounds, get back in fast," they said. Baltimore did not have a major league baseball team, nor did it have any other professional teams to follow. That left only one outlet for all of their zealotry: supporting their Colts. With the stadium under construction, these raucous fans could crowd close to the field. Taliaferro could feel their collective energy as soon as he stepped onto the field, but by the end of the game, they had also felt his.

Journalist Sam Banks later wrote about his performance for the magazine *Our Sports*. Taliaferro appeared on the cover in a classic football pose, left arm wrapped around the football, tucked tight

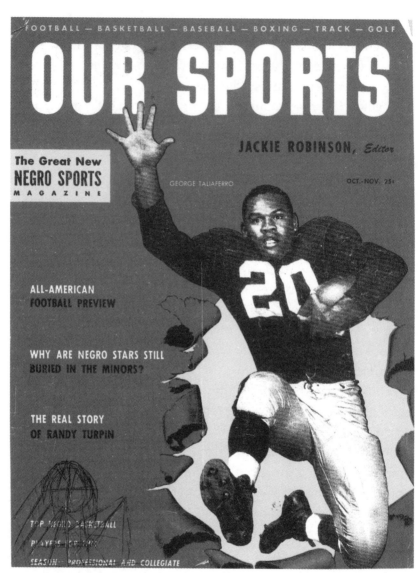

Fig. 8.3 Taliaferro bursts out of the cover of the October–November 1953 issue of
Our Sports, a magazine for black college and professional athletes that was edited
by none other than Jackie Robinson. *Photo courtesy George Taliaferro.*

against his side, right arm out, ready to stiff-arm anyone in his way. He appeared to be bursting through the cover of the magazine. Above his picture were the words *Jackie Robinson, editor*— the connection between the two of glaring historical significance. In the article, Banks wrote of Taliaferro, "The powerfully-built charger had what may have been his finest day in professional football. He passed, ran and punted the Dons to a lop-sided win over the Colts, and the thousands of fans who witnessed his performance went away 'oohing and ahing' and bemoaning the fact that Taliaferro was not a member of the under-manned Colts." Banks added, "His brilliant offensive play that day was nothing short of magnificent. And his defensive work only went to point up his all-around brilliance. For example, on two occasions he got off spiraling punts that soared some sixty yards, and then raced down the field to make the tackles himself."

In October, Taliaferro met another former Indiana player, Bob Hoernschemeyer, when the Dons played the Chicago Hornets. The game, not to be taken lightly, would decide which team would win a playoff berth in the All-America Conference. As he had so often done in the course of his football career, Taliaferro delivered. Robert Cromie of the *Chicago Daily Tribune* wrote the next day, "George Taliaferro, former Indiana All-American, last night made a strong bid for rookie-of-the-year honors as he passed the Los Angeles Dons to a 24 to 14 victory over the Chicago Hornets." Taliaferro scored two touchdowns, had fifteen carries for 48 yards, and completed twelve of twenty-four passes for 215 yards.

It is no wonder then that Taliaferro finished his rookie year with the Dons with postseason honors. He was, as Cromie predicted, selected Rookie of the Year in the AAFC. He had had a promising season in which, according to Banks, his total offense covered 1,249 yards, making him the leading rookie in the AAFC and winning him the honor of outstanding rookie back. He was also the number two rusher, with 472 yards; number two scorer, with forty-two points; and number two kickoff returner, with 313 yards. He had even run one punt back for a touchdown. He was enjoying his success in professional football, and he enjoyed living in Los Angeles. The fact that the Dons had recruited other black players helped put him at ease in his new environment.

Almost as quickly as it had begun, however, Taliaferro's career with the Dons was over. According to Peterson, by 1948, all of the AAFC teams, except for the Browns, were losing money. The ongoing player war with the NFL did not help matters. Chicago journalist Edward Prell wrote in April 1948, "One of the biggest headaches these days to professional football and baseball operators is the ever-recurring bonuses star athletes ask [for] before they sign on the dotted line." Taliaferro's $4,000 signing bonus was a significant amount of money in 1949. According to Prell, these bonuses, a product of the war between the NFL and AAFC, caused financial difficulties for the clubs. In fact, by the end of that 1949 season, the Dons' owners were forced to give the financially devastated team back to the AAFC. The only two stable teams in the struggling league were the Browns and the 49ers, but even their attendance was down, indicating trouble to come. Still, this financial trouble did not keep the two leagues from competing for players and for position, the AAFC commissioner going so far as to challenge the NFL to a playoff game. He wanted the champion of each league to vie for a world championship title. The NFL, however, continued its policy of ignoring the AAFC— and the challenge. Despite the NFL's best attempt, the refusal to respond to the AAFC did not make it go away, and the NFL was having attendance problems of its own. It became clear, Peterson wrote, that the two leagues would have to work something out and merge if professional football was to survive.

Rumors began to circulate that a merger was coming. Then, on December 20, 1948, an article in the *Gary Post-Tribune* alluded to one. The title, "Pro Grid Peace Meeting Today," was also a summary of the article. All anyone actually seemed to know about the meeting was that there was one. Once again, communication between the two leagues was at an impasse. Both leagues had ended their seasons the previous day. The Philadelphia Eagles were the NFL champions after beating the Chicago Cardinals. In the AAFC, the Cleveland Browns had beaten the Buffalo Bills for the title. The article reported a rumored world championship game between the two and even named the time and place: December 26 in New York. Newspapers the next day offered only a little more information. The meeting was, according to an *Indianapolis Star* article, the first between representatives from both leagues and the first time the NFL acknowledged the existence of the rival league.

Once again, however, discussions broke down, and the two leagues were unable to resolve the dispute. The AAFC commissioner indicated that, instead of merging, the two leagues would remain separate, and the AAFC would reduce its number of teams from eight to seven. Instead of playing two divisions, the teams would play a round-robin schedule. In January 1949, Edward Prell wrote, "The All-America's surprise announcement of a seven team set-up after four days of mysterious deliberations stamped out the last flicker of hope that peace would be attained with the National League." Because both leagues were losing money to the player and attendance war, it was assumed that at least a common player draft would happen in the hopes of salvaging the two leagues. When this did not happen either, according to Prell, Washington Redskins owner George Marshall said, "I prefer to let the All-America go another year. They will only get more tired." Marshall was right; nearly a year later, the two leagues were forced by their dire financial situations to come to an agreement.

Before the 1950 season began, the All-America Football Conference ended up merging with the National Football League. An article in the December 10, 1949, *Chicago Daily Tribune* read, "Professional football's four year war was settled across a conference table today. The All-America Conference merged with the National Football League." The war, the article explained, had cost owners from both sides more than $2 million because of the salary enticements and battle for attendance in cities where the two leagues were in direct competition. Horace Stoneham, owner of the New York Giants baseball team, was credited with the merger. He owned the polo grounds where the two New York NFL teams played, and he was tired of losing money because of the war between the rival conferences. He asked NFL commissioner Bert Bell and J. Arthur Friedlund, the AAFC's representative, to meet. Several such meetings later, the two leagues had merged. As per terms of the agreement, the NFL, which was divided into the American Conference and National Conference, agreed to take the AAFC's Cleveland Browns, San Francisco 49ers, and Baltimore Colts. The rest of the AAFC teams' players, including those of the Los Angeles Dons, were put into a pool for an NFL draft. The New York Yankees of the AAFC were also among the teams now defunct. Its players were to be distributed between the New York Bulldogs and the Giants. The Bulldogs, however, decided to rename themselves the Yankees, since that name was now available. Taliaferro was the second player in 1950 that the NFL's New York Yankees, or Yanks, a National Conference team, drafted.

During the off-season, Taliaferro stayed in Bloomington and continued to work. He and IU friends Jerry Stuteville and Casimir "Slug" Witucki decided to go to the Indy 500 together on May 30. Stuteville's roommate was also planning to go. Witucki was one of Taliaferro's former IU teammates, and Stuteville, who was going to do the driving, played basketball for Indiana with Bill Garrett. Leaving around four o'clock in the morning, they decided, would allow them to beat much of the heavy traffic. When Taliaferro, awakened by a loud banging, answered his door that morning, he noticed immediately that Stuteville, who had just come from a fraternity party, had been drinking. Taliaferro's attempts to get his keys failed. He didn't

GEORGE TALIAFERRO

Halfback—New York Yanks
Age: 23; Residence, Gary, Ind.
Height: 5-11   Weight: 195

This will be George's first year with Yanks. As rookie tailback with Los Angeles Dons last year, led all AAFC frosh in total offense with 1,294 yards. No. 2 rusher with 472 yards, scorer with 42, and kickoff return man with 313. No. 6 major college punter, U. of Indiana, 1948. All-American, 1948. All-Big Ten for 4 years.

No. 14 in a SERIES OF FOOTBALL PICTURE CARDS
© 1950 Bowman Gum, Inc., Phila., Pa., U. S. A.

Figs. 8.4a and 8.4b This 1950 Bowman football card is of George Taliaferro during his first season with the New York Yanks.

have a phone to call Witucki, but he thought that if he could get Stuteville to pick Witucki up first and then come back, the two of them could hold their friend down and wrestle the keys from him. When Witucki answered his door a few minutes later, he also noticed that Stuteville had been drinking. Like Taliaferro, he refused to get in the car, opting to forgo the race. Since Witucki didn't return with him, Taliaferro's plan to hold down Stuteville wouldn't work. He tried again to reason with him, but Stuteville refused to let anyone else drive. With attempts to keep his friend from driving to Indy unsuccessful, Taliaferro also opted not to go to the race. That left just Stuteville and his roommate. Just south of Indianapolis, Stuteville lost control of the car and sideswiped a bridge. Twenty-two years old and only one month from becoming a college graduate, Jerry Stuteville died instantly. His roommate sustained no serious injuries. Haunted by the fact that he had not kept Stuteville from driving that day, Taliaferro threw himself into football, finding the physical effort and familiarity of it to be, as it had been so many times, a source of comfort.

Playing for the Yanks in 1950 gave Taliaferro his first opportunity to play with Claude "Buddy" Young, who had been signed by the New York Yanks in 1947. Aside from their shared Big Ten experiences, Young and Taliaferro had also played against each other in high school, when Young had played for one of the few schools against which the Gary Roosevelt Panthers were permitted to play—another all-black school, Wendell Phillips High School in Chicago. Young was "a little guy," Taliaferro recalled. "He was about five foot four and weighed about 175 pounds. But he could flat out run. At one time Buddy Young was the fastest man in the world." Young had, in fact, held the world record for the forty-five-yard dash and had twice equaled the record for the sixty-yard dash while on the track team at the University of Illinois. A Colts football program would later describe Young: "At just 5 ft. 4 in. he is the shortest player currently active and,

Fig. 8.5 New York Yanks practice, circa 1950. While with the Yanks, George Taliaferro (number 20) had the opportunity to play for the first time with friend Buddy
Young (number 80). Young, despite being only five feet four, was once the fastest man in the world. Young and Taliaferro shared similar experiences as African American football players in the Big Ten. *Photo by Bob Olen, courtesy George
Taliaferro.*

because of his stature, is jokingly described as the only man in the
world who can block you at the knees without bending down."

Young's experiences paralleled Taliaferro's in many ways.
Like Taliaferro, Buddy Young had been a star athlete at an all-
black high school in the Midwest. He too had gone on to be All-
American for a Big Ten school, playing football and running track
for Illinois. Young and his Illinois teammates won the 1946 Big
Ten championship and the 1947 Rose Bowl, their only Big Ten
loss coming at the hands of Indiana. The 1945 Hoosiers were the
last Big Ten champions before the conference reached an agreement that would send its championship team to the Rose Bowl.

Illinois had had problems with returning servicemen and had suffered losses to Indiana and Michigan in 1945, prompting discussions of firing their coach. But by 1946 the Fighting Illini were faring better. Military service during World War II affected both Indiana and Illinois, and both Young and Taliaferro had stints in the service in the middle of their college careers. Playing professional football and raising families were other similarities the two would eventually share. With a dignity that made them role models for others, both managed to overcome the racism and segregation that defined their lives. It was no surprise, then, that they were close friends.

In college, Young, too, had been forced to live in a private residence because of the University of Illinois's segregated housing policy. Young lived at the home of Mrs. Ida Wells and her husband, a railroad worker who inspired the young men who lived in his home to be successful and hardworking. The residents of the Wellses' home were all black, male students, but Young was the only athlete. Later, in a 1967 interview, Young would describe athletics as "great equalizers." Sports, he believed, would help realize the constitutional ideal of equality. Little did he know that fifty years later, NFL athletes using the sport to fight for social equality would become the center of a national debate. Like Taliaferro's, Young's experiences with white teammates had not always been positive. During the first team shower, he remembered one white teammate who waited five minutes, just watching Young and another black teammate, Paul Patterson, before finally deciding he could get in the shower. Unlike Taliaferro, though, Young quit college after his sophomore year to go pro, and he never went back.

While with the Yanks in that 1950 football season, Taliaferro gained 411 yards rushing and scored four touchdowns, tying friend Sherman Howard's record. He also had five touchdowns as a receiver, completed three of seven passes for eighty-three yards, and threw one touchdown pass. As usual, he played both offensive and defensive positions. In December, he broke a record with eight kickoff returns in the game against the New York Giants. According to the Banks article, it was also during that season that Taliaferro began to earn the reputation of being a hot-and-cold player. His coach, Jimmy Phelan, who had been the head coach for Purdue for eight seasons, could tell what kind of a game he was going to have simply by his behavior at practice. If his manner was tense and nervous, Taliaferro would have a good game. A relaxed Taliaferro, however, often meant that a lackluster performance was to come. "Nevertheless, the slashing speedster managed to have enough good days to keep his rating as one of the finest runners in the game and, although his passing and punting fell off considerably, he could still pick 'em up and lay 'em down with the best," Banks wrote in *Our Sports* magazine. At the end of that 1950 season, the Yanks were 7–5, finishing in third place in the National Division.

Phelan was not always content with Taliaferro's performance, though. During one practice, Taliaferro threw a pass with his left hand instead of his right. He was playing halfback in the T formation. The quarterback received the ball and threw it to Taliaferro, who was then supposed to throw it to the receiver. He did, but being ambidextrous, and without thinking, he threw the ball with his left hand. "I don't want any Globetrotters on my football team," Phelan yelled in disapproval.

Occasionally, Taliaferro would go to the famed Red Rooster in Harlem, which was owned by George Edwin Woods, the "strangest man in Harlem," a *New York Times* article dubbed him. Woods dated a white actress from the South, Taliaferro recalled. The Red Rooster was a gathering place for famous black people in New York. Taliaferro ran into everyone but Jackie Robinson there. Robinson, he said, had endured so much, and had been made so miserable by the strong reaction to his breaking the color barrier in baseball, that he shunned the limelight. Taliaferro ran into just about everyone else at the Red Rooster, though, including Joe

Louis. Although he enjoyed socializing, Taliaferro did not drink and could not be persuaded to do so. One night, after a game against the Cleveland Browns, several members of the team were at the Red Rooster when someone offered to buy them a round. Taliaferro ordered a Shirley Temple with a cherry.

"What is a Shirley Temple?" the man asked.

"A ginger ale with fruit in it," Taliaferro said.

"I'm not going to buy any shit like that. Give him a double scotch. If he doesn't drink it, I'll pour it on him," the man told the bartender.

"They'll know where to find you on Memorial Day," Taliaferro told the man.

Taliaferro also met Malcolm X at the Red Rooster. Taliaferro was there with some football players, including Don Newcomb, Sherman Howard, and Buddy Young. Malcolm X was there with a group of people too. Everyone was mulling around talking about sports, which is how the two men ended up talking. They discussed trying to get more black college athletes involved in professional sports because there were so few black pro athletes. That, they felt, would open up more coaching and educational opportunities for black people too. Aside from that, Taliaferro said, he and the other athletes were shy to discuss politics with Malcolm X. "His plate was so full, we just wanted to be in his presence," he said.

About halfway through the season, Milton Purvis, Viola's play brother at Virginia State, came to New York for the day to see Taliaferro. The two men attended football practice together, went out to lunch, and took in a movie. Much had happened since Taliaferro had left the army, so the two had a lot of catching up to do. One topic, which seemed to be just below the surface of their conversation all day, finally came up after dinner, when Purvis finally asked the question that had been on his mind.

"When are you going to marry my play sister?" he asked.

Taliaferro wondered that too. Purvis's question prompted him to take action. He was ready to make it permanent, to set the date, but he was nervous. Later that night, Taliaferro had mustered enough courage to call her, to get a definite answer. Sometime after eleven o'clock, he picked up the phone and dialed the number. His heart beat faster as he heard the phone ring. Jones's roommate, Estelle, answered, but before agreeing to put Jones on the phone, she reprimanded Taliaferro for waking her and making phone calls in the middle of the night. After gleaning a sufficient apology from him, she reluctantly agreed to wake Jones.

The line went quiet for a long time, enough for him to wonder if Estelle hadn't just put the phone down with no intention of waking Jones at all, to teach him a lesson. Just when he was about to give up, he heard a familiar voice.

"Hello?" she asked groggily. He could hear the sleep in her voice, a huskier, rougher version of the familiar one.

"Will you marry me?" Taliaferro blurted out after identifying himself. He had to do it quickly, before he lost his nerve. It was the third time he had asked her to marry him. There was an uncomfortable pause.

"Yes," she finally said. She would work it out and call him later with all the details, she told him.

After the phone call, Taliaferro went to bed, contented that Jones would soon, finally, be his wife. Jones fell back asleep immediately, and when she woke up the next morning, she felt as if the proposal had been a dream. She wondered whether the conversation had actually taken place. She later said of that morning that two thoughts were running through her mind: *I must be dreaming* and *I must be out of my mind.* She picked up the phone and called Taliaferro to confirm that they had actually spoken the previous night.

The ringing telephone woke Taliaferro around seven o'clock in the morning. He shook the sleep off quickly when he realized that it was Jones and that she sounded a little worried. She asked whether he had actually called her the night before. She thought perhaps she had been dreaming and wanted to make sure that wasn't the case, she explained. She didn't ask what she really wanted to know, whether he had asked her to marry him. When he realized what she was digging for, Taliaferro's worry turned to amusement.

"What did we discuss?" Jones wanted to know.

"I asked you to marry me," he reminded her, matter-of-factly.

"What was my reply?" she asked.

He repeated their conversation for her, reminding her that she was going to work out the details and call him.

"I just wanted to be sure," she said and hung up the phone. Taliaferro smiled.

She did work out the details. They would be married on November 24, 1950 (the fifth anniversary of the game in which Indiana University beat Purdue University for the undisputed Big Ten championship), at quarter to four in the afternoon (the same time the game started). Taliaferro had a game the night before at Detroit. He would play the game and leave from Detroit to meet her in Washington, DC, for the wedding.

When the Detroit game began, Taliaferro had no idea just how crazy his night would get. With only about two minutes remaining in the game, it started to snow. It was not a soft dusting. No, snow dumped on the field by the inches. Crews had to come out with shovels just to spot the football. When it was finally over, the Yanks had lost the game. That night, Taliaferro did not dwell on the loss. He had other priorities: getting to DC for his wedding. After the game, the team went to the locker room to grab quick showers before getting their luggage on the bus and heading to the airport. At the airport, they boarded a snow-covered plane and waited for the windshield to be cleared before taking off. But they only made it about two hundred yards in the air before the captain realized that the radio was out and that they had no communication with the ground. They were forced to turn back around, land, and wait for crews to de-ice the plane. By that time, the coach had had enough. He decided that they would just go to a hotel and take a train out in the morning.

This plan would not work for Taliaferro. "Well, I'm being married at three forty-five tomorrow," he said. "They will find me walking. I have to get to DC." He wasn't alone. A *New York Times* reporter also on board needed to get back, and friend and teammate Sherman Howard, who simply didn't want to wait until the next morning, said, "Tell them I'm your best man." So, while the rest of the team went to a hotel, Taliaferro, Howard, and the reporter boarded a new flight to Buffalo, New York, which had "more snow than Alaska" when they landed, Taliaferro said. From Buffalo, they caught a connection to New York City and then a train to DC, and Taliaferro made it there with just enough time to spare to get about four hours of sleep.

That day, George Taliaferro married Viola Jones at her sister's home, with Milton Purvis standing as Taliaferro's best man. Despite several failed engagements and a blizzard, Viola Jones finally became Mrs. Viola Taliaferro. "It took a while for her to realize that life really couldn't go on for me without her," Taliaferro said of the long delay.

She alluded to this as well. "I don't know. He just came after me. That's all," she said of her decision to finally marry him. After the nuptials, the newlyweds lived in Gary for the rest of the football season.

Incidents of racism were fairly isolated while Taliaferro played for the Yanks in 1950. Teammate Sherman Howard said in a 2003 interview that racism was not a problem for him, George Taliaferro, or the other black players on that team. Of course, Jim Crow laws continued to beleaguer the black athletes, who had to stay in separate facilities, often with private families, when they played in places like Louisiana and Texas. That, however, was neither new nor unexpected. Most of their Yanks teammates, Howard said, many of whom were from the South, accepted them.

Fig. 8.6 Even a blizzard could not stop George and Viola Taliaferro from cutting their wedding cake on November 24, 1950, the fifth anniversary of the win against Purdue that earned the Hoosiers a Big Ten championship and undefeated season. The Taliaferros were married at 3:45 p.m., the same time the game had started. *Photo courtesy George Taliaferro.*

Because of their past football experiences, many of their white teammates had already heard of Howard and Taliaferro. The players who did not already know them soon discovered that these black men, despite having come from neighborhoods generally poorer than their own, were gentlemen with strong values. Howard found that in their relationships with teammates, he and Taliaferro were often judged by the content of their character rather than by the color of their skin.

However isolated, some incidents still happened. One such experience, Taliaferro remembered, occurred while he played for the Yanks. In a 1950 game against San Francisco, Taliaferro had a confrontation with a 49er from Louisiana State University who,

Taliaferro said, had not had much experience playing against black football players and wasn't keen to start. This particular player caught a kick, and as Taliaferro approached to tackle him, he jumped up and tried to kick Taliaferro in the face. Blocking the player's foot with his forearm, Taliaferro then proceeded to flip him onto his back and punch him in his jaw. The stunned 49er lay on the field as Taliaferro walked away, already readying himself for the next play. "Then it was over," Taliaferro said of the incident.

Taliaferro continued to rack up successful statistics. Howard said he was involved in almost every play of every game. "I would block for him, and he would block for me. It wasn't one for one; it was one for all," he said. Howard noticed Taliaferro's considerable pride and belief in excellence. "Whatever he does he wants to be the best, and he instills that in others too," he explained. If the Yanks needed a pass or a play, Taliaferro would tell him, "I'm going to do my part; you just do yours." One of the reasons for their strong bond may have been the attitude both men had regarding racism. Howard echoed Taliaferro's feelings when he said of racists, "They the person got a problem—when I start acting like him, then I got a problem—just be yourself."

Before Taliaferro's eyes, football was continuing to evolve, and in 1950, while Taliaferro and Howard played for the Yanks, professional football became a televised sport. Years later, at breakfast one morning, Viola Taliaferro told their daughters how their daddy had been a football player before there was television. "Mommy, there wasn't anything before television," Renée, their second-oldest daughter, replied. Other changes in pro football were also occurring in the 1950s. The experimental rule permitting unlimited substitutions, for example, was made permanent, which also led to the universal practice of having separate teams for offense and defense and the development of specialists like place kickers and punters. Unlike most professional football players, however, Taliaferro continued to play on both sides of the football.

When the 1950 season was over, the Yanks had a record of 7–5. The Taliaferros moved to Bloomington, Indiana, for the off-season, enabling Taliaferro to finally fulfill the promise he had made to his mother and father. In May 1951, he earned his bachelor's degree. Satisfied by the accomplishment, he was ready to focus solely on football during the 1951 season.

That season found Taliaferro with the New York Yanks again and making history again. Bob Gill, in an article for the newsletter of the Professional Football Researchers Association, wrote that Taliaferro and three other players shared the quarterback position during the 1951 football season after their quarterback, George Ratterman, defected to Canada. Taliaferro, who completed thirteen of thirty-three passes for 251 yards and one touchdown in the position, thus became the first African American to play quarterback in the National Football League.

In the article, Gill called Taliaferro a "forgotten" trailblazer. Willie Thrower, who quarterbacked three games for the Bears two years later, was sometimes mistakenly given the credit, Gill wrote, for being the first black quarterback in the NFL. On October 18, 1953, George Halas put Thrower in to replace George Blanda. He completed three of eight passes for twenty-seven yards, and Thrower's longest gain was twelve yards. He also threw one interception. This historic game is, according to some research, the one in which Thrower became the first black quarterback in the NFL. However, Taliaferro had already been in the NFL for two years by that time and had thrown ninety-six passes in the league before Thrower had even joined the Bears. Despite this, Taliaferro thought Thrower deserves the recognition of being the first African American quarterback in the NFL. This, Taliaferro said, is because Thrower was actually selected for the Bears as a quarterback. In an article he wrote for the *Coffin Corner*, Taliaferro explained, "The Bears listed Willie as quarterback on their roster. That's important. Because of the variety of plays used in a game and the changes caused by free substitution, a

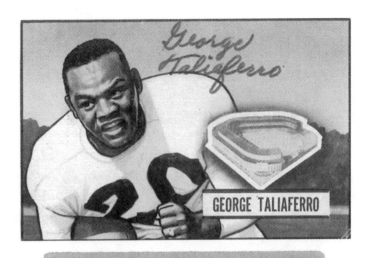

Figs. 8.7a and 8.7b A 1951 Bowman football card of George Taliaferro during his second season with the New York Yanks.

player might begin a play at almost any position. But, whatever a team lists as a player's position is what the team and his coach thought his position was. The Bears thought of Willie as a quarterback." Taliaferro went on to explain that even though he often took snaps in what is now known as the shotgun formation, he did not take snaps under center, which is "the thing that distinguishes a modern T-quarterback from those who came before." In the single-wing formation, which turned one hundred years old in 2006, the ball can be snapped to the tailback, the fullback, and sometimes the wingback. "The distinction of being the first black quarterback really does belong to Thrower," he said.

Thrower was more aptly named for the position, if nothing else. Although humble, Taliaferro does deserve recognition. While Thrower was the first African American quarterback in the NFL, George Taliaferro was the first African American to play the quarterback position in the NFL. Either way, Thrower, having been relegated for the most part to sitting the bench and not accustomed to doing so, ended up leaving the National Football League to play in the Canadian League for the Toronto Argonauts and then the Winnipeg Blue Bombers.

More important to Taliaferro than his history-making football achievements, though, was the birth of his first daughter, Linda Taliaferro, on September 28, 1951, in Washington, DC. At the time of her birth, Taliaferro was across the country playing a football game in Los Angeles against the Rams. Her birth was the highlight of an otherwise dismal night. The fact that Taliaferro established a single-game record of fourteen punts was indicative of the nature of the game and the Yanks' season in general. The team came in last place in their division with an abysmal record of 1–9. The Rams, on the other hand, won the NFL championship.

On the Los Angeles Rams that year was rookie Len Teeuws. Because there were only fifteen black players in the NFL and six of them played for the Rams, Teeuws said they were often called the "Black Rams." Among the six black players were Harry

STATE FAIR
STADIUM
SEPT. 14
SHREVEPORT

25c

New York
Yanks

vs.

Washington
Redskins

Fig. 8.8 A football program from Taliaferro's 1951 season with the New York Yanks. The Redskins were owned by George Preston Marshall, a man some believed to be responsible for the segregation of the NFL.

Thompson of UCLA, Bob Boyd of Loyola, and Hall of Famer Richard "Night Train" Lane. Lane actually preferred to be called Richard, Teeuws said, "But you know you've become a hero when you have a nickname." Even though the black players had separate sleeping facilities when they played games in the South, they were still part of the family to their white teammates. When there were team parties, for example, everyone was invited, including the black players, Teeuws emphasized. On the other hand, he said, there were other great black players who were not on the team because there were already "too many" black players. To emphasize the point, Teeuws said, "If Jesus had come down as a black man, he would not have made the team."

Although the Yanks had not fared as well as the Rams, Taliaferro's effort did not go unnoticed. *Los Angeles Times*'s Frank Finch wrote that Taliaferro "gave one of the greatest solo performances ever. Handicapped by a lackluster supporting cast, Taliaferro gained 172 yards in 12 tries for a 14.3 average, scored two touchdowns (one coming on a 65-yard run), and passed to Bob Celeri for another. He completed three of five passes, caught one himself, averaged 42.55 yards punting and doubled in brass as a defensive halfback." His statistics for the season were equally impressive. He had passed for 251 yards with two touchdowns, had rushed for 330 yards with four touchdowns, and had an average gain of 14 yards per reception. He also led the league in kickoff returns. And that was just on offense. On defense, he added four interceptions to the list. At the end of the season, Taliaferro was selected to the Pro Bowl, a game that gave him a chance to meet up again with former Indiana teammate Pete Pihos, who was representing Philadelphia in the Pro Bowl and who would go on to become a Professional Football Hall of Famer.

Accompanied by his wife, Taliaferro booked a room in LA for the Pro Bowl. Their friend Kenny Washington, the first black NFL player, was also in town. Washington had played college football at UCLA with Jackie Robinson and movie actor Woody

Strode. Strode had also played baseball with Robinson, who was a four-sport athlete for the Bruins, adding basketball and track and field. In fact, Robinson was UCLA's first four-sport varsity letter winner. That night Washington, already retired from football, invited the Taliaferros to meet a close friend of his, Nat King Cole, who was performing for a packed room at the Brown Derby. Before the performance started, Washington introduced Cole and his wife, Maria, to George and Viola Taliaferro. Taliaferro told Cole that he had seen him compete in high school track, against Taliaferro's older brother, James, in Chicago when he was a boy, and he explained that he was in town to play in the Pro Bowl. Cole dedicated the next half hour of his set to the Taliaferros and serenaded them with "Unforgettable," which had just been released in October. Also entertaining them that evening was a well-dressed white woman who let Cole know, "You can put your slippers under my bed any time." The woman, Taliaferro said, "had her drink and she had her foot tapping, and every time he terminated a song, she led the applause."

A couple of months later, rain fell on Bloomington, Indiana. It was March 31, 1952, the anniversary of famed Notre Dame coach Knute Rockne's death. It was also the day Bo McMillin, Taliaferro's Indiana University football coach and mentor, died of a heart attack in his Bloomington home. He was fifty-seven years old. He had retired early from coaching the Philadelphia Eagles because of health reasons when two operations had not succeeded at curing a severe stomach ailment. A month earlier, he had been hospitalized for a few weeks. He had returned home just ten days prior to his death. Bloomington had adopted McMillin, the man they credited with having the most significant overall impact on IU athletics. University leaders and former football players were among those who mourned the Texan. They remembered his ability to lead and inspire with colorful adages rolling off his tongue in a Texas drawl. Former players became pallbearers for the man who'd had such a significant impact on

Figs. 8.9a and 8.9b The Dallas Texans formed when a group of investors bought the financially downtrodden New York Yanks. Taliaferro was then drafted to play for the Dallas Texans, as shown in this 1952 Bowman football card.

GEORGE TALIAFERRO

89 BACK
Dallas Texans

Res.: Gary, Ind.
Age: 25
Height: 5-11
Weight: 195

All-American back from Indiana in 1948. Top rookie in 1949, he is now in third year with Texans (formerly Yanks). Used primarily on offense, George, nevertheless, intercepted 4 passes in 1951, with average return of over 18 yards. Led in kickoff returns, 12th in punting.

RECORD FOR LAST SEASON

CARRYING: Attempts, 62; Yards Gained, 330; Average Gain, 5.3.

PASSING: Attempts, 33; Comp., 13; Yds. G., 251; Td. P., 1; Int., 3; Av. G., 7.61.

RECEIVING: Number, 16; Yards Gained, 230; Average Gain, 14.4.

SCORING: Touchdowns, 5; Total Points, 30.

COLLEGE TO PRO *FOOTBALL* PICTURE CARDS
©1952 Bowman Gum Division, Haelan Laboratories, Inc., Philadelphia 44, Pa. Printed in U.S.A.

Figs. 8.9a and 8.9b *(continued)*

their lives. Taliaferro, unable to attend, mourned the loss of his mentor. McMillin, who had helped him through some of his most difficult times, would never be forgotten. In addition to mourning his mentor, Taliaferro was dealing, once again, with the pressure of playing for a team that was barely surviving.

For the Yanks, the end of the 1951 season had not brought an end to the NFL saga, despite its integration with the AAFC. The New York Yanks of 1950 and 1951 folded and in 1952 became the Dallas Texans. Taliaferro, then, became a Texan. Like its predecessors, the Texans' team was fraught with problems from the outset. In his article "Belly Up in Dallas," Joe Horrigan described the Texans' failings. Yanks owner Ted Collins, tired of spending money on a losing team, sold the franchise back to the NFL. That was when Texas millionaire Giles Miller and a group of investors decided to buy the troubled franchise to bring professional football to Dallas. Early on, there were critics of the move. Journalist Stan Grosshandler wrote later that some critics worried that a state so devoted to college football would not support a pro team.

Others were just bothered by the losing track record of the Yanks, which would make attracting fan support difficult. On the other hand, supporters of the move thought Dallas was ready for a professional football team precisely because they were so supportive of high school and college football. At the very least, the general consensus was that Dallas was a better bet than Baltimore was for the team. The board of directors of the old Baltimore Colts had also been bidding on the team, but when the final decision was made, the New York Yanks became the Dallas Texans, Texas's first professional football team, while Baltimore was left without a team.

The critics of the move to Dallas may have been right. According to Horrigan, while the Texans played in the Cotton Bowl, an arena that seated 75,000 people, on their best day they drew a crowd of only 17,499 people. On opening day a meager 15,000 fans turned out to watch their newly acquired team, Grosshandler wrote. The team's only shining moment of the season came minutes into the opening game, with a fumble that led to a Texan touchdown. After that, the season steadily declined. The Giants ended up winning the opening game 24–6, and each week, as the losses piled up, the crowds grew smaller. Coach Phelan even joked that rather than have the players announced over the public-address system before the game, he should just send them into the stands to personally introduce themselves to each fan. Sadly, in a state known for its obsession with football, it was a struggle to get anyone to attend the games.

Giles Miller and his investors were unable to cover the expenses of running the losing Texans, and even before the season was over, they returned the team to the NFL. Rarely getting a chance to stop and practice, and playing all games at the arenas of their opponents, the Texans became a road team without a home. Despite the obstacles his team continued to face as a whole, Taliaferro's individual performance continued to impress. He and Buddy Young were still teammates, and the duo was dynamite together in the backfield. This, according to Horrigan, was one of the few positive aspects of the team. He wrote, "After all, their roster did include future Hall-of-Famers Gino Marchetti and Art Donovan, and the potentially explosive backfield duo of Buddy Young and George Taliaferro." Even though the season had not been going well, Taliaferro's skill was not questioned. In the Los Angeles Rams vs. Dallas Texans football program, Frank Finch wrote of him, "The fact that every club in the National Football League would bid the limit for the former Indiana All-American is ample evidence of his pigskin prowess." At season's end, Taliaferro was, once again, on the Pro Bowl roster for the National Division, his second time. During the season, he had rushed for 419 yards in one hundred attempts and had one touchdown. He had also passed for 298 yards and two touchdowns. His average gain receiving was about 12 yards, with 244 yards in twenty-one attempts and one touchdown. His statistics, once again, were impressive even though he had played for a losing team, which ended its season with a record of 1–11.

Life in Dallas, on top of the losses and volatility of the team, was hard for the Taliaferros. The 1950s were difficult for African Americans, Viola Taliaferro said, no matter where one lived. Anywhere in the South, however, was "particularly awful." The segregation was worse in Dallas than it had been in the East. She could not even go shopping for a dress, she said, and there was not a day in Dallas that she felt they were treated with the respect and equality they deserved. "There was not a single day that we were not treated as being inferior in some way," she said. Even the Cotton Bowl, in the Texans' arena, was segregated. In other arenas, she and Buddy Young's wife, Geraldine Young, would sit with the other wives, but that was not the case at Dallas's Cotton Bowl. There, they sat in the segregated section. When the Texans' owners noticed where the two women were sitting, they did invite them to sit with the other wives. To make a point, the two women declined the offer, refusing to leave the "colored" section

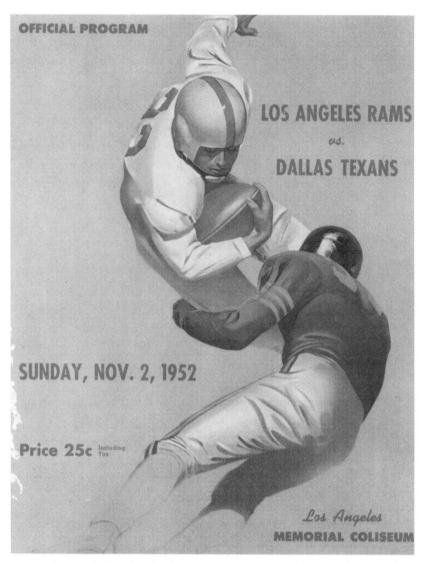

Fig. 8.10 In 1952, the Los Angeles Rams were on their way to the NFL championship. The financially devastated Texans won only one game.

Fig. 8.11 November 23, 1952: Dallas Texans versus Green Bay Packers. Number 20 (*left*) is George Taliaferro. Number 44 (*right*) is Packers rookie Bobby Dillon. *Photo courtesy George Taliaferro.*

of the field. "No, it is your practice that black people sit together, and that is exactly where I am going to sit," Viola Taliaferro told the owners. It was hard, she explained, to experience that kind of thing on a daily basis and not get to a point where she was just filled with hatred.

Originally, a plan had been designed to permanently segregate seating at the Dallas stadium. It was created, according to Horrigan, in anticipation of the heavy demand for tickets from Dallas's African American fans. But the segregated seating was not permanent. While the exact reason behind the change was not determined, there was some speculation. "Whether resulting from pressure from the Texans' management or a lack of ticket requests in general, a minor blow for social justice occurred when segregated seating never materialized," Horrigan wrote. Segregated seating was not the only plan that did not work out for the

Texans. The financially devastated team would not remain in Dallas, and ready to pick up the pieces was Baltimore. Although it had been spurned before, the city was still interested in the troubled franchise whose demise it had followed all season. But the NFL still had its reservations and was not convinced the team should move there. If Baltimore wanted the financially broken, homeless football team, it was going to have to prove it, and it wasn't going to be easy. The NFL had to minimize its risk.

To acquire the team, then, the city of Baltimore would need to sell 15,000 season ticket books in six weeks. The books, which cost $19.80, were sold at the worst time of year, around Christmas, and the tickets were for games that were nearly a year away. Add to this the fact that the team had ended its previous season losing all but one game and that the Colts' previous best advance sale had been 6,700 tickets. More than doubling that, selling 15,000 tickets in six weeks, was a monumental task. But Baltimore was also a city that had kept together the Colts Band, which had continued to meet every Sunday, even during all the years when the city did not have a team. The Colt Corrals, the unofficial gathering of Colts fans, also continued, even when the city was Colt-less. Baltimore had remained faithful to its football team even when it didn't have it. If any city could rise to the NFL's challenge, it would be this one.

Any lingering doubts were erased when the city met the 15,000-ticket challenge in only four weeks and three days. On January 23, 1953, the team that had been the Yanks, and then the Texans, officially became the second edition of the Baltimore Colts. A Colts team had existed in 1947 in the All-American Football Conference. The first edition of the Colts was formed when the Miami Seahawks folded. Those Colts had dressed in the predecessor's colors, green and silver. In 1950, the team became an NFL member, but it was disbanded after the 1950 season, following a losing streak of eighteen games over two seasons and a significant loss of money. With the orphaned Dallas Texans seeking a home, Baltimore saw its opportunity to adopt a professional football team again. Since the second edition of the Colts was formed from the Texans, whose colors had been blue, white, and silver, the new Baltimore Colts opted to keep those colors. They rarely wore the silver, however, and eventually their colors evolved to just blue and white. On the sidelines during the game, the players would wear reversible hooded capes that were cloth on one side and rain gear on the other. Just visible beneath the layers was stitched the outline of a star—the Dallas Texans' logo. They had simply sewn a new layer over it.

While Baltimore was going through the process of acquiring the Colts, the Taliaferros, eager to leave segregated Dallas, moved back to Los Angeles. Their experience in the City of Angels, while different from the one in Dallas, was not necessarily better. They wondered how they would feel about Baltimore. Hesitant to pick up and move everything again, only to end up somewhere else they didn't feel like they belonged, they decided to keep a residence in each city until they could be certain before moving there permanently. So in July, George Taliaferro left for Baltimore, while his family remained in California.

The support Baltimore had demonstrated when they purchased more than fifteen thousand season tickets did not wane in the intervening months, and when the Colts started their first season as an NFL team, the Colts Band was waiting for them. The old Colts Band would be playing in a new stadium, one that was being built as a new level above the old one. Ed Steers, who had moved from Philly to Baltimore in 1947, the same year the Colts came to Baltimore for the first time, was a water boy for the second edition of the Colts. He remembers those days well. The upper deck of Baltimore Memorial Stadium was being constructed during the 1953–54 season because the stadium was also going to be used for baseball, he recalled.

Under the stands, there were tunnels for the construction workers to bring in their materials. Steers, who lived just three blocks from the stadium, and his friends had explored every inch of those tunnels. They knew how to sneak into the stadium to watch the Colts on any given day. They also liked to sneak in to watch Notre Dame–Navy games when Navy used the stadium. In 1953, Steers and his friends would sneak in to watch their heroes, players like Buddy Young and George Taliaferro. On one such occasion, when the Colts were playing the Packers, Steers and his cousin discovered, to their utter dismay, that one of the tunnels was closed off, blocking their entry to the game. They weighed their options. They could climb the fence at center field, but it was so high that the police would usually catch the kids gate-crashing before they made it all the way over. Sometimes a group of forty kids would rush the fence, knowing that about ten of them would make it without getting caught, but that wasn't going to work with just the two of them. They were starting to run out of options, and they could hear the Colts Band playing, signaling that the game would soon begin. Panicked that they were going to miss the game, they ran around to the players' entrance to see if it was open. As they were hanging out by the door waiting to see if they could somehow get in, a taxi pulled up. Out stepped a black man, about five foot four, in pajamas, a robe, and leather slippers. They recognized him at once as Buddy Young, the smallest man on the team. They called to him, begging to be let in the player door. At first Young just looked at the boys in surprise, taking in what they were saying. Then he shook his head, shrugged, and waved them in, saying, "Okay, come on."

Young led them to the locker room and asked equipment manager Freddy Schubach to give them something to do. Schubach accommodated Young, handing the boys water and towels. Not only had they gotten into the game for free, but they were even able to stand on the sidelines with the players in their new role as water boys. These water boys didn't have paper cups and plastic coolers, though. They scooped water from a galvanized bucket and lifted the metal ladle to the lips of their thirsty heroes.

Although it hadn't occurred to him at the time, years later Steers was struck by the fact that Buddy Young let them into the game that night. "Two white kids, why in the hell should he bother with us? It was such an unusual thing to do, but he said, 'Sure kids, come on,'" Steers recalled. But Young had a reputation for being charitable, and things like that went on in Baltimore all the time, Steers said. The NFL, even professional sports in general, weren't the same as they are today, he explained. In the 1950s, the players were accessible to the fans. The Colts were a part of Baltimore, not just something to be worshipped from afar. Steers said he would run into the players at the local pizza parlors and laundromats. Fans would attend the Colts' practices and then sit and talk to the players afterwards. Steers had lived just down the street from Clifton Park, where the Colts held practices during the years 1947 to 1949, and he went to practice every day to watch. He was one of the fans who would stay and talk to players. He also watched when they practiced at Westminster Maryland College.

At that time professional football was struggling, Steers explained. It had nowhere near the following baseball had. Teams used patched-up equipment and played on public fields. "They weren't superstars," Steers explained, just guys who had played college football; they all had jobs on the side. They were a part of Baltimore, and the fans knew them. For that reason, there was a real connection between the fans and the players, who didn't disappoint when they started off the 1953 season well enough to prompt pennant dreams. The Colts already had two wins against the Bears and had played a close game with Detroit, the defending champions. Even a disappointing loss to the winless Green Bay Packers, 37–14, may have been a fortunate event for the Colts.

Watching the game that day was Carroll Rosenbloom, a wealthy textile manufacturer and former collegiate football player. The Penn alum had been asked to serve as the financial backer of the Baltimore Colts. Reluctantly, and only out of a sense of obligation to the city, Rosenbloom had agreed. His reluctance

Figs. 8.12a and 8.12b There to pick up the pieces of the Dallas Texans was Baltimore. The city met an NFL challenge to earn the team, making Taliaferro a Baltimore Colt, as seen on this 1953 Bowman football card.

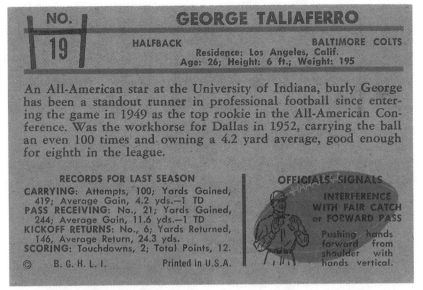

NO. 19	GEORGE TALIAFERRO	
	HALFBACK	BALTIMORE COLTS
	Residence: Los Angeles, Calif.	
	Age: 26; Height: 6 ft.; Weight: 195	

An All-American star at the University of Indiana, burly George has been a standout runner in professional football since entering the game in 1949 as the top rookie in the All-American Conference. Was the workhorse for Dallas in 1952, carrying the ball an even 100 times and owning a 4.2 yard average, good enough for eighth in the league.

RECORDS FOR LAST SEASON

CARRYING: Attempts, 100; Yards Gained, 419; Average Gain, 4.2 yds.—1 TD
PASS RECEIVING: No., 21; Yards Gained, 244; Average Gain, 11.6 yds.—1 TD
KICKOFF RETURNS: No., 6; Yards Returned, 146, Average Return, 24.3 yds.
SCORING: Touchdowns, 2; Total Points, 12.

© B. G. H. L. I. Printed in U.S.A.

OFFICIALS' SIGNALS

INTERFERENCE WITH FAIR CATCH or FORWARD PASS

Pushing hands forward from shoulder with hands vertical.

Figs. 8.12a and 8.12b *(continued)*

changed, ironically enough, when he watched the first loss of the season to one of the league's worst teams. At the end of the game, with no hope up of making up for the deficit in points, George Taliaferro continued to play as if they could still win it. On a Green Bay punt the last play of the game, Taliaferro ran about forty yards and was tackled just past the Colts' bench. Carroll Rosenbloom leaned over and asked him why he hadn't just run out of bounds.

"That's not how I play football," Taliaferro responded.

"Even when they had you cornered," Rosenbloom said, impressed, his voice trailing off in thought.

Stuart McIver wrote for *Sport* magazine, "The game was nearly over and the Colts hopelessly beaten when George Taliaferro, their negro halfback, ran a punt back for good yardage. He was at the sidelines when the Packers closed in on him. He had only to step out of bounds to avoid the tackle. Instead he piled into the Packers and picked up two extra yards. 'If they want to play that hard,' said Rosenbloom, 'I want to go with them all the way.

Fig. 8.13 The Taliaferro family dressed for Easter, April 18, 1954: Linda stands in front, and baby Renée is held in Taliaferro's arms. *Photo courtesy George Taliaferro.*

If they've got that kind of spirit, I can't sit back, can I?'" Rosenbloom came away with a renewed sense of confidence and a total willingness to back his team. The Baltimore fans must have
shared his feelings. When the losing Colts returned to the airport, four thousand fans were there to greet them. Rosenbloom
knew he was no longer a reluctant participant in the Baltimore
Colts. The Colts, for their part, didn't disappoint the following
Sunday, when they beat the Redskins.

To Taliaferro, the most humorous incident of the season occurred during this Washington Redskins game. It began, he remembered, with a comment by Redskins owner George Preston
Marshall, the man who was still refusing to integrate his football
team (and would continue to refuse for nearly a decade), despite
the fact that other teams already had done so. Marshall, who was
standing just behind Taliaferro during the team introductions,
said loudly enough for Taliaferro to hear, "Niggers should never
be allowed to do anything but push wheelbarrows." Although the
comment itself wasn't funny, Taliaferro laughed telling the story,
"because then I went out and scored three touchdowns!" he said.

Excitement continued to grow as the season progressed. In
a late-November game against the Rams, they played in fog so
heavy that the players couldn't see from one end of the field to
the other. To make matters worse, it was to be Taliaferro's first
time as quarterback for the Colts. Taliaferro supposed his experience at Indiana University, during which he often threw passes as
a running back in the old single-wing formation, earned him the
quarterback position. The Tuesday before, with his other quarterbacks injured, Coach Molesworth, or "Moley" as the players
called him, had begun preparing Taliaferro for the role. Molesworth focused on a few basic plays during practice to initiate
Taliaferro into his new position. They kept practicing these plays
until they were confident that Taliaferro had them down, not
realizing at the time that Taliaferro's initiation into the position
would include heavy fog.

The game started with the Colts receiving first. They picked up a first down, and the first series of plays, which had been determined before the game, went smoothly for Taliaferro. But when he got in the huddle to begin the second series, he couldn't remember a single play. He looked at the players in the huddle, hoping the plays would come to him, but they didn't. Realizing he was in trouble, he knew that his only option was to call a quick time-out. "I can't remember the plays!" he gasped to Coach Molesworth, who burst out in a hearty laugh before grabbing the playbook and refreshing Taliaferro's memory. That was all Taliaferro needed. Having been reintroduced to the second series, he began calling plays as if he had been quarterbacking for years. His performance, which included running, passing, and kicking, could have earned the Colts another win if Taliaferro hadn't thrown a long pass that was picked off to give the Rams a 21–13 win. Still, Taliaferro had put on a show in the heavy fog and proved he was worthy of the quarterback position. PR director Sammy Banks later wrote about the game, "Who will ever forget the brilliant display put on by George Taliaferro as he took over the quarterback chores for the injured Fred Enke? And how about that fog? Remember? You couldn't even see the fans in the upper deck during the second half."

Unfortunately for the Colts and their fans, the pennant dreams had faded by the end of the season. They had made only a slight improvement on the Texans' record, with three wins and nine losses, finishing in fifth place in the West Division of the NFL. The record book hadn't recorded the team's other successes, though. The fans had proved that Baltimore was an NFL city with their record-breaking season ticket purchases. Rosenbloom had been inspired by his team's determination, and it turned out to be the first year the team had finished the season with a profit. The players and coaches were even awarded $500 Christmas bonuses. And Taliaferro had, for the third time in a row, earned a position on the Pro Bowl roster. His triple-threat abilities were apparent in his other statistics as well. He rushed for 479 yards that season. His average kickoff return was 19 yards. And he established a rushing record of 95 yards for the longest run ever by a Colt. More importantly, though, Taliaferro had a happy addition to his family with the birth of his second daughter, Renée Angela, who was born at around seven o'clock in the evening on December 15, at Cedars of Lebanon Hospital in Los Angeles.

Football continued to modernize. The Colts and Rams game was played in Boston on a Saturday instead of Sunday in order to telecast it to eighty-eight stations in forty-three states. Like an early version of pay-per-view, the game, blocked out locally, could be viewed by owners of video sets, who would drop two-bit coins into an attachment to see the game on a closed circuit. As many as thirty-five thousand fans were expected to attend. But as much as the game was modernizing, segregation was still stringently enforced even in the NFL. Games in the South continued to be difficult for the black players in the league, players like George Taliaferro and Buddy Young, even though they were two of the stars of the team. In fact, Taliaferro and other black members of the Colts were still unable to use the same hotel accommodations as the rest of the players. Taliaferro could not be complacent. As he had at Indiana University, he decided to use his position as a leader on the team to do something about the widespread discrimination so pervasive in the NFL.

Taliaferro first tried enlisting the help of the Colts' general manager. Appealing to reason, Taliaferro explained, "Segregation is expensive." Taliaferro tried to convince him to let managers of pro football teams in the South know that if they wanted professional football in their states, they were going to have to change the Jim Crow laws; otherwise, the professional football teams in the North would simply stop going to play them. In theory, this probably could have worked. But it required the cooperation of those in charge of the teams in the northern states too, something Taliaferro could not count on. When his general manager did not offer further help, Taliaferro decided to accomplish his goal in another way. For an exhibition game against the Pittsburgh Steelers, the Colts traveled to Tulsa, Oklahoma, where one of the worst race riots in the United States had taken place in 1921. Upon arrival, they were taken directly to a local high school to practice. After, the players dressed and got ready in the school locker room. There the road secretary, who arranged everyone's travel, began calling out the names of players with their assigned roommate for the hotel. Taliaferro went ahead and asked for keys for the black players' rooms, knowing they would be rooming together.

"You're not staying in the hotel with the rest of the team. You're staying in the black hotel," the road manager said.

Knowing, then, that the bus would be going to the white hotel, Taliaferro replied, "How are we going to get to the hotel?" In answer, Coach Weeb Ewbank put his hand in his pocket and pulled out several bills. "I snatched up the bills and said we would take a taxi," Taliaferro recalled. Taliaferro and six other black players ended up at a hotel owned by a black friend of his who had graduated from the School of Law at Indiana University. Normally, the man would have allowed the players a free stay at his hotel, but instead Taliaferro asked him to bill the Colts. The bill, which came to over $300, was an impressive sum for the 1950s. For their part, the black players were thrown a party by some black professionals also staying there. "We enjoyed ourselves like you cannot believe," Taliaferro said, so much so that the white players wanted to join them. Later, when the hotel owner received the money from the Colts, he sent it back to the players who had stayed there. He had just wanted to help Taliaferro make the point that segregation was costly. It was a beginning, something that would hopefully get team managers talking about segregation. If people wouldn't look at the issue from a moral perspective, maybe they would consider the financial ramifications of the practice. At the very least, it was a place to start.

Taliaferro, though sensitive to racial discrimination and active in using football to help facilitate social change, never became consumed by the impact racism had on his life. Instead of focusing on his color, he focused on his other qualities, like his intelligence and education. He chose to focus not on his identity as a black man but instead on his roles as father, husband, and professional football player. Of those roles, the only one that would not last was that of a professional football player; his career was already nearing its end. Having had a good season despite another losing record, Taliaferro stayed with the Colts in 1954, the same year a new rule requiring all players to wear face masks was adopted. The Colts had a new head coach, Weeb Ewbank, who immediately began working on a winning football team. Taliaferro refers to this period of time for the Colts as BU, "Before Unitas," and Ewbank's success was not to come for a couple more years. By then, Taliaferro would no longer be with the franchise.

Ewbank had issues to work out in his team before the Colts could become a success. Among those issues were the injuries. Taliaferro had an impressive preseason showing, and a Colts program predicted, "Taliaferro is a key man in the Colts' plans for 1954. With four year[s] of NFL pro football behind him and a fine statistical record to boot there is no reason 1954 cannot be his finest in the game." That may have been true if not for a series of injuries at the beginning of the season that plagued him throughout. He injured his hand and sprained his ankle early on, and at the end of the season, he had to have cartilage removed from his right knee. The effect of the injuries was apparent in his personal statistics for the season. He played only three games and had negative two yards on three rushing attempts. He was held to just 457 yards for the season. The Colts, who had been hopeful about the Taliaferro and Young combination, ended the season with a disappointing three wins and nine losses, and for the first time in years, Taliaferro was not on the Pro Bowl roster.

Fig. 8.14 This picture appeared in the December 1954 issue of *Sport* magazine. The caption read: "Former Indiana all-purpose back, George Taliaferro has been the team's big gun in recent seasons. He runs, passes, does punting." Taliaferro was still a Baltimore Colt at the time.

His injuries didn't keep him from playing another year. A Baltimore Colts news release in June 1955 indicated that the Colts had signed Taliaferro to play again for the franchise. Taliaferro's injuries had healed, and he had been working out regularly during the winter and spring. Optimistically, the news release reported that the twenty-eight-year-old Taliaferro "would report to camp in the best shape he has been in in several years." Dr. Dan Fortmann, Taliaferro's new surgeon, was a former Chicago Bears lineman. He had Taliaferro exercising every day, and it looked as if he was gearing up for a comeback. He was expected to resume his punting duties, which had been covered by Cotton Davidson, who had left for the service. The reality of the situation was quite different. Unfortunately, Taliaferro's injuries had not healed as fully as Dr. Fortmann had anticipated, and Taliaferro was unable to meet the expectations of his team. In the middle of the season, the Colts traded the injured Taliaferro to the Philadelphia Eagles. His family, whose house had been swallowed by the Santa Monica route of Los Angeles's new expressway system, had just moved to join him in Baltimore.

While Taliaferro was playing for the Colts and Eagles that season, the civil rights movement was commencing. The National Association for the Advancement of Colored People (NAACP), of which Taliaferro was a lifetime member, had helped end school segregation by winning a court ruling on its unconstitutionality. While the courts had mandated that segregation was acceptable as long as schools were "separate and equal," the NAACP provided information elucidating that the amount spent on white schools was nearly three times that of black schools, an average of $37.87 per pupil for white students compared to $13.08 spent on black students. On May 17, 1954, the US Supreme Court case of *Brown v. the Board of Education of Topeka* overturned *Plessy v. Ferguson*, the case that in 1896 had sanctioned racial segregation in public schools. In 1955, Rosa Parks was arrested for not giving up her seat to a white person on the bus, beginning the Montgomery Bus Boycott. Shortly after her arrest, Dr. Martin Luther King Jr. was elected president of the Montgomery Improvement Association, making him the boycott's spokesperson. Ultimately, the boycott led to an important 1956 Supreme Court ruling that deemed bus segregation illegal and set a precedent for desegregation.

In the midst of this, Taliaferro made the difficult decision to stop playing professional football. He had always kept in the best possible condition in order to perform to his utmost ability for his team. No longer able to do that, he felt that retirement was his only option. No longer able to play to his full potential, Taliaferro did not want to be remembered for playing what he referred to as "a poor brand of football." His pride and team loyalty were not

Figs. 8.15a and 8.15b Taliaferro is still with the Colts in this 1954 Bowman football card. That season he was plagued by injuries.

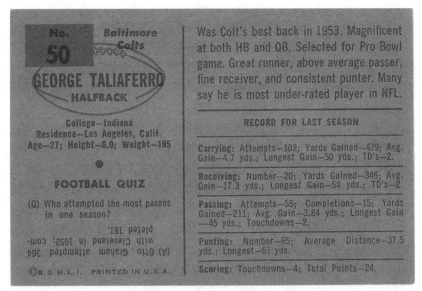

Figs. 8.15a and 8.15b *(continued)*

his only considerations, though. He also took into account the risk of exposing himself to further injury and ultimately doing more permanent damage to his already-injured knee. It was a difficult decision to make. The difficulty of the situation was allayed somewhat by the birth of his third daughter, Donna, in Baltimore, Maryland, on November 20, 1955, a reminder that family would always be his priority.

His trailblazing football career, which included impressive statistics, was coming to an end. Taliaferro was also one of the last professional football players to play on both sides of the ball, offense and defense, in the old "iron man" days of professional football. Arguably the most versatile player to have ever played in the NFL, Taliaferro had performed in an astonishing seven positions. More than a triple threat, Taliaferro was a passer, runner, receiver, punter, punt returner, kickoff returner, and defensive halfback. Yet he finished his professional football career having been shuffled from one team to another, none having anything beyond a mediocre season. Despite his strong individual statistics

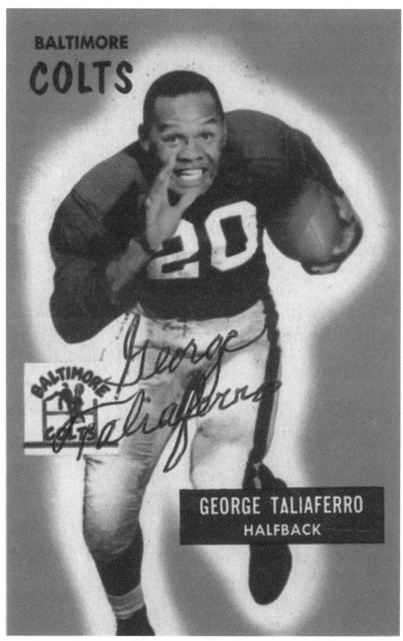

Figs. 8.16a and 8.16b Taliaferro's last season of professional football. He was with the Colts for half of the season before being traded to the Philadelphia Eagles. This 1955 Bowman football card shows him still with the Colts.

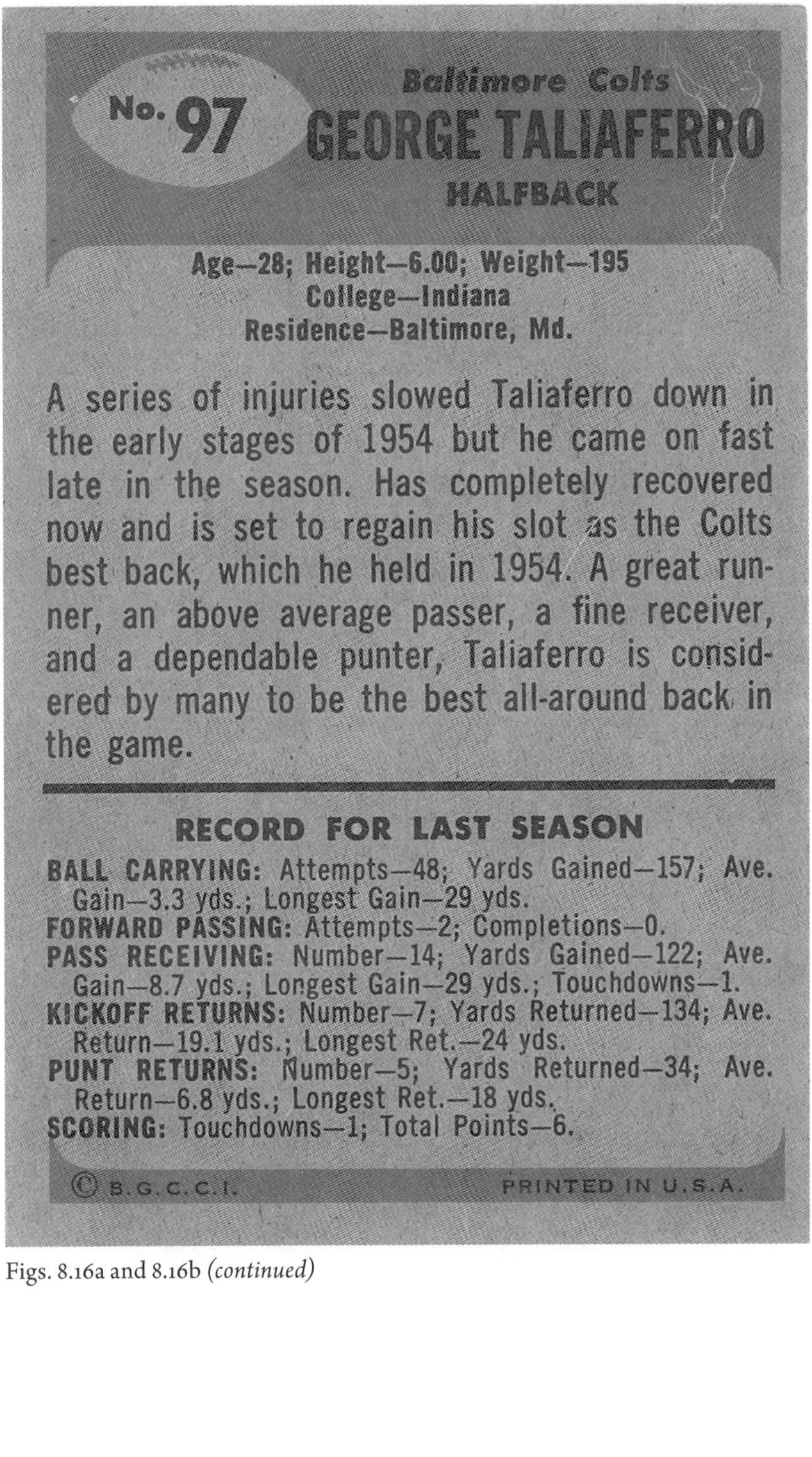

No. 97

Baltimore Colts

GEORGE TALIAFERRO

HALFBACK

Age—28; Height—6.00; Weight—195
College—Indiana
Residence—Baltimore, Md.

A series of injuries slowed Taliaferro down in the early stages of 1954 but he came on fast late in the season. Has completely recovered now and is set to regain his slot as the Colts best back, which he held in 1954. A great runner, an above average passer, a fine receiver, and a dependable punter, Taliaferro is considered by many to be the best all-around back in the game.

RECORD FOR LAST SEASON

BALL CARRYING: Attempts—48; Yards Gained—157; Ave. Gain—3.3 yds.; Longest Gain—29 yds.
FORWARD PASSING: Attempts—2; Completions—0.
PASS RECEIVING: Number—14; Yards Gained—122; Ave. Gain—8.7 yds.; Longest Gain—29 yds.; Touchdowns—1.
KICKOFF RETURNS: Number—7; Yards Returned—134; Ave. Return—19.1 yds.; Longest Ret.—24 yds.
PUNT RETURNS: Number—5; Yards Returned—34; Ave. Return—6.8 yds.; Longest Ret.—18 yds.
SCORING: Touchdowns—1; Total Points—6.

© B.G.C.C.I. PRINTED IN U.S.A.

Figs. 8.16a and 8.16b *(continued)*

Fig. 8.17 A cartoon depicting George Taliaferro with the Baltimore Colts. *Photo courtesy George Taliaferro.*

and three Pro Bowl appearances, Taliaferro had never played for a winning football team in the National Football League. "I was never able to get on a club where I wasn't the whole offense," he explained. The Colts, under the new leadership of Weeb Ewbank, ended up breaking the .500 mark for the first time in 1957 with "the Golden Arm" Johnny Unitas at quarterback. It didn't take long after that for the Colts to actually win the NFL championship. In fact, they were back-to-back champions in 1958 and 1959. By that time, Taliaferro was no longer playing professional football.

Even though he had never played for a winning team, Taliaferro did not regret his decision to play for the Los Angeles Dons instead of the Chicago Bears. "I sometimes speculate I would have gotten greater press coverage, more money, and a stable career," he said. "Then I wonder about my social life and the opportunity to learn and grow by traveling and meeting new people and experiencing the changes brought on by being on my own far from Gary," he continued. There was no doubt that if Taliaferro had decided to realize his childhood dream and sign with the Chicago Bears, he would have played for a better football team under the outstanding coaching of George "Papa Bear" Halas. Still, Taliaferro said, "I was truly happy just to be playing professional football!"

His overall career statistics are impressive, especially given the abysmal teams he played for. During his career, Taliaferro had rushed for more than 2,200 yards in 436 attempts, caught 95 passes for 1,300 yards, returned 27 punts for 251 yards, and had another 2,000 yards in 67 kickoff returns. He also threw 248 passes with 92 completions for 10 touchdowns and 1,633 yards, a statistic that Gill said defined him, "in fact if not in reputation, the NFL's first black quarterback." More important than his personal statistics and the win/loss records of his various teams was Taliaferro's role in the NFL as a trailblazer. His status as the first African American drafted by an NFL team and as the first black quarterback may not have immediately opened doors for other black football players, but it was something.

1955–PRESENT:
LIFE AFTER FOOTBALL

TALIAFERRO'S DECISION TO RETIRE FROM professional football was made easier for two reasons. First, he had already accomplished what he had wanted: to play professional football and have fun doing it. Second, Taliaferro was educated. His education, however, did not ensure the smooth transition from professional football to career that he had envisioned. Unlike many of today's professional athletes, Taliaferro had not signed multimillion-dollar contracts, did not have mega endorsement deals, and did not have a future in sports broadcasting. So life after football was more challenging than it would be today. Having a college education should have made the transition a smoother one, but he had not anticipated that the color of his skin would be a factor.

"The American Dream was still eluding me because I was black," Taliaferro said. Until that time he had been able to manage the obstacle. He had always fought racism and discrimination to some degree of success. That changed upon his retirement from the NFL. With his family, he returned to Baltimore, where he applied for a job as a high school football coach. He had a degree in health, physical education, and recreation (HPER) and seven years of experience playing professionally, which should have put him in high demand. He wanted to be like Bo Mallard, his football coach at Gary Roosevelt High School. He had always credited Mallard with being a positive influence on his life and with teaching him everything he knew about football. Now he wanted to pass on what he had learned through his own experiences to other young football players. His versatility as a player, professional football experience, and degree made him highly qualified for the position. Sadly, none of those seemed to matter.

The first obstacle Taliaferro encountered was with the public school system in Baltimore, which would only hire black teachers and coaches for one of its two all-black schools. There were no positions open in either one. That made Taliaferro's dream of becoming a role model considerably more difficult to achieve. Not new to obstacles and not one to shy away from them, Taliaferro decided to use his Indiana University connections. He contacted the dean of HPER at IU and explained the problem he was having with the Baltimore school system. "I am open to suggestions," he told the dean, who suggested that Taliaferro pay a visit to Baltimore's superintendent of physical education, an Indiana University alum who might be willing to help a fellow IU grad. It was a promising lead.

With a renewed sense of confidence that came from having a connection to someone with the position to help him, Taliaferro went to the superintendent's office. "I walked in with my little diploma in hand and my little dressed-up self," Taliaferro said, his tone bitter. He introduced himself to the superintendent, explaining that he was also an Indiana University alumnus, that he had spoken to the dean, and that the dean had suggested he come to explain his situation. The superintendent appeared to be listening, giving Taliaferro hope. When he finished explaining his plight, however, the superintendent merely repeated what Taliaferro had been told before: "Well, we only have two high schools that are all-black, and those are the ones that you would qualify to teach at." Once again, Taliaferro was reminded that his skin color meant that he could not obtain something for which he had worked hard and which he was highly qualified to do.

"I almost choked. I almost died. I'm sure I didn't hear much of what he said after that. I was so angry that here I had persevered to get this degree over a five-year period . . . and then to have a man to tell me the only place I could work would be in a black school. I just couldn't believe it. I simply could not believe it. And so there I was with a family and now with no way to support my family," Taliaferro said. In an article by Chuck Crabb, an assistant at IU's Athletic Publicity Office, Taliaferro related the story: "One problem I had was I am black. Before that time, I was able to surmount and hurdle this problem. The Baltimore area black schools had sufficient staffs. There was no compelling rush to help George Taliaferro get a job."

Taliaferro was angrier and more frustrated than he had been in a long time. There he was, a man with professional football experience who had played in three Pro Bowls, and he wanted nothing more than to pass on his knowledge and experience to young Baltimore football players. How could they turn him down solely on the basis of his skin color? "It was simply beyond my comprehension," he said. In frustration, anger, and desperation, he went to some known gangsters, actual gangsters, and asked for work. He thought that if he worked for them, he would be able to adequately provide for his family. The gangsters, who presumably knew of his career, turned him down, not because of his skin color but because they recognized his character.

"You're throwing your life away because you're angry," one of them told him, explaining why they wouldn't give him any work.

"I must do what I need to do to care for my family," Taliaferro insisted, growing angry. Despite his pleas, he was sent away still jobless.

He didn't tell Viola about this desperate yet futile attempt, but she sensed that he was frustrated. She was both encouraging and firm. "So you can't teach in Baltimore. So what? Let's do something else," she said. Forced to pursue another means of support for his family, Taliaferro took the only job he could find, selling cars, which turned out to be a better situation than he had anticipated. Because his name was so well known in Baltimore, the car business actually proved quite successful. However, his pay was based on commission and wasn't steady, so he found other ways to supplement his income for times when the checks were too paltry. He managed to do some substitute teaching in the two black high schools when he was not at the car dealership, and he did a little golf hustling on the side. Golf had been a hobby of his for many years, likely because he was so good at it. His hustle would be to find businessmen who had money but who couldn't match his golf skills, then take advantage of that by wagering on golf matches between them.

The combination of all of those meant relative financial stability for his family, but it brought little satisfaction to Taliaferro, who felt he had so much more to offer. He wanted to help people, and he didn't think his skin color should bar him from doing that. He finally decided, with encouragement from his wife, to pursue a degree in social work, a degree that would allow him "to work with people, period." He was finally going to do something about the dissatisfaction he felt at being unable to work in education.

In 1957, Jackie Robinson retired from baseball, and Dr. King, who spoke to a crowd of fifteen thousand people in Washington, DC, formed the Southern Christian Leadership Conference to fight segregation and obtain civil rights. It was also the year Taliaferro began working as director of the Lafayette Square Community Center in Baltimore while pursuing a master's degree in social work. He had found a position that provided financial stability for his family and satisfaction for him. While he still golfed on the side, now it was solely for enjoyment. He would sometimes buy crabs or a bushel of oysters for the family to share for dinner. And when Taliaferro took Viola out for an evening to places like Lenny Moore's nightclub, where Viola loved to eat the chitlins, they would have Sonny Liston babysit for the girls. The whole family would attend the annual picnic Art Donovan threw at a local country club.

Having almost let the anger and frustration of racism ruin his life when he sought employment with known gangsters, Taliaferro had learned a valuable insight. "People who are winners are engaged in making things happen and do not have the time to be consumed with hatred or putting others down," he said. He was going to keep himself busy by making things happen. At the community center, Taliaferro was the only paid staff member. He set up the program, taught the volunteers, and raised the funds. When he left, it took three people to replace him.

In 1958, Walter Carter, the president of the NAACP in Baltimore, lived across the street from the Taliaferros. Like the Taliaferros, Carter had two little girls, and he was a social worker. He asked Taliaferro to participate in a civil rights celebration that the organization was planning in downtown Baltimore. Taliaferro, of course, agreed. Carter suggested involving some of the Colts' players too. Although Taliaferro was no longer playing, he had connections with the Colts and knew many of the players, including Johnny Unitas. Knowing what Unitas's presence would do for the cause, Taliaferro asked him to join him on stage. He wouldn't even have to say anything; just his presence would be enough. Unitas turned Taliaferro down, indicating that he didn't get involved in things like that. After that, Taliaferro said, "I put him on my list of people not to befriend. I didn't hate him, but we weren't friends."

Taliaferro's community-mindedness was evident in his subsequent career choices as well. In 1959, while working on his degree, Taliaferro became a caseworker for the Prisoner Aid Association in Baltimore. He was also a psychiatric social worker at the Clifton T. Perkins Hospital and senior caseworker at the Shaw Residence in Washington, DC. These were paid positions, but they also provided scholarships toward his degree. That was when he first met Muhammad Ali, who was in town for a fight. After class at Howard University in DC, where he was working on his master's degree, Taliaferro would head back to Baltimore, driving right past the golf course designated for black golfers. "So I'd just stop," he said. That's exactly what happened that day. Taliaferro had stopped to play golf at the course, which was surrounded by a chain-link fence. A chauffeur-driven limo came around the corner, and Ali stuck his head out the top.

"Hey, you with the white cap on—I'll take you on any time," Ali yelled to him.

"If you get out of the car, I'll take you out with this driver," Taliaferro said.

"I think you would, too." Ali laughed. Later, when Taliaferro finished golfing, he found Ali at the clubhouse. The two began to talk.

"Where are you from?" Ali asked. Taliaferro told him and talked about a boxer from Gary, Booker Beckwith. At one point, Taliaferro had aspired to be a boxer, and Beckwith was the one he "most wanted to be like." Beckwith had fought and lost to Ezzard Mack Charles, from Cincinnati, who was a heavyweight champ. Ali knew Charles. The conversation then switched to football. Ali explained that he had once been interested in football but chose boxing instead. Taliaferro's course had been the opposite. Looking back at their conversation decades later, Taliaferro said, "Almost everything was fun with Muhammad Ali. He was effervescent—I mean bubbly." Years later, the Taliaferros would run into Laila Ali in Vegas or LA, he couldn't remember which. Taliaferro introduced himself to her and told her how he had met her father that day. He said, "We talked about fighting each other. I was going to use a golf club." A few years later, Taliaferro would note Ali's ideas regarding the Vietnam War. "He said no Vietnamese ever called him a *nigger*, and that he had no reason to fight them. I thought that was the way the world ought to be looked at," Taliaferro said.

In DC, Taliaferro continued to work with prisoners until 1964. In the Virginia penal system, he saw people who reminded him of the person he had been on the day he went to the gangsters. They were angry people who had let their anger and frustration dictate who they would be, people who had made the decision to become products of the racism they faced. He understood how easy that line was to cross. His own life turned out differently from theirs.

Taliaferro's youngest daughter, Terri, was born on December 21, 1962, the same year Taliaferro earned his master's degree from Howard University. With this degree, he had more than fulfilled the promise he made to his father. His experiences leading up to the accomplishment taught him that "you have what it takes to be anything you want to be if you are willing to make the sacrifice," Taliaferro said. He now understood what separated him from the men in prison he helped. Every day Taliaferro's mom and dad had said, "We love you. You must be educated," instilling in him the value of education. Now, he understood that it was this education that kept him from becoming like the prisoners he helped. "Remember two things about me," Taliaferro said. "First, I am educated. Second, I am educated. In spite of all odds I have beat the system. I have four daughters and a wife who have beat the system. And I have seven grandchildren who are preparing to beat the system."

Helping others overcome obstacles became a passion that went beyond a job in social work. He knew that he had energy to give and that there were worthy causes that could use his help. While still living in Baltimore, he got involved in Big Brothers/Big Sisters. His first Little Brother was Clarence Clark, or CC. CC lived on an alley street in a row house downtown with his mother and three sisters. There was no father in the home. CC, a thirteen-year-old seventh grader, had a juvenile record for missing school, shoplifting, and breaking and entering. He had been on the list for a Big Brother for over a year. A caseworker introduced Taliaferro to him, and they made arrangements for Taliaferro to pick him up the following morning at eight thirty. Excited to finally have a Big Brother, CC dressed neatly in his nicest clothes for

Fig. 9.1 George Taliaferro watches TV at his home in Baltimore circa 1962 with his daughters. Linda sits next to him on the couch, Renée kneels, and Donna reads a paper. Daughter Terri was not yet born. *Photo courtesy George Taliaferro.*

the meeting. But upon discovering that CC had spent little time on grass because his entire neighborhood was concrete, Taliaferro decided they should spend the day outside. So they found a change of clothes for CC and spent the day working outside together.

The next morning, they met again. With his mother's permission, CC attended church with the Taliaferros and then spent the remainder of the day at their house. They talked, ate, watched TV, and made plans for the following weekend. Those plans never happened. That Wednesday, CC was caught in the warehouse two doors down from his home, stealing twenty cartons of cigarettes and five hams. He was sent to the Youth Correctional Facility in Hagerstown, Maryland, for eighteen months. Fortunately for him, at the time Taliaferro was doing an internship with the institution as a graduate student at Howard University, so they were still able to continue their relationship while CC served his time there. When the eighteen months had passed and CC returned home, they began regular weekly visits. Often, they included the Taliaferros' daughters and CC's sisters in their outings, visiting parks and zoos, holding picnics, going to ball games, and finding quiet times to talk.

In May 1963, following the mass demonstrations against segregation that led to the arrest of Dr. Martin Luther King Jr. for demonstrating without a permit, the Birmingham Truce Agreement was announced. Stores, restaurants, and schools were to be desegregated. That same year, 250,000 people attended Martin Luther King's Freedom Walk in Detroit, Michigan. The rights Taliaferro had made small strides toward in football were finally becoming a reality throughout the country. Of course, the struggle was far from over. In fact, according to research by Pitts and Yost, Darryl Hill became the first African American to play football in the Atlantic Coast Conference that year. Pitts and Yost wrote that Hill remembered playing at Clemson: "Not a black person in the stands anywhere. The black people had to sit outside the stadium on a red, dirt hill called 'Nigger Hill.'"

In 1964, the Taliaferros moved to Washington, DC, where he continued his work with the prison population at a halfway house for rehabilitating convicts. At the same time, he worked as a director of the Prince Georges County Community Action Programs for the United Planning Organization, a community outreach program aimed at providing services for the needy as well as developing job programs. He also served as the executive director of a drug abuse counseling center. From 1966 to 1968, Taliaferro was an assistant professor at the University of Maryland Graduate School of Social Work, and he received a certificate in criminology from the University of Montreal, something he felt would help with his work in the penal system.

Taliaferro went back to Bloomington in 1967 for celebrations of the Indiana University football team, which had been selected to represent the Big Ten Conference in the 1968 Rose Bowl. He attended several parties and celebrations and visited old friends while he was back in Indiana. At one point, he passed through Linton, Indiana, where he took down their welcome sign: "Black people—don't let the sun going down catch you in this town." He never stopped fighting discrimination. His 1945 teammate, Howard Brown, who was an assistant football coach at Indiana, was also there for the celebration. Although the weekend had reestablished some of his Indiana University connections, it wasn't quite time for him to return to the Hoosier state. Nevertheless, each career move was bringing him closer to Indiana.

For two years, from 1968 to 1970, Taliaferro was the vice president and general manager of the Dico Corporation, a subsidiary of Martin-Marietta Corporation in Washington, DC. The goal of the Dico Corporation was to integrate the seriously unemployable into the private sector. As manager, Taliaferro developed a rapport with local law enforcement and correctional agencies, as well as other community members. That is where he was on April 4, 1968, when he heard on the radio the news out of Memphis that Dr. Martin Luther King Jr. had been shot. "I was sick. I mean I was sick. I didn't throw up, but I felt like I was going to throw up," he remembered. Tears welled in his eyes. He walked out of his office into the corridor and looked out a window for at least half an hour. Then he went back to his office and just sat there for the rest of the day. The other social workers must have realized how upset he was, and they didn't send him any more clients for the rest of the day. By that evening, King had been pronounced dead, and Taliaferro wondered, *Will there ever be a time in the United States when black people can be worry free about dying because of the color of their skin?* Almost fifty years later, this question would prompt protest by NFL players.

There were only two people Taliaferro ever wanted to meet, both of whom were assassinated before he had the chance: Martin Luther King Jr. and John F. Kennedy. He did meet some other legendary civil rights activists, though, including John Lewis. Lewis, the youngest speaker at the 1963 March on Washington, was arrested dozens of times while taking part in the nonviolent protests of the era. It may have been his association with the bloody attacks on peaceful protesters marching from Selma, Alabama, during which time Lewis suffered a skull fracture, that made him most famous. His particular focus on voting rights would eventually lead him to a successful run for Congress. Taliaferro met Lewis during a civil rights event in Baltimore, and Taliaferro was "thrilled to be in his company." Years later, John Lewis would visit the Taliaferros in Bloomington, Indiana, and ask them to participate in a lecture series. Although George Taliaferro would end up too ill that day to participate, Viola Taliaferro would take part.

In 1969, the one hundredth anniversary of college football, while he was with Dico, Taliaferro was honored by IU fans who selected him to the first team of the IU All-Time Football Team, reminding him of fond memories and important people in his life. Three members of the 1967 Rose Bowl team were named with him: Harry Gonso, John Isenbarger, and Jade Butcher.

A short time later, Taliaferro changed careers again to become dean of students at Morgan State University in 1970, a position considered challenging with the activism so prevalent on college campuses at the time. In a Hammel article, Taliaferro explained why he didn't find it that difficult: "All you have to do is listen. I can honestly see in these students the George Taliaferro of 25 years ago, and I'm just like everyone else. We are supposed to learn from history, but the paradox has been that we do not. I have tried to make an effort to defy that paradox and show those students that I have learned something from being on this earth." Aside from his duties as dean, Taliaferro was also an unpaid assistant football coach, and he became, around this time, the first

Fig. 9.2 At Mt. Pleasant golf course in Baltimore, circa 1971, with other pro trailblazers. *From left*: Jackie Robinson (baseball), Cliff Brown (golf), Joe Louis (boxing), female admirers, and George Taliaferro (football). *Photo courtesy George Taliaferro.*

"Negro" vice president of the association of former players for the Baltimore Colts. In a 1971 golf tournament, Taliaferro was partnered with Jackie Robinson, Joe Louis, and the first African American golfer in the PGA, Clifford Brown—an elite group of trailblazers.

An opportunity he credits Howard Brown with bringing about, in 1972 Taliaferro was asked to go to Indiana University to serve as a special assistant to IU president John W. Ryan. As a student and athlete, Taliaferro had experienced segregation, racism, and discrimination at Indiana University. He had not been permitted to live on campus, eat in certain restaurants, visit a barbershop, or sit in the front of the class. Nearly thirty years later, Taliaferro was offered a position at Indiana University with an office just across from President Ryan's. As Ryan's assistant, Taliaferro would primarily be responsible for an affirmative action plan that included all eight Indiana University campuses. The need for this position may have been prompted by events such as the 1969 boycott and an incident with a professor that had occurred earlier that year.

Fig. 9.3 George Taliaferro golfs in Las Vegas, circa 1972.

In 1968 came Indiana University's first and only appearance in the coveted Rose Bowl game. Coach John Pont's previous head coaching engagements, seven years at Miami of Ohio and two years at Yale, had earned him a 55–27–3 record. During the 1967 season, the Hoosiers lost only two games, to Minnesota and Southern Cal. Similar to the storybook ending Taliaferro's team had earned with a win over Purdue, the 1967 team's Old Oaken Bucket win to end the season earned the Hoosiers a trip to Pasadena, California, for the Rose Bowl. Even the 14–3 loss to USC, during which O. J. Simpson rushed for 128 yards and two touchdowns, was not altogether disappointing for IU. The appearance in Pasadena was an honor for a team that had fought all season through close games to eke out wins, earning them the name "Cardiac Kids." Hoosier fans were already looking ahead to a possible return to the Tournament of Roses the next year, and at the beginning of that season it looked like a good possibility. However, a boycott midseason and three subsequent losses kept that from becoming a reality. Fourteen black players decided midseason not to attend practice because of racial issues they wanted to bring to the attention of Coach Pont, 1967's national Coach of the Year Award winner. Calvin Snowden, a defensive end on that Rose Bowl team, explained why they felt the need to take such action.

Indiana University, he said, was a microcosm of society, and just as they were in society as a whole, black people at IU were being treated as second-class citizens. In Indiana football, that translated to coaches stacking black players behind each other, so they would be competing with each other for position instead of starting in other positions. Snowden pointed to Cordell Gill as one example. Gill, he said, was a talented linebacker who should have been starting in that position. Instead, he played behind Snowden as a defensive end, a position that wasn't suited for his five-foot-nine, 230-pound body. Black quarterbacks were changed to running backs, according to Snowden, in order to keep the black players from starting in too many positions. But stacking, he said, wasn't the only issue. By 1969 there were twenty thousand students at Indiana University, and his roommate was black. "Get my inference?" he asked. "I was faceless." White students would talk to him or study with him in private, but they wouldn't go to lunch or dinner with him, and on campus they wouldn't acknowledge him. Sometimes the racism was more out-right, like when the word *nigger* was leveled at him on campus. He also pointed to the fact that black players had been instrumental in getting to the Rose Bowl but had not reaped the same rewards from it as the white players had, including postseason honors. Finally, there were comments that bothered him. One of the trainers, Snowden said, often made comments that offended the black players. For example, before the Rose Bowl game, he asked Snowden if he had been dating Caucasian girls.

"I always see you with some bitch," the trainer said.

"If I called the woman you loved a bitch, how would you feel about that?" Snowden asked. The trainer continued, ignoring the question, saying that he didn't think the pro scouts watching Snowden would appreciate him dating white girls.

"I don't think the pros care who I date," Snowden replied.

"The reality was we were a commodity to be used," Snowden explained. Issues like the ones he experienced had finally prompted black players to boycott practice. The boycott, in turn, forced Coach Pont to have a meeting with his coaches to discuss the situation. They decided to meet with the players and give them the option to return to practice without penalty. Only four of the fourteen returned. Among them was John Andrews, who went on to play for the Baltimore Colts. One reason he returned, he said, was that the black players had originally only agreed upon a one-week boycott. However, with the intrinsic atmosphere of student protests in the 1960s, the boycott ended up lasting longer than had originally been anticipated. Also, unlike some of those who weren't going back, Andrews was a starter, the only black starter on offense his junior year. That didn't mean he couldn't empathize with the protesters, though. Players who had been starting quarterbacks and running backs in high school, he said, were moved to defense when they came to Indiana University, and the black players on defense were stacked behind one an-other, as Snowden had indicated, increasing their frustration and hindering their desire to return to the team. Finally, most of the players not returning to practice were seniors and would only be missing half the season. Andrews, on the other hand, a junior, would have had to sacrifice much more.

According to Andrews, Larry Highbaugh, a sophomore, had made that sacrifice. He had done so because, unlike Andrews, Highbaugh was not a starter. He was one of the players, Andrews said, who should have been starting as a wide receiver but who was stacked behind another player on defense. Highbaugh also ran track for the Hoosiers, where he clocked a 4.2 forty and once won three events at the Big Ten championships. Unlike some of the players who did not return to practice, Highbaugh went on to play professional football, starting in the Canadian Football League. The players who chose not to return to practice were consequently dismissed from the team. The Hoosiers ended the season, anticipated to be a repeat trip to the Rose Bowl, with a losing 4–6 record, a blow to IU athletics and to a football team that had once been ahead of its time in race relations. According to Andrews, the entire incident probably made it difficult to recruit talented players, especially black players, in the next few years.

The idea that Indiana's football team was a microcosm of society was reinforced by the Syracuse 8, a group of football players at Syracuse University who boycotted football practice to protest racism at Syracuse. According to Given and Springer, it was actually nine players, not eight, who, despite wanting to play for the team that had achieved much success, felt that they had to speak out against the racism they endured. Givens and Springer described how running back Greg Allen was warned not to date any white girls and was told he didn't have time for biology labs even though he wanted to major in biology. Similarly, Givens and Springer explained, Abdullah Alif Muhammad was pushed into general education classes rather than the classes he needed for the engineering degree he wanted because math was during football practice. They said that this policy apparently did not apply to white players. Like the players at Indiana, the Syracuse 8 faced being stacked behind other black players. Another Syracuse 8 player, Dana Harrell, told Givens and Springer, "You could have three outstanding halfbacks, but you wouldn't play them all together, because you didn't want the 'big money boosters'—that's what I call them—the big money boosters to accuse the program of going black."

The nine players ended up drafting a petition asking for the same academic access as their white peers, better medical care for the entire team, and a black assistant coach—something they felt would help mitigate some of the racial issues they had been facing. The petition garnered media attention, but not in the way they wanted. The men were suspended from the team, and white fans, players, and alumni threatened to boycott if the players were allowed to return. Like Taliaferro, whose father had stern words for him when he wanted to leave Indiana, according to Givens and Springer, Harrell's father told him, "Dana, when you're 40 years old and have a family and a mortgage and things you want to do for them, you're going to need that college degree."

Givens and Springer wrote that the nine returned home for summer break uncertain of where they stood, wondering if they would be welcomed back or would retain their scholarship in the fall. They did return to practice, but when it became clear that nothing was actually going to change, they determined to boycott, sitting out the season. They were supported by the chancellor and a group of faculty members who fought for the players to keep their scholarships. Eight of the nine ending up graduating from Syracuse, and the university began to change. However, as Colin Kaepernick would discover decades later, the NFL wanted nothing to do with players who used football as a vehicle for social change. Greg Allen, for example, Harrell and Springer wrote, had been contacted by scouts from every NFL team after his sophomore season. He ended up playing his senior year at Syracuse, "but he didn't hear from a single NFL scout," they wrote.

Nearly fifty years later, the university made a formal apology and awarded the men with the Chancellor's Medal and letter jackets. Givens and Springer said, "It took 36 years for the Syracuse 8 to meet again on that football field . . . 36 years for Syracuse to apologize and recognize the players were on the right side of history."

Like Syracuse, Indiana was facing racial strife around that same time, and it went beyond the football field. In fact, it was an issue with a professor on IU's campus, which may have prompted the hiring of George Taliaferro as President Ryan's assistant. A letter of complaint about Professor Stanley Rafalko stated, "In Doctor Rafalko's course (Anatomy of the Ear and Vocal Cords), he had no syllabus, no required texts; he made frequent derogatory remarks about the physically handicapped and racist remarks about people of color all over the world." The letter included a quote by Rafalko: "All colored people have overdeveloped buccinator muscles and enlarged lips, which is why colored children have difficulty articulating and trouble in speech therapy. And what's worse, they're colored." A group of students protested Rafalko's racism with a teach-in, but according to the letter, it wasn't until two hundred black students assembled on President Ryan's lawn that something was done about the situation. The letter stated that the Rafalko case was just one example among many. Indiana University was facing the same problems in race relations that were being felt across the country, and as Ryan's assistant, Taliaferro would perform duties that included endeavoring to better these relations.

The IU Affirmative Action plan wasn't his only duty. He also handled any special assignments from Ryan, recruited and counseled minority students, and served as an assistant professor in the Graduate School of Social Work. Somehow, he also found time to mentor student athletes as a faculty adviser to the Big Ten. One such athlete was John Dudeck, who met Taliaferro on his first recruiting visit to Bloomington. Legendary track and field coach Sam Bell, one of Indiana University's most accomplished coaches, had offered Dudeck, a high schooler who threw both discus and shot put, a scholarship. Bell was intrigued with Dudeck's size, at six feet, six and a half inches and 245 pounds; athleticism; and quickness. He ran a 4.68 forty-yard dash. Upon Bell's request, it was Taliaferro who picked Dudeck up from the airport. As they drove to campus, Taliaferro told Dudeck that he had been an athlete at Indiana too, although he did not mention the accolades he had received while there. Taliaferro started the campus visit at his office in Bryan Hall, across from President Ryan's office. Taliaferro's office was meticulously clean and orderly, with a seating area, couch, and coffee table, on which was prominently displayed a copy of the Big Ten records book. After a brief chat in his office, Taliaferro excused himself, explaining that he wanted the recruit to meet someone.

Years later, Taliaferro confessed to Dudeck that he would leave that book out when he was escorting a recruit around campus. He used it to predict an athlete's motivation. Taliaferro was gone about ten minutes, enough time for Dudeck to read through the records book, where he saw names like Olympic swimmer Mark Spitz, golfer Jack Nicklaus, Olympic track star Jesse Owens, and more. When Taliaferro came back, he asked Dudeck what he thought. "I don't think it could get any more impressive than that," Dudeck replied. At that moment, Taliaferro was confident in his ability to succeed as a student/athlete at IU. Taliaferro was accompanied by IU president John Ryan, whom Taliaferro introduced to the track recruit. Dudeck recalled that the three of them spent about twenty minutes talking about Indiana University and Taliaferro's background as a student athlete there. The statement that struck Dudeck, though, came when Ryan referred to Taliaferro as the Jackie Robinson of professional football and said he was the first black player to be drafted.

It wasn't Dudeck's first time meeting a university president. The track athlete, who was accomplished in several events as well as football, was being recruited by a number of schools. Ryan hoped, he said, that Dudeck would make the decision to attend Indiana. During this brief encounter, Dudeck felt Ryan's sincerity when he said he would be there for him if Dudeck ever needed anything or just wanted to stop by for a chat. "I really mean that," Ryan said. When the conversation was over, Ryan walked Taliaferro and his protégé to the stairs. The two of them were going on a tour of the campus and athletic facilities. Within hours Dudeck knew he was going to Indiana, ending what had been a painstaking two-year process of decision-making for him.

Later, when Taliaferro heard that Dudeck had arrived on campus, he found out his number and called him at his dorm to welcome him. He told Dudeck, "This is the right decision for you. My door is always open," and he said that he wanted to remain in contact. So Dudeck checked in with him on occasion. Over the Thanksgiving and Christmas holidays, when Dudeck had nowhere to go, except back to "the neighborhood," the Taliaferros invited him to stay with them instead. Dudeck grew up in the racially divided South Side of Chicago, in which gangs like the Disciples, Blackstone Rangers, and others flourished in the historically troubled thirteenth police district. Gang warfare had been an everyday part of his life. Although Dudeck was unaccustomed to spending time in the homes of black people, the Taliaferros put him at ease. "They provided a roof, food, warm place to stay, generosity, and graciousness," Dudeck said. "They made it easy. They radiated love." So he began to attend their Sunday dinners and helped Taliaferro with chores, like organizing the garage, washing and waxing cars, and raking leaves. This was how he had discovered Taliaferro's love of golf and remarkable athleticism. Taliaferro, as a scratch golfer, was constantly coming home with trophies and awards; prizes like golf bags and clubs filled his garage on a regular basis. In his backyard, he had built a chipping green, complete with hole and flag, where he would practice after dinner. He had a zero handicap for many years. Years later, when Taliaferro was in his seventies, he was frustrated by a handicap of 6, his highest ever. During campus vacations when the dorms were shut down, the Taliaferros knew that Dudeck was exposing himself to significant risk simply by returning to his old neighborhood. They routinely offered him the opportunity to stay with them, which he did on occasion. Their relationship grew as Dudeck continued his track career at IU, eventually seeing the Taliaferros as surrogate parents. He remembered the couple, whom he refers to as Papa and Mama T, using unspoken communication, quick glances to check in with one another, before speaking with a unified voice. Their role in his life would become particularly significant during Dudeck's junior year.

During this period Dudeck had been through his third major knee reconstruction after shattering his patella twice, tearing his ACL and MCL. With fewer options for such injuries available at the time, the doctors did what they could to repair his knee. He spent several months after each surgery in casts that went from his ankle to his crotch. When the casts finally came off after eight or nine weeks, his leg muscles had severely atrophied, and he had lost much of the muscle tissue that he had worked for years to develop. The rehabilitation processes were brutal. Once recruited by Corso for the football team, he ultimately chose to focus all of his efforts on track and field. During the rehab process, however, he was unable to compete or travel with his team. The isolation and frustration of constantly rehabbing his knee began to wear on him. He was working with trainers, but he questioned whether he would be able to throw again, much less do it with any proficiency. After each major knee operation, he was left with only 15 percent of normal flexibility in his left leg. He struggled to sit, stand, or do anything normally, much less squat, throw, or lift properly. He compensated for the physical restrictions by watching endless hours of film, attempting to maximize his ability. With substantially less medical knowledge, trainers, coaches, and Dudeck himself were desperate to get movement back in the knee. After the last two surgeries, trainers attempted to snap the adhesions that had formed while the leg was in the cast for so long. In these instances, trainers would attempt to snap the adhesions without a surgical cut, an extremely painful endeavor. The process involved trainers stationed one at each shoulder, one at each hip, and one at the ankle. They gave him three large tongue depressors to bite as they tried repeatedly, without success, to snap the adhesions. They would count down and push with all their might, eventually deciding to stop this tactic after the pain caused him to lose consciousness. The doctor told him that he would need another surgery to cut away the adhesions. Although Dudeck was a proficient student, the feelings of guilt and inadequacy were taking an emotional toll.

One morning, at two thirty, he picked up the phone. "Papa T, it's me," he said when Taliaferro answered the phone.

"What's up?" Taliaferro asked.

"Things aren't going well here. I'm wasting people's time and resources," Dudeck answered. Because of his scholarship, he felt an obligation to perform. Unable to do so, he felt like a failure.

"Stay right there. Don't move. I'll pick you up in twenty minutes," Taliaferro replied.

They talked for almost two hours, Taliaferro giving Dudeck a review of his accomplishments at Indiana. Dudeck, one of eight children, had lived in five step homes and had lived in friends' basements, crashed on their couches, and slept on their floors. He had been in a gang. Now, he had a high grade point average in a difficult major, and he was well on his way to becoming the only college graduate in his family, which would enable him to obtain a career that would prevent him from repeating the cycle of poverty.

"What would you do? Where would you go? Do you have a job? A place to stay? Do you want to go back to the two-bedroom apartment with nine other people on the South Side of Chicago?" Taliaferro asked. "Dig deep. This is one of the biggest decisions of your life. I am not going to let you go. Do you understand that?" Taliaferro told Dudeck to look at the possible ramifications thirty to forty years ahead. "I want to look at you and say, 'Wow, look at all he has accomplished,'" he finished. Two hours later, Dudeck was back at his IU residence.

He red-shirted his senior year in order to continue to reha- bilitate his body. By his second senior year, though, he was ready to compete again. Nervous the night before the Big Ten Out- door Track and Field Championships at Northwestern, he called Taliaferro, once again needing reassurance from his mentor. Taliaferro responded, "You're already prepared. Do me one favor, and things will work out all right. Think of one thing; focus on what you already know. You've already got the top fifteen marks in the discus in the Big Ten this year. Don't think of changing a thing. Clear mind. No extra effort. No change to the speed or velocity. Smooth and easy."

The next morning, Dudeck did not just break but shattered the Big Ten Conference meet record by more than fifteen feet. He threw the discus 184 feet, 4 inches, destroying a record set by Olympian Fortune Gordien thirty-eight years before. The only older record in the Big Ten was held by Jesse Owens. Months later, at the in-state summer AAU meet, he threw 197. Coach Tom Pagani, who would later be the head throws coach for Team USA at the Seoul Olympics, called Dudeck the Phoenix. "I have never seen another one like you," he said. Dudeck ended up in the Big Ten records book not once but twice, about which Taliaferro said, "Well, now you're getting into rarified air, because there's not a lot of names that are in that book twice."

Dudeck's success after college is more notable, however. His first job after graduation was at the largest commercial real estate firm in the world, CBRE, where he was one of the top thirty bro- kers internationally for his final decade. He did that for twelve years, earning more by his late twenties than most CEOs of major corporations. After that, he became a consultant to small and

Fig. 9.4 George Taliaferro taught IU track and field star and Big Ten record holder John Dudeck how to golf. The two of them in August 1977. *Photo courtesy John Dudeck.*

medium-sized businesses and entrepreneurs. He said that Taliaferro is "the closest thing I have to a dad. I've always wanted to make him proud. From early on, he was always one of my first calls for major events that took place [in my life]." Dudeck continued, "He changed my paradigm forever about race and race relations but most importantly taught me about manhood and living a principle-centered life."

Although Taliaferro often helped athletes, particularly black athletes, adjust to life at Indiana University, he was there, in an unofficial capacity, to mentor any student he saw in need. In his official duty as coordinator of the Affirmative Action plan, Taliaferro developed a plan for all eight campuses to help prevent discrimination on the basis of race or gender. As Ryan's assistant, Taliaferro could provide support to any department at Indiana

University, and he was pleased when the athletic department began using him in a small recruiting role. To add to his duties, Taliaferro chaired the Big Ten Advisory Committee at this time as well. The committee, made up of one black athlete from each school, made recommendations regarding athletics and academics in the Big Ten and in the NCAA. Taliaferro's past contribution to his alma mater as an athlete himself did not go unrecognized. In 1976, he was inducted into the Indiana Football Hall of Fame.

His athletic and affirmative action duties collided in 1978 when Taliaferro criticized football coach Lee Corso for not abiding by affirmative action laws when hiring a replacement for an assistant coach. In an *Indiana Daily Student* article by Jane Ransom, Taliaferro said he was angry that the university had not advertised nationally in publications chosen to reach minority applicants as the law required. Normally, Taliaferro attended every football game, but in the article, he explained why that would not continue: "I decided not to purchase season tickets. I do not wish to support anything or anybody that is not going to abide by the law." Taliaferro's outspoken criticism forced Corso to defend himself. At first, he insisted that he actually had advertised for the position, but he later claimed that he could not remember. Athletic Director Paul Dietzel, however, said that he had already advertised for the assistant position when they had hired two other coaches four months earlier and that it was not necessary to repeat the advertising. To that, he added that the abrupt departure of this assistant coach so close to spring training had not left them with enough time to advertise. It would not be the only conflict between Taliaferro and Corso.

While Taliaferro kept busy in his numerous roles at Indiana, Viola Taliaferro was engrossed in her own pursuits. John Dudeck remembers when Mama T applied to law school. Her decision to attend came about in part because of the example set by her parents, who had always encouraged community involvement. "They made things happen," she said of her parents, who had also been actively involved in improving their community. Like them, she wanted to play a more active role. "We have that responsibility to make a contribution in some way," she said, adding that everyone does this in a different way, but that each should give as much as possible in whatever way possible. To do her part, in 1974 she enrolled part-time in the School of Law at Indiana University, and she started full-time in 1975. Offering his full support, at a time when it was not popular to do so, Taliaferro said he became "Mr. Mom" to their four girls. By 1977, Viola Taliaferro had earned a law degree. Upon finishing that, she took and passed the state bar exam and then began her private practice.

In 1981 George Taliaferro received a letter that left him humbled. He was, the letter indicated, one of eleven men selected to be inducted into the College Football Hall of Fame that year. There he joined the ranks of other greats like Coach Bo McMillin, who had been enshrined in 1951, and Pete Pihos, who had been enshrined in 1966. With Taliaferro on the list of inductees for 1981 was Navy quarterback Roger Staubach. Inductees to the Hall of Fame have to have an outstanding collegiate football record and must have continued to progress as contributing citizens. Taliaferro certainly had accomplished both. President Ryan and three other IU delegates attended the induction ceremony, which took place at the Waldorf Astoria in New York. "You stand for everything that is good in the game," the congratulatory letter, which was signed by Executive Director James L. McDowell of the National Football Foundation, stated. According to a Hammel article in the Bloomington newspaper, Taliaferro said to his wife, "Isn't it ironic I would get an honor of this kind, just for having fun?"

Despite accolades like those he received in 1981, there had been some difficult times, and more were to come. A run-in with IU basketball coach Bob Knight was just one example. The Taliaferros had made a vow that they would make Bloomington a welcoming place for black athletes. As long as he could help it,

Fig. 9.5 George Taliaferro stands as he is honored as an inductee into the College Football Hall of Fame in 1981. Navy quarterback Roger Staubach (*to his right*) was also being inducted. *Photo courtesy George Taliaferro.*

Taliaferro explained, none would leave Memorial Stadium or Assembly Hall without someone to say, "I'm glad you're here." Because of this, the Taliaferros became surrogate parents to some of the black athletes who came through Indiana University. It was in that role that they were invited by a couple of these players to a party thrown by some of the parents to celebrate the end of the 1981 basketball season, which had ended with the Hoosiers' fourth national title. The Taliaferros went to Assembly Hall to wait for the players. They were standing at the edge of the basketball court near the dressing room when, according to Taliaferro, the door was flung open and Bob Knight yelled to him, "And I don't want to see your face at the parents' party."

"You son of a bitch, you better be there, 'cause that's where I'm going!" Taliaferro replied, not one to back down, even from Bob Knight's infamous temper.

Viola Taliaferro finally managed to calm down her husband, talking him out of attending the party, where he was certain to have a confrontation with Knight. "Where do you think we're going?" she asked. "Do you have a son [on the team]?" They went home.

Still angry, Taliaferro decided to tell President Ryan what had transpired. "I will knock him out if he ever points at me in public," Taliaferro informed Ryan. "You either get a new coach or a new assistant." Ryan calmed Taliaferro and convinced him to stay in his capacity as assistant. He was too valuable to lose, and it would be some time yet before Bob Knight's temper would finally get him fired from his position as head coach, especially since he had just won his second NCAA championship with the Hoosiers. Knight would lead them to another title, his third with the team, their fifth overall, in 1987.

Taliaferro would remain Ryan's assistant for less than a year after that. Shortly after another run-in with football coach Lee Corso, in 1982, he resigned. Ironically, when Corso was hired, parallels had been drawn between him and legendary IU football coach Bo McMillin, Taliaferro's mentor. Both men had inherited unsuccessful teams and turned them around. Taliaferro had even been a member of the team Ryan put together in 1972 to hire a replacement for retiring coach John Pont, choosing Corso. Ten years later, however, at a luncheon of the Downtown Evansville Quarterback Club, Taliaferro publicly criticized Corso's coaching style and handling of players. He told the club that Louisville, Corso's previous coaching engagement, had painted a favorable picture of him to Indiana's committee because they wanted to get rid of him. The story of Taliaferro's public criticism of Corso was all over the papers the next day. Although he publicly apologized for anything that might have hurt the Corso family, he said he still stood behind his remarks.

Apparently, there were some people who agreed. One Bloomington resident wrote a letter to the editor of the *Bloomington Herald-Times* to voice his support of Taliaferro's remarks. Despite speculation by local reporters that Taliaferro would be fired, Peter Fraenkel, another Ryan assistant, indicated that would not be the case. However, after implementing and overseeing the Affirmative Action programs at Indiana University for more than a decade, Taliaferro felt that it was time for a change. There was some media speculation that the reassignment request was prompted by the public controversy surrounding Corso and Taliaferro, but that was confirmed neither by the university nor by Taliaferro. Regardless, he was subsequently reassigned to the dean's office of the School of Social Work, where he would be an assistant to Beulah Compton, the school's acting dean.

While Taliaferro was shaping future social workers, his wife was continuing to make her mark on Bloomington. In 1989, she became the first African American to serve as magistrate in the Circuit Court of Monroe County, Indiana. Then, in 1995, she was the first appointed as a Monroe Circuit Court judge. This meant new pet names from Taliaferro, who began referring to her as "her ornery" or simply "the judge." He remembered being in the courtroom one day because he had driven her there. His cell phone began ringing, and unfamiliar with it, he had a difficult time turning it off. "Mr. Taliaferro, could you approach the bench?" she said, and then proceeded to reprimand him. As circuit judge, according to the Judicial Family Institute, "she handled all county juvenile, paternity, probate, and mental health commitment cases." As a juvenile court judge, she chose the best rehabilitation options for Monroe County's juvenile offenders. Judge Taliaferro's belief that there are no bad children and her commitment to do everything in her power to aid and rehabilitate them led to much success. In fact, the Judicial Family Institute reported that she served as a consultant to US Attorney General Janet Reno and was on the National Research Council on Juvenile Crime. In 2004, the same year she retired, she was named Judge of the Year by the National Court Appointed Special Services Association. "The Judge" retired in December of 2004, leaving a legacy. She had performed the state's first same-sex adoption, one of her proudest accomplishments; was named Bloomington's Woman of the Year for 1999; and won the Book of Golden Deeds Award for 2001. She was also very involved in the community through organizations like the Human Rights Commission, the Bloomington Safe and Civil City Project, and the Boy Scouts, just to name a few. She had served in organizations for juvenile justice and family issues at the local, state, and national levels. Her focus, in and out of the courtroom, was on children. There is even an annual award named after her, the Judge Viola J. Taliaferro Award, through the Indiana State Bar Association, which is given out to Hoosiers who work on behalf of children. So renowned was her work with juveniles that Indiana University's Maurer School of Law dedicated the Viola J. Taliaferro Family and Children Mediation Clinic in 2008. In her retirement, she continued to do special projects for the Indiana Supreme Court. Taliaferro, who often drove her there, continued to call the transportation "driving Miss Daisy."

Taliaferro also continued to be recognized. He was inducted into the Indiana University Athletic Hall of Fame in November 1992, an honor he probably would have been given earlier had he not been ineligible because he was employed by the university. In 1995, he was elected to the NFL Players Association's Retired Players' Steering Committee, a nine-man policy committee that represented 2,500 former players. The three-year term he would serve on the committee was only one of many engagements for Taliaferro. In 1995 or 1996, Taliaferro boarded a bus that would take him and other retired players to a golf tournament at the University of Notre Dame. Legendary Iowa coach Hayden Fry, who won 143 games and took his team to 17 bowl games between 1979 and 1998, was sitting in the front. He told Taliaferro that when he called for the off tackle right running play, which involves the halfback running the ball, he called it "George"—"because," he explained, "you executed it better than anyone I have ever seen."

More importantly, he was actively involved in charity and in giving to the community through his work in at least a dozen community organizations. He started the Monroe County chapter of Big Brothers/Big Sisters in Bloomington, Indiana, where he served the organization as a Big Brother, as its president, and on its board of directors. Children's Organ Transplant Association (COTA) was another of Taliaferro's charities, one that has helped thousands of sick children. He helped raise millions of dollars for the organization. He hosted the George Taliaferro Open in Bloomington each year, an annual celebrity golf tournament and charity auction, and made celebrity appearances to raise money for COTA.

Outside of the specific organizations he belonged to, Taliaferro impacted his community in other ways. The way he lived his life provided an example to others. He treated people with respect and thought it important to remember people's names and to address them by name. "It makes people feel special," he said. His goal of meeting someone new every day made this an especially difficult task, but it was one he accomplished fairly well.

After retiring from Indiana University in 1992, Taliaferro continued to learn and to help others. There is a long list of people who credit Taliaferro for the positive role he played in their lives. For example, Taliaferro never lost touch with Sydney Cummings, his Gary, Indiana, neighbor who used to follow his hero around their hometown. When Taliaferro played football at IU, he was never too busy to write Cummings. He reminded him to obey his parents and to stay out of trouble. Cummings would go to the movies to see the highlight films of the IU football team, "just to see Fat [Taliaferro] on the screen playing for Indiana,"

Cummings said. And when Taliaferro played pro football, he sent tickets to Cummings to come watch him play. Cummings remembers Taliaferro introducing him to Buddy Young at one of those games.

"Because of him, I went to school," Cummings said of Taliaferro. Cummings, who received a master's degree from Indiana University, went on to teach in Gary, Indiana, where he, like Taliaferro, could inspire people. Taliaferro had a similar effect on CC, the boy from Baltimore who had been his first Little Brother. CC also ended up doing well in school and graduated from college. He got married, worked at a steady job, and joined Big Brothers/Big Sisters and had a Little Brother of his own. Another Gary, Indiana, youth who watched Taliaferro play football was Fred Williamson, who played football for Northwestern and went on to play professionally for the Kansas City Chiefs, after which he went into the film industry. Taliaferro saw him at a golf outing, where Williamson told others around them that Taliaferro was "the man that was my inspiration to get out of Gary."

Taliaferro also collected golf balls, which for years he sent by the dozens to the Dayton Youth Golf Academy, which gives underprivileged kids the opportunity to play golf. Over the course of several years, he estimated that he sent over 5,000 packages, with a dozen golf balls in each. One year he took seven sets of regripped and polished golf clubs and 215 packages of a dozen balls each to the organization. Because golf was an important part of Taliaferro's life, he wanted to help share the sport with others.

Others have noticed Taliaferro's impact as well. New York Yanks teammate Sherman Howard, for example, said about Taliaferro, "Whatever he does he wants to be the best, and he instills that in others too." Howard added that Taliaferro had integrity, that he was "a man of his word," something that no doubt would have pleased Taliaferro's father. Howard said that Taliaferro's actions tell others, "Judge me by the content of my character, not by my color." Taliaferro's contributions were also

Fig. 9.6 Former teammate Sherman "Chet" Howard (*left*) and former head coach of the Indianapolis Colts Tony Dungy (*center*) with George Taliaferro (*right*), the recipient of Methodist Sports Medicine's 2010 Brady Lifetime Achievement Award for athletics and sportsmanship. *Photo courtesy George Taliaferro.*

noticed by his alma mater again in 1998, when the Indiana University Athletic Department honored him with the Clevenger Award, the honor given to a former IU athlete who has continued serving the athletic department.

Roger Wilkins, a commentator for National Public Radio who, as an editorial writer for the *Washington Post* during Watergate, helped earn the *Post* its 1973 Pulitzer, considers Taliaferro his all-time hero. However, one does not have to be a Pulitzer Prize winner to recognize Taliaferro. A Bloomington, Indiana, second grader wrote him a letter requesting that he come speak at his school. It was Black History Month, and his teacher had assigned each child a famous black person to research. The young student had been disappointed to be assigned Isom Dart, a cowboy who got into a lot of trouble and then managed to turn his life around, only to be killed by a bounty hunter. Because he and his parents were unimpressed by the message of that particular story, they requested that the teacher allow him to choose another research topic. Despite their pleas, she denied the request. The boy wrote a letter to Taliaferro anyway, and Taliaferro ended up speaking at his school.

Taliaferro continued to inspire. That is why, on June 17, 2006, Indiana University awarded him with a Distinguished Alumni Service Award. The program for the awards dinner read, "An inspiration to tens of thousands of young people, George Taliaferro has exhibited throughout his life the courage and determination that made him an All-American both on and off the gridiron. . . . For his stalwart advocacy of a level playing field, we proudly celebrate the life and work of George Taliaferro and bestow upon him the title of Distinguished Alumnus."

He isn't forgotten in Gary, Indiana, a city renowned for its athletics, either. Al Hamnik wrote for the *Northwest Indiana Times* that the city, which celebrated its centennial in 2006, compiled a list of Gary's fifteen greatest athletes to recognize as part of its celebration. Taliaferro was one of the fifteen, and he was in good company. Tom Harmon, a Michigan graduate, was the nation's leading scorer in 1939, Heisman winner in 1940, and he had graced the covers of both *Time* and *Life* magazines. Boxing champion Tony Zakm, football great Alex Karras, and Olympians Charles Adkins, Lee Calhoun, and Willie Williams were also on the all-star list.

George Taliaferro spent a lifetime overcoming obstacles. His determination, athleticism, positive attitude, and steadfast conviction of the importance of education enabled him to break color barriers as a student and athlete in Bloomington, Indiana; in professional football; and beyond. As the first black man to be drafted by an NFL team and as the first black professional quarterback, he paved the way for those who would follow. As an educator and as a person, he continued to be an inspiration. Today, the African American athletes and coaches in the NFL can continue to look at his example as the league continues its integration and its players continue to use football as a vehicle for social change.

TEN

—ᘓ—

1949–PRESENT: INTEGRATION OF THE NFL

FORMER INDIANAPOLIS COACH TONY DUNGY, one of only three African American head coaches in the NFL in 2005, described the role of George Taliaferro as a trailblazer in the league. In a 2004 interview, Dungy, who was a quarterback in his college career at Minnesota, said, "While growing up, it was important to see guys like George. It allowed you to dream that one day you could do it. Had I not had that example, I don't know that I would have persevered." As a pioneer in professional football, Taliaferro helped open doors for other black quarterbacks. These transformations of the league, however, took years to become widely accepted.

Although Taliaferro had been a quarterback as early as 1949, and Willie Thrower had quarterbacked one game in 1953 for the Chicago Bears, completing three of eight passes, the position was not immediately integrated. According to an article by Cliff Christl, Charlie "Choo Choo" Brackins was a successful black quarterback from all-black Prairie View A&M College in Texas, and at six foot two and 220 pounds, he was the perfect size for the position. Like Taliaferro, Brackins had a successful college career, starting all four years and playing positions on offense and defense. The Green Bay Packers drafted him in the sixteenth round of the 1955 draft, making him the third black quarterback in the NFL, the only black quarterback of the thirty quarterbacks in the league in 1955. Brackins was also a kickoff returner and receiver. Despite his impressive college record, size, and versatility, however, Brackins did not remain with the Packers for long. He played seven games and threw two incomplete passes before he was dismissed for a curfew violation, Christl wrote. He continued, "Whether Brackins was a victim of the times or a victim of his own indiscretions is open to debate." Taliaferro figured it was the former. "As a black quarterback, if you didn't come in and win the Super Bowl, you weren't staying," he said. That, he explained, was also what happened to Willie Thrower. Whatever had happened with Brackins, it would be more than a decade before there would be another black quarterback in the NFL.

In 1960, Sandy Stephens, who was the first black All-American quarterback and who had led the University of Minnesota to a national championship, never quarterbacked in the NFL despite being a second-round draft pick of the Cleveland Browns and a first-round pick of the American Football League's New York Titans. The American Football League (AFL) existed from 1960 through 1969, but like the AAFC, it ended up having to merge with the NFL. Because these teams had indicated that they would change Stephens's position to a running back or defensive back, he decided to play in the Canadian Football League instead. There, the Montreal Alouettes gave him the opportunity to play the quarterback position.

Six more years would pass before a black quarterback was successful in the position. According to Bob Gill, Charlie Green played for the minor league Pasadena Pistols of the Texas Football League. In his first season with the Pistols, Green threw for 2,209 yards and twenty-four touchdowns. He was even more successful the following year, with 3,133 yards and thirty-five touchdown passes. Green was on the all-league team both years. While an injury kept him from playing much in 1968, Marlin Briscoe and

Eldridge Dickey were just starting their careers. Dickey became the first African American to be drafted by the AFL or NFL in the first round when he was selected by the Oakland Raiders. A record-breaking quarterback at Tennessee State, it looked hopeful that he would become the first established black quarterback. That did not happen. The Raiders offered Dickey more money to switch to wide receiver and practice with the quarterbacks in training camp, where he hoped to earn a position as quarterback anyway. Although he made a strong showing during training, he was placed permanently at wide receiver.

At the same time, University of Omaha quarterback Marlin Briscoe was making his mark on professional football. On October 6, 1968, Briscoe, whose nickname was "the Magician" because of his ability to escape defenders to make a play, made history as a Denver Bronco when he became the first black starting quarterback in a major football league. Initially, Briscoe was a defensive back, despite having had an impressive tryout for the quarterback position. He was put in as quarterback the third game of the season after backup quarterback Joe Divito, who had been the replacement for injured first-string quarterback Steve Tensi, failed to make an impression. Briscoe impressed the coaches, almost pulling off a win despite a thirteen-point deficit, thus earning the starting position. According to a College Football Hall of Fame article, at first, he was concerned that his primarily white offensive line, many of whom were from the South, wouldn't block for him. But they did, and Briscoe started seven games and set a Broncos record of 1,589 yards passing, fourteen touchdowns, and 308 yards rushing. At the time, the Broncos belonged to the AFL, which was considered the more tolerant league of the two. Briscoe's impact, while a sign of progress, still did not make for immediate change. The following year, despite his record-setting season, Briscoe was traded to Buffalo, where he was once again moved from quarterback to wide receiver. He played that position for several teams, including Coach Don Shula's 1972 Super

Bowl champion Miami Dolphins, the only team to win the championship with a perfect season.

The NFL's treatment of black players frustrated Taliaferro. While serving as vice president of the Association of Former Colts Players, Taliaferro said he did not think there would be an African American quarterback or coach in the NFL during his lifetime. Despite his own trailblazing, integration was happening only gradually. Before the 1969 draft, James "Shack" Harris, who had set records as a starting quarterback at Grambling University, decided he would not be among those who had to switch positions in the pro arena. Like Taliaferro, he was frustrated by the attempts to keep black players from leadership positions in the NFL. He made it clear that he did not want to be drafted by any teams unwilling to keep him at the quarterback position. In a College Football Hall of Fame article, he said, "It was totally unrealistic to think you had a chance to play. There were all kinds of reasons why blacks weren't playing quarterback, saying we weren't smart enough or we ran too much, or we couldn't read a defense . . ."

While it was a risk for Harris to be so adamant, something which could have kept him out of football altogether, he ended up being drafted by the Buffalo Bills in the eighth round as a quarterback. Harris attracted national attention when he started the opening game of the season as the Bills' quarterback, relieving the injured Ron Jaworski. Ironically, Briscoe, whom the Bills had previously switched to wide receiver, was now receiving passes from a black quarterback. Unlike the black quarterbacks before him, Harris became the first black established quarterback in NFL history, and in 1975 he became the first black quarterback in the Pro Bowl. Although he faced periods during which he was plagued by injuries or benched, he was a successful quarterback for most of his career, until his retirement in 1980.

By 1974, Joe "Jefferson Street" Gilliam Jr., another Tennessee State University product, proved Taliaferro's prediction wrong again when he quarterbacked for the Pittsburgh Steelers. Gilliam, whose father was on the 1945 champion Indiana team with Taliaferro, was picked by the Steelers in the eleventh round of the 1972 draft. A players' strike led to Gilliam's starting position. In 1974, quarterback Terry Bradshaw went on strike with other players, leaving the position open for Gilliam. He continued as the starter even after the strike had ended, but when his performance level declined, Bradshaw took back over, leading the team to a Super Bowl championship. Gilliam's success was short lived, and like Harris's, it was too slight to completely integrate the position. Sadly, Gilliam died young, at the age of forty-nine, having struggled with drug problems that kept him from getting his career back together.

Thus, even in the mid-1970s, after the civil rights movement had peaked, the African American quarterback was a rarity in professional football. According to a *Los Angeles Times* article by Robyn Norwood, this is because mainstream society was just not comfortable with African Americans as leaders, and the quarterback position was the key leadership position on the field. "The white-dominated football hierarchy often labeled blacks as 'athletes' who should play cornerback, receiver, or running back, sometimes suggesting that they lacked the passing and cognitive abilities to play quarterback," Norwood wrote.

Tony Dungy said this change may have been slow "because of people's perceptions of what that [the quarterback position] is and what it should look like." It takes a while, he said, to break through such preconceived ideas. African American quarterbacks, Dungy pointed out, were still a novelty even in college football in the 1960s. When he played college football in 1973, his position was fairly well accepted in the Big Ten, but not nationally. That is one of the reasons he decided to attend Minnesota, he explained. In 1977, when Dungy turned pro, there were not many black quarterbacks in the league. In fact, he was another example of one whose success as a college quarterback did not equate to professional work in the position. Instead, he played defensive back.

In the late 1980s, Doug Williams of the Washington Redskins became the only African American quarterback to lead his team to a Super Bowl victory. In fact, Williams's life had been a series of firsts. At Grambling University, the same historically black college that had produced James Harris, he became the first black quarterback from a predominantly black school to be named to the Associated Press All-America team. He also became the first black quarterback chosen in the first round of the NFL draft when the Tampa Bay Buccaneers picked him seventeenth in the 1978 draft, and he was not asked to switch from the quarterback position to other positions, unlike many of the black quarterbacks before him. However, like his predecessors, Williams received taunting from some white fans, which intensified when fans blamed him for the inability of his team to defeat Dallas in the playoffs. His volatile relationship with both fans and team owners eventually led to his decision to play for the rival United States Football League (USFL), which folded almost as quickly as it started. His outspoken manner kept him from returning to the NFL, so he started a new career, coaching receivers at Southern University. Williams had resigned himself to that role when the Redskins contacted him in 1987, looking for a backup quarterback. He accepted, and during the playoffs, when starting quarterback Joe Schroeder struggled with injuries, Williams started. Under his leadership, the Redskins made it to the Super Bowl, adding another first to his list, the first black quarterback to start in the Super Bowl. He added more firsts when his team won 42–20 and he was named the MVP. Still, his career was not without its problems. A couple of years later, he was out of the NFL again, and while he had managed to blaze a trail as a black quarterback, overall black quarterbacks were still not accepted in the league.

At the same time as Williams, Warren Moon was asserting himself in the position. He had performed admirably at the position at his Southern California high school but was unable to interest the bigger universities in playing him. Instead, he attended Pasadena Junior College, where he proved himself worthy of a position. There, he earned the attention of Washington, which, unlike USC and UCLA, offered him a scholarship to play quarterback. Washington made the right decision. In 1978, Moon led them to a Rose Bowl victory. Still, he went undrafted in 1978, so he played in the Canadian Football League, where he remained, racking up more than twenty-one thousand passing yards and leading the Edmonton Eskimos to five titles in his six seasons in the league. These numbers garnered the attention of the Houston Oilers, who subsequently signed him in 1984. The Oilers were in the playoffs for seven years with Moon as their field general, after which he played for other NFL teams, not retiring until 2000. Unlike other black quarterbacks before him, Moon finished his career with impressive statistics, never having the lackluster seasons others had sometimes experienced.

Randall Cunningham was also making his way as a black quarterback at that time. Like Moon, he found that most Division I colleges that were interested in him wanted him to switch positions. The University of Las Vegas (UNLV), however, would give him the opportunity to play quarterback, so his decision was an easier one. Impressive statistics there earned Cunningham a look from the Philadelphia Eagles, who picked him in the second round of the 1985 draft. It took a couple of years, but Cunningham became the starting quarterback for the Eagles by 1987, and by 1989 he was one of the NFL's highest paid players. Cunningham struggled during a few seasons, but his career, which spanned sixteen years, was an impressive one overall.

Although the cumulative effect of these players' accomplishments helped change the culture of the NFL, in 1992, Moon and Cunningham were among just five black quarterbacks in the league, with Jeff Blake, Rodney Peete, and Vince Evans. As the decade progressed, however, this began to change too. Kordell

Stewart, a 1994 second-round draft pick of the Pittsburgh Steelers, was one reason. He played wide receiver and running back as
well as quarterback occasionally, although he was not the starter.
Steve McNair was then drafted by the Titans in the first round of
the 1995 draft. He would become the second black quarterback
to lead his team in the Super Bowl in 1999, when the Titans lost
to the Rams. In 1998 the ten black quarterbacks on NFL rosters
added up to more than there had been at any other time in NFL
history, according to journalist Cliff Christl. While only four of
them were starters at the beginning of the season, three others
were starting by season's end. The momentum continued in 1999
when Daunte Culpepper and Donovan McNabb were selected
in the first round of the draft. In fact, in 2000, sportswriter John
Posey wrote that the press had nicknamed the season "Year of
the Black Quarterback." By that time, five of the twelve starting quarterbacks in the league were African American, and at
least fourteen had started at least one game during the season,
according to Norwood. The 2001 draft further indicated change
when Michael Vick was selected as the number one overall draft
pick by the Atlanta Falcons. A short time later, Vick would make
history again when he faced McNabb in the title game, the first
time two black quarterbacks had started against each other in a
conference championship.

The strides in integrating the quarterback position took decades, but the quarterback position was not the only one to integrate too slowly. Although African American players, including
quarterbacks, now star throughout the NFL, black coaches are
still a minority. The next step toward integration is for more mi-
norities to get opportunities to coach, Tony Dungy said. Lenny
Moore, a Hall of Famer who holds the record for eighteen consecutive games scoring a touchdown (Baltimore Colts 1963–65),
agreed in a 2002 USA Today article. In the piece, Moore indicated
that he was disappointed in the lack of black head coaches in the
league. He referred to individuals from his era as "a lot of good

folks with great minds, going down the drain," who would have made good head coaches but were prevented from doing so because of their skin color. Among them was George Taliaferro. Taliaferro knew that despite his hard work and impressive statistics, he could not have had a career in coaching. During his football career, he didn't know any African American coaches, on the collegiate or professional level. At least his social work career had enabled him to "help people from the cradle to the grave," he said.

In 1980, there were 14 black assistant coaches in the NFL, but by 1997, there were 103. By 2003, 154 of 547 assistants were black. The NFL, perhaps ploddingly, is at least moving in the right direction. In 2003, there were only three African American head coaches in the league, but by 2006, that number had doubled. According to Frank Woschitz, director of the NFL Players Association, fifty to sixty black assistant coaches attend a training camp put on by the NFL each year, so that number should continue to improve.

Super Bowl XLI—which was played on February 4, 2007, and pitted Lovie Smith's Chicago Bears against Tony Dungy's Indianapolis Colts—was not only the first time a black head coach coached a team in the Super Bowl but also the first time two black head coaches faced off in a Super Bowl. The Colts' victory, then, assured Dungy's place in history as the first black head coach to win a Super Bowl. Interestingly, it was with those same teams that Taliaferro had blazed his trail. First, the Chicago Bears drafted Taliaferro, making him the first black man drafted by an NFL team, and later he became the first black man to play quarterback in the NFL when he played for the Colts.

In 2013, Joshua D. Pitts and Daniel Yost's research on racial segregation in position when players transition from high school to college indicated the importance of football as a vehicle for social change. Pitts and Yost warn of the negative impacts of stacking black players in peripheral positions, something their research indicated was still occurring today, decades after Tony Dungy experienced it. They referenced another study to indicate the so-cietal impact this practice could have. In some ways, football is a microcosm of society, they explained. To Pitts and Yost, this means that stacking can have an "indirect impact on perceptions of African Americans' leadership ability outside of the sports la-bor market." So can perceptions of black athletes, then. In their study on Richard Sherman's media portrayal, Page, Duffy, Frisby, and Perreault review other studies that indicate that black foot-ball players are often "characterized as exceptionally athletic" while their white counterparts are "described in terms of intel-ligence." Findings like these are especially significant considering Pitts and Yost's finding that "suggests that racial strides made in the sports labor market precede similar strides made in the gen-eral market." In fact, Pitts and Yost believe it "is hard to overstate the importance and impact of sport on a society in which it is so ingrained."

These pioneers on the football field, then, may have implica-tions on society as a whole, even affecting how Americans view race. At the very least, George Taliaferro and other trailblazers in the integration of the NFL represent hope and inspiration to those who follow them. Like these trailblazers, today's football players are continuing to change the perception of race in the United States. More black men are taking on leadership positions in the sport, and they are continuing to use their positions as elite athletes to fight for social equity.

ELEVEN

—ᗗᗗ—

2016–PRESENT:
THE NEW TRAILBLAZERS

ON SEPTEMBER 12, 1983, BLOOMINGTON, Indiana, police shot to death twenty-four-year-old Denver Smith. Smith, a black man, was finishing his last semester at Indiana University, where he was also a member of the football team. He was married and had a three-week-old daughter. According to a *New York Times* article, the police said that the incident began when they received a complaint that Smith was threatening employees of a garage. They said that he took a tire iron from the garage and used it to threaten motorists. Five white officers who responded ended up in a scuffle with Smith, who managed to take both a revolver and a nightstick from them. At that point, one officer shot him twice in the back. When the gunshots did not stop him, another officer shot Smith two more times, the final shot hitting him in the chest.

Smith's family and friends were puzzled by the story. According to the *Times* article, President John Ryan, for whom Taliaferro worked as an assistant, had released a statement saying that Smith was considered a gentle giant by his friends, a sentiment echoed by the football team faculty. The coroner found evidence of swelling in the brain, not a result of blows to the head. He was unsure whether that could be responsible for Smith's aggressive behavior. The coroner found no evidence of drugs or alcohol. Many black members of the community speculated that the shooting was race related. However, there were white voices too, like a Republican mayoral candidate. The incident seemed to prompt more questions than answers: What really happened that morning, and was the killing racially motivated? Perhaps the best way to summarize the incident is a statement by a white Bloomington minister, Robert Epps. According to the *New York Times*, he said, "Possibly, even probably, no one will ever know the answer to that question. But, we do know that we live in a world where people hate each other on the basis of skin color alone." Viola Taliaferro, a lawyer at the time, represented Smith's family in a wrongful-death suit.

Incidents like this one have continued. However, they began prompting protests as more people became aware of them. The Rodney King trial sparked a national debate that continued through the deaths of Trayvon Martin, Eric Garner, and Michael Brown, among others. These events prompted San Francisco 49er Colin Kaepernick to remain seated during the national anthem at a preseason game on August 26, 2016. Kaepernick remained seated on the bench, away from his team, to protest such incidents. *Atlantic* writer Megan Garber reported Kaepernick's reason. He said, "I am not going to stand up to show pride in a flag for a country that oppresses black people and people of color. To me, this is bigger than football and it would be selfish on my part to look the other way." At first, his silent protest went largely unnoticed. Then, a fan who noticed posted a picture of him seated that went viral, setting off an interesting chain of events that would include Kaepernick becoming a free agent without a football team but also the recipient of *Sports Illustrated*'s Muhammad Ali Legacy Award. Together, these depict the polarization of the issue.

It is fitting that Kaepernick, a fraternity brother of Taliaferro, receive an award that honors the legacy of Muhammad Ali. At a time when the fight for civil rights was at its zenith, Ali used his platform as an elite athlete to protest social issues. An outspoken

Fig. 11.1 George Taliaferro wearing the Greek letters of the Kappa Alpha Psi fraternity at a 2007 Juneteenth celebration in Bloomington. According to the *Indiana
Daily Student*, the holiday originated in 1865 when slaves in Galveston, Texas, finally
heard about the Emancipation Proclamation two years after Lincoln had issued it.
Photo by Brandon Foltz, courtesy Indiana Daily Student.

critic of the Vietnam War, Ali refused the draft. He was also a
member of the Nation of Islam, and he spoke out against economic oppression and for social equality for black Americans.
Ali's protests were controversial, and he met with significant criticism and vilification.

He was not the only athlete using his platform for protest. For
example, 1968 Olympic gold medalist Tommie Smith and bronze
medalist John Carlos raised black-gloved fists during the playing
of the US national anthem in Mexico City on the medal podium
for the 200 meters. The raised fists were a gesture of black power
associated with the Black Panther organization and silent protest
of the social injustices black Americans faced. The third man
on the podium, a surprise silver medal winner, was Australian
sprinter Peter Norman. According to James Montague, Norman

had heard about the protest the Americans were planning. To show solidarity, he asked an American rower for his Olympic Project for Human Rights badge, which was from an organization fighting racism in sports. Montague wrote about rower Paul Hoffman's reaction to the request: "If a white Australian is going to ask me for an Olympic Project for Human Rights badge, then by God he would have one. I only had one, which was mine, so I took it off and gave it to him." Carlos, Smith, and Norman all paid a price for their act of defiance. None were invited onto their respective countries' teams again, despite their success. They did become lifelong friends, however, and according to Montague, Norman did not regret the decision that ended his running career, saying, "On the contrary. I have to confess, I was rather proud to be part of it."

Protests like these can be risky. According to Cooper, Macaulay, and Rodriquez in a study on African American sport activism, significant risks and consequences came with social activism: "Consequently, the actions resulted in mental health deterioration, economic deprivation, family dissolution, and distorted reputations for the individual activist athletes and, at times, their families." However, the risks may have been worth it. They also explained that "African American sport activism was beginning to be viewed as a serious threat to oppressive norms in society." And history, it seems, may be kind as well. By the time of Ali's death in June 2016, he was a national treasure, revered for his athleticism and largely respected for his activism.

Perhaps history will also be kind to Colin Kaepernick. Like Ali, Kaepernick knew that his protests to raise awareness of social injustices against black Americans were of significant risk to him. The picture of Kaepernick seated during the anthem was met with an immediate outcry on social media. While there were supporters, the photo also met with harsh criticism, vilification, and downright hatred. Kaepernick's protest prompted former Green Beret and NFL kicker Nate Boyer to write an open letter to

Kaepernick on Armytimes.com. Like many Americans, Boyer took issue with Kaepernick's decision to sit during the anthem. However, he acknowledged the very real injustices that had prompted it. Rather than contributing to what he felt was polarization and hate, Boyer wanted to take a different approach. He wanted to listen to Kaepernick, to see if he could come to an understanding.

According to ESPN writer Nick Wagoner, Kaepernick was listening too. Having read the open letter, he invited Boyer to meet with him before the final game of the preseason, against San Diego, to discuss the issue. After, they would go to the game together. San Francisco 49er teammate Eric Reid joined the discussion. It started, Wagoner described, with Kaepernick first making clear his respect for the military and thanking Boyer for his service. The men exchanged ideas about the racial injustices that moved Kaepernick to action and the best way for him to raise awareness while remaining respectful to the military. Boyer shared text messages from fellow soldiers about their disapproval of Kaepernick's decision to sit. The honest discourse left Kaepernick in a quandary. While he did not want to disrespect the military, and had been moved by the messages, he also did not feel that he could, in good conscience, stand while the injustices were occurring. Reid suggested a compromise. Kaepernick could kneel. According to Wagoner, Boyer weighed in, agreeing that kneeling was a symbol of respect. He said that if Kaepernick were to take a knee and remain with his teammates rather than sitting away from them, it would signal respect for the military while still calling attention to the protest. Gerald Early, a professor of English and African and African American Studies wrote that the custom of standing for the anthem is a demonstration of "our solidarity as Americans." He continued: "The genuflection does not deny this larger solidarity . . . but simply distinguishes how black people see themselves figuring into it." Kneeling made sense.

Even the president weighed in. Senior editor Adam Serwer reported for the *Atlantic* that President Donald Trump had told an Alabama crowd he would love to see NFL owners punish the kneeling players. He wanted owners to say, "Get that son of a bitch off the field right now, out. He's fired. He's fired!" While this drew cheers from the crowd at a Republican Senate primary campaign event, it drew criticism from other circles. Just weeks before the NFL protests, white supremacists had marched in Charlottesville, North Carolina, with torches, chanting a Nazi rally cry: "Blood and soil!" A counterprotester speaking out against the hate-charged rhetoric of the crowd was killed when one of the supremacists drove his vehicle into the crowd. Trump's refusal to speak out against the hateful rhetoric and violence was widely criticized. His only offering was that there were good people "on both sides." On the heels of this, as Serwer called it, "sluggish reaction to the white supremacist protest in Charlottesville," Trump's vehement reaction to kneeling players was notable. In fact, it inspired more NFL players and teams to join the protest, scores of them choosing to kneel or link arms together during the anthem. According to Megan Garber, by mid-September the AP estimated that about 130 players were involved. White players like Green Bay Packers quarterback Aaron Rodgers protested too. This act of solidarity was even joined by some coaches and owners, like Baltimore Ravens coach John Harbaugh and Jacksonville Jaguars owner Shahid Khan. According to the BBC, even a couple of owners who had been big Trump donors joined the protests or criticized the president's response to them.

According to Intravia and others, "Professional athletes, and NFL players in particular, occupy a unique position in American culture. Their visibility gives them a platform on which they can draw attention to significant social issues." They continued, "Anthem protesting players have commented that they are using their platform to call attention to a variety of social justice issues including excessive use of force, poverty, limited educational opportunities, and other problems that dispropor-tionately plague minority communities." The support of dozens of other players throughout the NFL did not diminish the criti-cism. But this is not necessarily surprising, either. *USA Today* sports columnist Nancy Armour wrote, "Protests, by their very nature, are not meant to be popular or even comfortable."

In some ways, this reaction was an essential part of the pro-test. "Activist expression," as Early wrote, "demands risk and it demands cost, as it should. It is only through risk and cost that the activist can convince the public that his or her devotion to the cause is indeed worth the public's attention. Otherwise, without risk and cost, how would anyone really be able to distinguish the frivolous from the authentic?" As it turned out, the consequences were very real. After the season, Colin Kaepernick became a free agent, and he has not been offered a position on any teams to date. According to Coombs, others, like Denver Broncos linebacker Brandon Marshall and outside linebacker Von Miller, lost spon-sorship deals. Players faced very real risks for their participation in the protests.

But there was also support, even from big brands. Accord-ing to *Business Insider*'s Dennis Green, some of the NFL's brand sponsors weighed in on the controversy, many of them finding space between the sides. Ford's statement, Green wrote, said that the company does "respect individuals' rights to express their views, even if they are not the ones we share. That's part of what makes America great." Others statements similar in sentiment included those from Nike and Under Armour. And the protests were prompting change. Several of the NFL players met with league representatives, Coombs and others reported. The out-come, they indicated, was "a letter written on 16th October 2017 from NFL Commissioner Roger Goodell and Seattle Seahawks player Doug Baldwin to members of congress urging the nation to attend to criminal justice reform." For his part, the teamless Kaepernick turned his focus completely to his cause. He pledged to donate a million dollars of his own money to charities focused on the specific issues he was protesting, and he started a foundation with the mission "to fight oppression of all kinds globally, through education and social activism." One arm of the foundation is the Know Your Rights Camp, with a focus on empowering youth. Whether one agrees with his methods or not, Kaepernick's motives behind the anthem protests seem to be sincere, and his actions inarguably brought awareness to social issues. In August 2018, Nike made him the face of a new advertising campaign: "Believe in something. Even if it means sacrificing everything."

Kaepernick is not alone in using football as a platform for social change. Numerous athletes are involved in various charities that promote social equity. The NFL's My Cause My Cleats week highlighted this. Players wore cleats of special designs to pay homage to their favorite causes. According to Christine Brennan with *USA Today Sports*, these athletes included Cincinnati Bengals defensive end Michael Johnson, whose cleats included images of children and police holding hands and the words "I am part of the solution." Johnson, Brennan wrote, wants to help open dialogue between kids and police. Brennan reported that he said, "With Colin Kaepernick doing what he did, taking a knee, he opened up a conversation."

Colin Kaepernick's protest may have been controversial, but it certainly raised awareness and started honest discourse. Perhaps Boyer and Kaepernick can serve as an example to a polarized country. It is possible that, as the two men discovered, we are closer together on the issues than it appears. The mutual exclusivity that currently divides the country is flawed. It is not a matter of choosing between the Black Lives Matter movement, which originated to protest the deaths of black men at the hands of police, and Blue Lives Matter, which grew in response to it and supports the police. It is entirely possible to do both. One can respect and support the police, who put their own lives at risk to serve and protect. However, some very real issues, like innate prejudice and the need for better training, need to be addressed to protect young black men. In this same vein, it is entirely possible that one may support the military while still agreeing that there are social inequities, like the ones Kaepernick is protesting, that need to be addressed. Somewhere in the space between the two sides, there is growth and understanding.

For decades, black players have used football as a vehicle for social change. While most of their support came from the black community, there were also those who went against the social norms of the time to support them. There were coaches who started black players and refused to stay in segregated hotels and teammates who refused to play if their black teammates were not welcomed. They held concerts to support integration of schools. They wore a badge on the medal stand. They knelt. Sometimes the gestures were smaller, like being the lone player to cross the field to shake the hand of a black opponent after a football game.

Despite their similarities, Taliaferro avoided discussing the criticism Kaepernick encountered. He said, "I don't think about it. And the reason I don't think about it is I know what he's going through." Taliaferro did not dwell on the negative, though. As he had since he was a teenager, he chose optimism. Of the controversy and the polarization of the country that surrounds Kaepernick's protest, Taliaferro said, "The one word I could use and really mean is *hopeful*."

EPILOGUE: 2017–18

AFTER A SERIES OF HEALTH-RELATED issues, George and Viola Taliaferro moved from their longtime home of Bloomington, Indiana, to a retirement home in Ohio, where they would be near their daughter Renée. Viola had already begun showing signs of dementia, often oscillating between past and present. In August 2017, I arrived for a visit, this time with Lori, the roommate who had prompted me to take Taliaferro's class nearly thirty years earlier. Taliaferro was sitting on a bench outside the retirement home when we arrived. Lori and I greeted him, but before we could start a conversation, he ushered us inside, as quickly as one who shuffled along on a walker could.

"I want you to see my girl," he said as he led us to the elevator that would take us to their apartment on the fourth floor. At their door, Taliaferro fumbled with the keys before letting us in. A naked Viola met us.

"Put your robe on," he reminded her, gently embracing her as he turned her around and pointed her toward the bedroom. A short time later, she walked out, tying her robe. She put her hands on her hips and eyed Lori and me with both recognition and confusion. She had known us for years, so we looked familiar, but she no longer remembered our names or how she knew us.

"Your friends are here!" I said, to head off any uneasiness at us being there. That reassurance must have worked. She smiled, and we hugged. Her straight hair, black and silver, fell just past her shoulders. She was still the slender beauty she had always been, the campus queen, but now she was frail and girl-like, the athleticism and self-assurance of the revered judge no longer apparent.

She wasn't doing well enough to go out to lunch, so Lori and I went out to pick some up. When we came back, we visited for a bit before I began asking Taliaferro some interview questions I had prepared. Viola was pushing the food around on her plate, not really eating, and distracting herself by reading Tom Archdeacon's article in the *Dayton Daily News* about Taliaferro's trailblazing football career. She was curious about a picture in the article in which she sat next to her husband on their coach. She wanted to know why she was in the picture too.

Taliaferro stopped our conversation to explain to her that they had been married for sixty-seven years, then added, joking, "It's about time I find somebody new."

She continued reading aloud from the article: "I took one look at her and said, 'Where has she been all my life?'" She smiled, looked at her husband, and said, "That's what you said."

Taliaferro and I stopped talking and listened. It was a window into the mind of someone with dementia, struggling to remain in the present and to remember the past. Her proud tone was often mixed with surprise. She was reading fond memories of her own life, much of which she could not remember.

She read about Carl Biesecker, who had crossed the field to shake hands with Taliaferro after a high school football game, and said, "Just imagine, George, how far that has gone."

She read the list of the positions Taliaferro had played, seven in all, and exclaimed, "Very busy there!" She teased him, "All right, old man, you still making it."

She read about their daughters. "I forgot something. All of our daughters have degrees from IU." Like their parents before them, the couple had instilled in their children the importance of getting an education. Her tone indicated her pride in knowing that all of their children had college degrees.

About her career as a circuit court judge, also mentioned in the article and which she seemed to remember fairly well, she said, "Janet Reno was one of my favorites."

She became upset when she read about someone who had used the word *nigger*. To that, she said, "If I'd have heard that little jigaboo say that, they'd have been repeating it forever. I would have slapped his ass upside down and inside out."

This one prompted Taliaferro to address her again. "No, you wouldn't," he replied, clipped, clearly agitated. He wasn't used to the colorful language that sometimes escaped his wife's lips since the dementia had worsened.

"All right," she said, matter-of-factly.

"Vi, go ahead and eat your sandwich, and then we'll put the rest away," I offered. She hadn't been eating or drinking much, so aside from trying to change the subject, I was also genuinely interested in getting her to eat more.

"You can go ahead and put it away now," she replied.

"How about just a little bit more of it," I suggested.

She picked at the food a little but then went back to reading the article.

"Taliaferro stared for all-black Roosevelt," she read. "*Stared?*" she asked.

"*Starred,*" Taliaferro explained.

"How do you spell *starred?*" she asked. He spelled it patiently, but Lori and I could see the pain on his face. His wife had been brilliant. He knew he was slowly losing her.

"Why the hell do you need two *Rs?*" she asked, annoyed.

"'Cause that's the way the word is spelled," he explained.

"Have you seen these pictures?" she asked me, pointing to a bulletin board that sat propped up on the kitchen table. A friend had put it together for her with pictures of her and George, their daughters, and close friends as a way for her to try to remember important people in their lives. For the third time that day, she pointed out the various people in the photos. Although she knew her daughters, she could not remember their names. She knew her husband. Everyone else was simply a friend. She pointed to a child in one of the pictures. "I spent so much of my life around children. I don't know why I still love to be around them."

"Because you love them," Taliaferro explained, because she could no longer remember that detail about herself.

Viola went back to reading, and Taliaferro and I continued talking. We spent hours discussing the way Taliaferro had caddied for Joe Louis, the time he and Viola met Nat King Cole, the Frank Sinatra concert at Gary Froebel High School, and his obsession with golf. We discussed how he would walk Indiana University's golf course in the 1990s, early in the morning before it got crowded, and handpick the crabgrass. He called it "My contribution to the golf course that I loved to play." When his wife wasn't listening, we talked about how he was dealing with the move to Ohio and her dementia.

"The difficulty is the loneliness," he explained. "The tragedy is that Vi is as she is. The moment the door closes, she won't remember the food. You will become 'the girls.'" He explained that she would ask him, "Who are the girls? Where are they from?" He had to put away a picture of the two of them because she would throw it away, and he put a note on his walker because she would move it. One night, she was found wandering outside, dressed only in a sheer nightgown, in twenty-five-degree weather, asking, "Where's George?" He hadn't slept well since, worried she would wander again.

"I put my hands on her all the time so she knows it is I," he said. As we discussed their life together, Vi made her way back to their bedroom. We could hear her chattering to herself.

"What the hell was she doing?" we heard her ask, angrily, and I wondered if I had upset her. I saw the weariness on Taliaferro's face, the toll it had begun to take on his health. His daughters had already begun to look for a solution that would allow the couple to remain together in a facility but would place Viola in a wing with special support for dementia patients.

By the end of the year, the Taliaferros had moved to just such a place. Even on my first visit there, Taliaferro's health seemed to show significant improvement. He was able to sleep again, and he was doing physical therapy. What had been a shuffle had turned into a brisk walk on the walker. And because he did not feel responsible for watching Viola, he was able to leave the facility and join another friend, Helen, and me for lunch rather than have us bring it in.

During lunch we talked about Muhammad Ali, Joe Louis, the 1951 Pro Bowl and Nat King Cole, the NFL protests, Colin Kaepernick, and Donald Trump. We talked about Taliaferro's parents, the importance of education, segregated movie theaters, work ethic, and the Red Rooster restaurant in Harlem. We talked about making his way through a blizzard to get to his wedding. At one point, our server interrupted the conversation to ask if we would like coffee.

Taliaferro immediately responded, "Coffee makes me black" and laughed. Eventually we returned to the facility. On the same floor as Taliaferro, on the opposite end of the hall, is the dementia wing where Viola's room is located. Taliaferro, Helen, and I went to the door and rang the bell. We had to wait for one of the caretakers to let us in—a safety measure to ensure that the residents of the area can't wander away. We made our way past a library and den area, Viola's apartment, and then to the cafeteria, where we found her. She recognized Taliaferro, and they leaned in for a kiss. We sat with her at a table and visited for a short time before Helen and I had to go.

By January 2018, Taliaferro explained during a phone call, her condition had further deteriorated. She no longer knew who he was, he said. To Taliaferro, it was a devastating loss. Aging was

Fig. A.1 George and Viola Taliaferro, December 3, 2017. *Photo courtesy Dawn Knight.*

one of the most difficult obstacles he faced, and he faced many in his ninety-one years. With the same combination of determination, humor, and hopefulness as he faced all the others, however, Taliaferro faced that one. He continued to visit Viola, his girl, several times a day, every day, until he passed in his sleep on October 8, 2018.

His was "a life well lived," a segment on the *Today* show after his death noted. For more than twenty-five years after he had written it on the board during his social work class, Taliaferro continued to be the embodiment of the phrase "All sickness ain't death" and an inspiration to those fortunate enough to have been in his orbit.

BIBLIOGRAPHY

AAC. "Life Short, but Turbulent: Competition Was Healthy for Pro Football." *Chicago Daily Tribune*, December 10, 1949. ProQuest Historical Newspapers.

AcePilots. "The Tuskegee Airmen 332nd Fighter Group." Accessed January 12, 2003. http://www.acepilots.com/usaaf_tusk.html.

Adams, Lehman. Phone interview by author. June 16, 2004.

Amato, Sara. "Juneteenth Celebrates Its 9th Year in Bloomington." *Indiana Daily Student*, July 1, 2007. https://www.idsnews.com/article/2007/07/juneteenth -celebrates-its-9th-year-in-bloomington.

Andrews, John. Phone interview by author. July 20, 2006.

Archdeacon, Tom. "Reminiscing with the NFL's First Black Quarterback." *Dayton Daily News*, August 20, 2017.

Arnold, Robert D. *Hoosier Autumn*. Indianapolis: Guild Press of Indiana, 1996.

Banks, Calvin. Phone interview by author. June 16, 2004.

Banks, Sam. "George Is Real George." *Our Sports*, October/November 1953.

Baumgartner, Jim. Phone interview by author. December 28, 2006.

BBC. "Trump NFL Row: US President Denies Comments Were Race-Related." September 25, 2017. http://www.bbc.com/news/world-us-canada-41384053.

Bell, Jarrett. "Circus Acts Mock the Game." *USA Today*, October 24, 2002.

Berman, Eliza. "When Frank Sinatra Took a Stand for Civil Rights in Schools." *Time*, May 18, 2015. http://time.com/3857736/frank-sinatra-civil-rights/.

Bigler, Matthew, and Judson L. Jeffries. "'An Amazing Specimen': NFL Draft Experts' Evaluations of Black Quarterbacks." *Journal of African American Studies* 12, no. 2 (2008): 120–41. http://www.jstor.org/stable/41819165.

Bloom, Jack. Phone interview by author. September 29, 2017.

"Bo McMillin Wins Big Ten Title: After 46 Years of Trying, Indiana Finally Wins Football Championship." *Life*, December 10, 1945.

Bolding, Mark. "The Chicago Charities College All-Star Game 1934–1976: The Night the Stars Came Out." August 8, 2006. http://www.mmbolding .com/BSR/The%20Chicago%All-Star%20Game_1949.htm. Page no longer available.

Boyer, Nate. "An Open Letter to Colin Kaepernick from a Green Beret-Turned-Long Snapper." *Army Times*, August 30, 2016. https://www.armytimes.com /opinion/2016/08/30/an-open-letter-to-colin-kaepernick-from-a-green-beret -turned-long-snapper/.

Brennan, Christine. "Meet 5 NFL Players Whose Cleats This Week Will Take On Social Injustice." *USA Today*, November 28, 2017. https://www.usatoday .com/story/sports/columnist/brennan/2017/11/28/meet-5-nfl-players-whose -cleats-week-take-social-injustice/902911001/.

Brown, Jeff. "Re-integration of NFL Is Focus of Black Athlete Lecture." February 20, 1997. http://dmolemiss.edu/archives/97/9702/970220/970220N4nfl .html. Page no longer available.

Brown, T. J. "IU, Wells Played Role in Sports Integration, Too." *Indiana Daily Student*, April 15, 1997.

CBS Sports Digital. "Hall of Fame S–Z." Accessed November 17, 2018. https://www .cbssports.com/collegefootball/history/halloffame/S-Z.

Christl, Cliff. "Black QBs Find More Opportunities." *Journal Sentinel Online*, November 8, 1998. http://www.jsonline.com/packer/sbxxxiii/news/qb110898 .asp. Page no longer available.

Cook, Bob. *Finally, Bob Cook Book on Bo McMillin*. Bloomington: Indiana University Varsity Club, 1995.

Coombs, Danielle Sarver, Cheryl Ann Lambert, David Cassilo, and Zachary Humphries. "Kap Takes a Knee: A Media Framing Analysis of Colin Kaepernick's Anthem Protest." Kent State University. 20th International Public Relations Research Conference. March 8–12, 2017. http://www.instituteforpr .org/wp-content/uploads/IPRRC20-proceedings_Final.pdf.

Cooper, Belle Beth. "Events That Changed History: How Fighting for Racial Integration Cost Frank Sinatra a $10k Gig, but He Did It Anyway." Attendly. January 9, 2013. http://www.attendly.com/events-that-changed-history-how-fight ing-for-racial-integration-cost-frank-sinatra-a-10k-gig-but-he-did-it-anyway/.

Cooper, Joseph N., Charles Macaulay, and Saturnino H. Rodriguez. "Race and Resistance: A Typology of African American Sport Activism." *International Review for the Sociology of Sport* (July 7, 2017). http://journals.sagepub.com /doi/abs/10.1177/1012690217718170.

Crabb, Chuck. "George Is Home and He Loves It Here." Athletic Publicity Office, Indiana University. Provided by George Taliaferro; publication information unknown.

Cromie, Robert. "Hornets and Dons Renew an Old Feud." *Chicago Daily Tribune*, October 27, 1949. ProQuest Historical Newspapers.

———. "Hornets Beaten by Dons, 24–14: Coast Eleven Keeps Alive Play-Off Hope—Taliaferro's Passes Bring Victory." *Chicago Daily Tribune*, October 29, 1949. ProQuest Historical Newspapers.

———. "Hornets to Battle Dons Tonight: Los Angeles Must Win for Play-Off Bid." *Chicago Daily Tribune*, October 28, 1949. ProQuest Historical Newspapers.

Cummings, Sidney. Phone interview by author. March 28, 2004.

Drummond, Herbert. Phone interview by author. June 15, 2004.

Dudeck, John. Phone interview by author. August 19, 2017.

———. Phone interview by author. January 1, 2018.

Dungy, Tony. Phone interview by author. November 5, 2003.

Early, Gerald. "Colin Kaepernick, Kneeling, and the Meaning of Gratitude: A Reflection on Resistance, Race, and Popular Culture." *Common Reader*, October 16, 2017.

Encyclopedia of Chicago. "Gary, IN." Accessed August 30, 2005. http://www.encyclopedia.chicagohistory.org/pages/503.html.

ESPN. "We Are." 30 for 30 Shorts. ESPN Stories. Accessed November 17, 2018. http://www.espn.com/video/clip?id=15695869.

Fullerton, Hugh, Jr. "Both Loops to Hold Player Drafts Today." *Indianapolis Star*, December 21, 1948.

———. "Pro Grid Peace Meeting Today." *Gary-Post Tribune*, December 20, 1948.

Garber, Megan. "They Took a Knee." *Atlantic*, September 24, 2017. https://www.theatlantic.com/entertainment/archive/2017/09/why-the-nfl-is-protesting/540927/.

"George Taliaferro Is 'Drafted' by Chicago Bears." *Chicago Defender*, January 1, 1949. ProQuest Historical Newspapers.

Gill, Bob. "Five Forgotten Trailblazers." *Coffin Corner* 24, no. 6 (2002). Professional Football Researchers Association Pro Football History. Accessed November 17, 2018. http://profootballresearchers.com/archives/Website_Files/Coffin_Corner/24-06-960.pdf.

Gilliam, Frances V. Halsell. *A Time to Speak: A Brief History of the Afro-Americans of Bloomington, Indiana, 1865–1965*. Bloomington, IN: Pinus Strobus, 1985.

Given, Karen, and Shira Springer. "Long before Kaepernick, the 'Syracuse 8' Took a Stand against Racial Injustice." *Here and Now*. WBUR. November 17, 2017. http://www.wbur.org/hereandnow/2017/11/22/syracuse-8-racial-injustice.

Gordon, Ed, and Robin Washington. "Naked in High School: Bad Dreams Do Come True." *News and Notes*. NPR. August 1, 2006. http://www.npr.org/templates/story/story.php?storyId=5597441.

Graham, Tom, and Rachel Graham Cody. *Getting Open: The Unknown Story of Bill Garrett and the Integration of College Basketball*. New York: Atria Books, 2006.

Green, Dennis. "Here's How Brands Are Responding to Trump's Criticism of the NFL Anthem Protests." *Business Insider*, September 27, 2017. http://

www.businessinsider.com/nfl-anthem-protests-brand-response-2017-9?
    pt=385758&ct=Sailthru_BI_Newsletters&mt=8&utm_source=Triggermail
    &utm_medium=email&utm_campaign=email_article.
Gross, Jane. "Police Killing of Student Stuns Indiana Residents." *New York Times*,
    September 25, 1983. http://www.nytimes.com/1983/09/25/us/police-killing
    -of-student-stuns-indiana-residents.html?emc=eta1.
Grosshandler, Stan. "A Disgrace." *Coffin Corner* 4, no. 10 (1982). Professional Foot-
    ball Researchers Association Pro Football History. Accessed November 17,
    2018. http://profootballresearchers.com/archives/Website_Files/Coffin
    _Corner/04-10-112.pdf.
Hackett, David. "Taliaferro Full of Memories." *Indiana Daily Student*, October 14,
    1982.
Hammel, Bob. "All You Have to Do Is Listen: Ryan Aide Taliaferro." Indiana
    University archives. Provided by George Taliaferro; publication information
    unknown.
———. "IU Stops Michigan in Opener." *Herald-Times*, September 22, 1995.
———. "Taliaferro Joins College Football Hall of Fame." *Herald Telephone*, De-
    cember 8, 1981.
Hammel, Bob, and Kit Klingelhoffer. *Glory of Old IU: 100 Years of Indiana Athletics.*
    Champaign, IL: Sports Publishing, 1999.
Hamnik, Al. "Gary's Top 15 Athletes Sure to Create Interest." *Northwest Indiana
    Times*, July 6, 2006.
———. "Taliaferro Continues His Battle." *Gary Post-Tribune*, January 20, 1993.
Horrigan, Joe. "Belly Up in Dallas." *Coffin Corner* 7, no. 3 (1985). Professional Foot-
    ball Researchers Association Pro Football History. Accessed November 17,
    2018. http://profootballresearchers.com/archives/Website_Files/Coffin
    _Corner/07-03-225.pdf.
Howard, Sherman. Phone interview by author. September 15, 2003.
Indiana Humanities Council. "Hoosier History: This Far by Faith; Black Hoosier
    Heritage." Accessed November 17, 2018. http://www.indianahumanities.org
    /pdf/ThisFarByFaith.pdf.
Indiana University. "Alma Pater: Herman B Wells and the Rise of Indiana Univer-
    sity." Accessed November 17, 2018. http://archive.li/a1e2R.
Indiana University Athletics. Accessed June 20, 2005. http://www.iuhoosiers.com
    /football/history. Page no longer available.
Intravia, Jonathan, Alex R. Piquero, and Nicole Leeper Piquero. "The Racial Di-
    vide Surrounding United States of America National Anthem Protests in the
    National Football League." *Deviant Behavior* 39, no. 8 (2017): 1058–68. https://
    doi.org/10.1080/01639625.2017.1399745.
IUHoosiers.com. "1992 Hall of Fame." Accessed November 17, 2018. https://iuhoo
    siers.com/sports/2015/4/1/GEN_20140101405.aspx.
Judicial Family Institute. "Football Great Admires Judge Spouse." Accessed Janu-
    ary 24, 2018. http://www.judicialfamilyinstitute.org/~/media/Microsites
    /Files/JFI/Resources/Football-Great-Admires-Judge-Spouse.ashx.

Kaepernick, Colin. Official Website for Colin Kaepernick. Accessed January 20, 2018. https://kaepernick7.com.

Kennedy, Tom. "Taliaferro Tallies Twice as Roosevelt Beats S.B.C." *Gary Post-Tribune*, November 2, 1944.

Kish, Bernie. Interview by author. June 27, 2003. College Football Hall of Fame, South Bend, IN.

Kutch, Joe. "No Foolin', Panthers Trip Rough Riders, 13–9." *Gary Post-Tribune*, October 7, 1944.

Lehman, David. "When Sinatra Campaigned for FDR." Excerpt from *Sinatra's Century*. *Daily Beast*, October 25, 2015. https://www.thedailybeast.com /when-sinatra-campaigned-for-fdr.

"Letters to the Editor." *Life*, December 3, 1945. https://books.google.com/books ?id=xkgEAAAAMBAJ.

Lewis, Carl. "The Old Bucket, Coveted Football Trophy, Speaks." *Indiana Daily Student*, November 22, 1947.

Long, Howie. *Football for Dummies*. With John Czarnecki. 2nd ed. Indianapolis: Wiley, 2003.

Longfellow, Henry Wadsworth. "Psalm of Life." Poetry Foundation. Accessed November 17, 2018. https://www.poetryfoundation.org/poems/44644/a -psalm-of-life.

McIver, Stuart. "Pro Football Club History #11 the Baltimore Colts." *Sport*, December 1954.

Michelson, Herb. "Campus Mourns Passing of Bo." *Indiana Daily Student*, April 1, 1952.

Montague, James. "The Third Man: The Forgotten Black Power Hero." CNN. April 25, 2012. https://www.cnn.com/2012/04/24/sport/olympics-norman -black-power/index.html.

Montieth, Mark. "Indiana's Best Football Season Ever." *Indianapolis Star*, October 6, 1995.

"Moore: 'Circus' Acts Mock the Game." *USA Today*, October 24, 2002.

National Football League. *The NFL's Official Encyclopedic History of Professional Football*. New York: Macmillan, 1972.

Nicholls, Shawn. "The Rise of Black Quarterbacks." *Sports Illustrated for Kids*, September 1, 2003.

Norwood, Robyn. "Black Quarterbacks Scoring in the NFL." *Los Angeles Times*, December 30, 2000.

Overmyer, Jack. Phone interview by author. December 30, 2005.

PBS. "Newspapers: The Chicago Defender." Accessed January 30, 2018. https:// www.pbs.org/blackpress/news_bios/defender.html.

Perdomo, Yolanda. "When Frank Went to Gary." WBEZ. October 30, 2015. https:// www.wbez.org/shows/wbez-news/when-frank-went-to-gary/f386bd26-9ce3 -4f59-8cd8-e868b50d019a.

Peterson, Robert W. *Pigskin: The Early Years of Pro Football*. New York: Oxford University Press, 1997.

Pimlott, Ben. "It's All in the Life." *New Statesman*, November 6, 1996.

Page, Janis, Margaret Duffy, Cynthia M. Frisby, and Gregory Perreault. "Richard Sherman Speaks and Almost Breaks the Internet: Race, Media, and Football." *Howard Journal of Communication* (May 2016). https://www.tandfonline.com /doi/pdf/10.1080/10646175.2016.1176969.

Pitts, Joshua D., and Daniel M. Yost. "Racial Position and Segregation in Intercollegiate Football: Do Players Become More Racially Segregated as They Transition from High School to College?" *Review of Black Political Economy* 40, no. 2 (2013): 207. https://doi.org/10.1007/s12114-012-9149-z.

Posey, John. "Black Quarterbacks in Vogue in the NFL." 2000. http://www.black athlete.com/nfl128.htm. Page no longer available.

Prell, Edward. "All-America to Operate with Seven Teams." *Chicago Daily Tribune*, January 22, 1949. ProQuest Historical Newspapers.

———. "All-America Will Continue: Lindheimer." *Chicago Daily Tribune*, January 20, 1949. ProQuest Historical Newspapers.

———. "Bonuses Cause Headaches for Club Owners." *Chicago Daily Tribune*, April 4, 1948. ProQuest Historical Newspapers.

———. "2 Football Leagues Hurt by Cash War Several Teams Hit Hard." *Chicago Daily Tribune*, November 1, 1948. ProQuest Historical Newspapers.

Pro Football Hall of Fame. "History." Accessed November 17, 2018. https://www .profootballhof.com/visit/hall-of-fame-history/.

Pro Football Reference. "George Taliaferro." Accessed June 5, 2003. https://www .pro-football-reference.com/players/T/TaliGe00.htm.

"Pro Leagues Merge; End 4 Year Fight." *Chicago Daily Tribune*, December 10, 1949. ProQuest Historical Newspapers.

Rampersad, Arnold. *Jackie Robinson: A Biography*. New York: Alfred A. Knopf, 1997.

Ransom, Jane. "Ryan Aide Faults Sports Hiring." *Indiana Daily Student*, March 31, 1978.

"Relationships of Sinatra with Blacks That Book about Him Does Not Highlight." *Jet*, October 13, 1986. https://books.google.com/books?id=5LADAAAAMBAJ.

Robinson, Rachel. *Jackie Robinson: An Intimate Portrait*. New York: Harry N. Abrams, 1996.

Schurz, John. "Alumni Enjoy True Homecoming." *Herald-Times*, October 8, 1995.

Serwer, Adam. "Trump's War of Words with Black Athletes." *Atlantic*, September 23, 2017.

Sheer, Harry. "Pro Grid Player War Rages on A.A. Leads Bidding for Stars." *Chicago Daily News*, January 4, 1949.

Shub, Seymour. "Bears Hold NFL Draft Rights: Dons Ink Taliaferro but Halas Not Upset." *Chicago Sun Times*, January 3, 1949.

———. "Not Upset over Dons Signing Taliaferro: Halas Eyes Pact with '2nd Bronko.'" *Chicago Sun Times*, January 3, 1949.

Simon, Scott. "'One More' for Sinatra, Who Took a Stand in Gary, Indiana." *Weekend Edition Saturday.* NPR. December 12, 2015. http://www.npr.org/2015/12/12 /459414244/one-more-for-sinatra-who-took-a-stand-in-gary-indiana.

Simpson, Isabella. "Scoop." In "Sports in the Calumet Region." Special issue, *Steel Shavings* 10 (1984). Provided by George Taliaferro.

Snowden, Calvin. Phone interview by author. June 20, 2005.

"Sports Illustrated Muhammad Ali Legacy Award." *Sports Illustrated,* accessed January 20, 2018. https://www.si.com/specials/muhammad-ali-sportsman -legacy-award/index.html.

Steers, Ed. Phone interview by author. August 22, 2005.

"Trailblazing Football Player George Taliaferro Dies at 91." *Today.* October 14, 2018. https://www.today.com/video/trailblazing-football-player-george-taliaferro -dies-at-91-1343932483847.

Taliaferro, George. "I Didn't Do It!" *Coffin Corner* 27, no. 5 (2005). Professional Football Researchers Association Pro Football History. Accessed November 17, 2018. http://profootballresearchers.com/archives/Website_Files/Cof fin_Corner/27-05-1098.pdf.

———. Interview by author. September 30, 1996. Bloomington, IN.

———. Interview by author. June 27, 2003. College Football Hall of Fame, South Bend, IN.

———. Interview by author. July 16, 2003. Bloomington, IN.

———. Interview by author. July 22, 2003. Bloomington, IN.

———. Phone interview by author. June 20, 2005.

———. Phone interview by author. June 27, 2006.

———. Phone interview by author. July 14, 2006.

———. Interview by author. August 26, 2017. West Chester, Ohio.

———. Interview by author. September 16, 2017. West Chester, Ohio.

———. Phone interview by Mackenzie Knight. November 1, 2017.

———. Interview by author. November 12, 2017. Mason, Ohio.

———. Interview by author. December 3, 2017. Mason, Ohio.

———. Phone interview by author. January 29, 2018.

Taliaferro, Renée. Interview by author. October 13, 2018. Avon, IN.

Taliaferro, Viola. Interview by author. June 29, 2004. Bloomington, IN.

"Taliaferro of Indiana Signed for '49 by Dons." *Chicago Daily Tribune,* January 3, 1949. ProQuest Historical Newspapers.

"Taliaferro Signs Contract with Dons." *Chicago Defender,* January 8, 1949. ProQuest Historical Newspapers.

Teeuws, Len. Phone interview by author. November 3, 2003.

University of Illinois. *Sports Interviews.* General Publications. 1967.

University of Notre Dame Official Athletic Site. "The Four Horsemen." Accessed November 17, 2018. https://und.com/sports/2018/8/7/trads-horse-html.aspx ?id=2038.

Vance, Lloyd. "The Complete History of African American Quarterbacks in the NFL." Black Athlete Sports Network. Accessed November 17, 2018. http://www.bqb-site.com/bqbhist.htm.

Wagoner, Nick. "From a Seat to a Knee: How Colin Kaepernick and Nate Boyer Are Trying to Effect Change." ESPN NFL Nation. September 6, 2016. http://www.espn.com/blog/san-francisco-49ers/post/_/id/19253/from-a-seat-to-a-knee-how-colin-kaepernick-and-nate-boyer-are-trying-to-affect-change.

Walsh, Steve. "Social Change Plays Out on Front Page." *Gary Post Tribune*, February 26, 2011.

Warren, Harry. "N.F.L. Ends Conference with Draft." *Chicago Daily Tribune*, December 22, 1948. ProQuest Historical Newspapers.

Werry, Norman S. "Fumbles Rule as Roosevelt Gets 7–0 Win off Froebel." *Gary Post-Tribune*, October 20, 1944.

———. Moleskin Musings. *Gary Post-Tribune*, September 12–November 25, 1944.

———. "Taliaferro's Touchdowns Beat Blue Raiders, 19–6." *Gary Post-Tribune*, November 10, 1944.

Whicker, Mike. "The Birth of a Juggernaut." Reitzfootball.com. Accessed November 17, 2018. http://reitzfootball.com/the-tradition/legendary-game-series/the-birth-of-a-juggernaut/. Originally published in *Reitz Football History*, October 1, 1948.

Whirty, Ryan. "A Hoosier Trailblazer: Taliaferro Overcomes Obstacles to Excel at IU, in Professional Ranks." *Inside Indiana* 12, no. 9 (2002).

———. "Making a Difference: Count to 30. How Has IU Changed the World in Which We Live? Let's Begin to Count the Ways." SICE News. Indiana University Alumni Association. March/April 2003. https://www.sice.indiana.edu/news/story.html?story=Making-Difference-Count-30-How-has-IU-changed-world-which-we-live-Let-begin-count-ways.

Williams, Maryann. Phone interview by author. January 29, 2018.

Woschitz, Frank. Phone interview by author. November 4, 2003.

"Yankees Halt Rally by Dons to Win, 17–16." *Chicago Daily Tribune*, November 25, 1949. ProQuest Historical Newspapers.

Ziegler, Valerie H. "C6-H0: The Centre Harvard Game of 1921." Provided by George Taliaferro; publication information unknown.

INDEX

Numbers in italics refer to illustrations.

DAWN KNIGHT received her BS in English from Indiana University and her MA in journalism from Ball State University. She teaches English at Westfield High School in Westfield, Indiana.